Praise for *Someday Is Today*

"*Someday Is Today* is a real, honest, and thinking solution for hacking your productivity. This book was absolutely inspiring for me, as someone who needs to make the most of his time. If you're looking for ways to streamline your life, this is a must-read!"

— **Nelson Dellis**, USA Memory Champion and author of *Remember It!* and *Memory Superpowers!*

"This is one of the most inspiring books I've ever read. Matthew Dicks is an incredible writer and storyteller, and this book has made me feel like I can do anything I set my heart to. His strategies are simple, profound, and eminently doable — and they deliver the results they promise."

— **Dr. Ali Abdaal**, productivity YouTuber

"Folks often ask me, 'How have you been so productive and written fifty books?' I've been a bit too busy to answer ☺. Fortunately, Matthew Dicks has supplied the complete answer in his wonderful new book. Want to be really productive and, more importantly, live your life purposes every day? Then *Someday Is Today* is the book for you."

— **Eric Maisel**, author of *Coaching the Artist Within* and more than fifty other books

"A practical and stimulating map to *carpe diem*. With wit, warmth, hard-earned wisdom, and a narrative that jumps off the page with signature style, Matthew Dicks leads us step-by-step with a fail-proof plan to rescue and reclaim our time and attention, harness our energy efficiently, and get us moving in the direction of our dreams. He then kindly kicks us off the couch to make the most of our lives, not *someday*, but *today* and every day. Seize this book!"

— **Meredith Heller**, author of *Write a Poem, Save Your Life*

"You're going to learn how to make productivity nuggets out of your black holes, and you're going to learn how to have the mindset of a person who gets things done without having your goals hijack all your free time.... This book will inspire you and give you the tools to turn your inspiration into accomplishment."

— from the foreword by **Elysha Dicks**, cofounder of Speak Up

"*Someday Is Today* is the most frustrating, inspiring, uncomfortable book. It is, without a doubt, one of the best books I have ever read."

— **Kate Norris**, public speaking consultant, mother, and person who desperately wants to do more with her time

"It is amazing how much time we can make for the things that really matter.... [Matt] has absolutely made me more conscious of what I *do* want and what I need to do to be there. That is a gift we can all benefit from."

— from the afterword by **Matthew Shepard**, communications consultant

"Brisk, upbeat, and slightly subversive, this book bats away every single excuse and leaves you inspired to get busy creating a life that matters to you. You'll even discover why it's good to be a chicken."

— **Sam Bennett**, author of *Get It Done*

Praise for *Storyworthy* by Matthew Dicks

"I laughed, gasped, took notes, and carried this book around like a dear friend."

— **Sarah McCoy**, *New York Times* bestselling author of *Marilla of Green Gables* and *The Baker's Daughter*

"Holy moly! Mathew Dicks is right — every one of us has a story to tell. And whether onstage or on the page, this master of the craft pulls us into his world, entertaining, instructing, and inspiring with every word."

— **Susan Gregg Gilmore**, author of *Looking for Salvation at the Dairy Queen*

"Matthew Dicks is dazzling as a storyteller and equally brilliant in his ability to deconstruct this skill and make it accessible to others."

— **David A. Ross, MD, PhD**, director, Yale Psychiatry Residency Training Program

SOMEDAY IS
TODAY

Also by Matthew Dicks

FICTION

Memoirs of an Imaginary Friend

The Other Mother

The Perfect Comeback of Caroline Jacobs

Something Missing

Twenty-One Truths about Love: A Novel

Unexpectedly, Milo

NONFICTION

Storyworthy: Engage, Teach, Persuade, and Change Your Life through the Power of Storytelling

SOMEDAY IS
TODAY

22 Simple, Actionable Ways
to Propel Your Creative Life

MATTHEW DICKS

Foreword by Elysha Dicks
Afterword by Matthew Shepard

New World Library
Novato, California

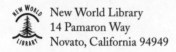 New World Library
14 Pamaron Way
Novato, California 94949

Text design by Tona Pearce Myers

Library of Congress Cataloging-in-Publication Data

Names: Dicks, Matthew, author. | Dicks, Elysha, writer of foreword.
Title: Someday is today : 22 simple, actionable ways to propel your creative life / Matthew Dicks ; foreword by Elysha Dicks.
Description: Novato, California : New World Library, [2022] | Includes bibliographical references. | Summary: "A noted storyteller and novelist offers strategies to help creative people of all kinds — including writers, musicians, artists, and entrepreneurs — increase their creative output, manage time effectively, and achieve long-term goals in their chosen field"-- Provided by publisher.
Identifiers: LCCN 2022003586 (print) | LCCN 2022003587 (ebook) | ISBN 9781608687503 (paperback) | ISBN 9781608687510 (epub)
Subjects: LCSH: Creative ability. | Time management. | Goal (Psychology)
Classification: LCC BF408 .D533 2022 (print) | LCC BF408 (ebook) | DDC 153.3/5--dc23/eng/20220315
LC record available at https://lccn.loc.gov/2022003586
LC ebook record available at https://lccn.loc.gov/2022003587

First printing, June 2022
ISBN 978-1-60868-750-3
Ebook ISBN 978-1-60868-751-0
Printed in Canada on 100% postconsumer-waste recycled paper

 New World Library is proud to be a Gold Certified Environmentally Responsible Publisher. Publisher certification awarded by Green Press Initiative.

10   9   8   7   6   5   4   3   2   1

For Plato,
the boss I always wanted,
the mentor I always needed,
the friend I never expected.

"Only put off until tomorrow what you are willing
to die having left undone."

— **PABLO PICASSO**

Contents

Foreword by Elysha Dicks..xiii
Prologue: A Boy Finds a Future..xvii

PART 1: TIME

Chapter ½: The Worst Word...3
Chapter 1: The One-Hundred-Year-Old Plan..............................4
Chapter 2: 86,400 Seconds..15
Chapter 3: Sleep Correctly...60
Chapter 4: The Eagle and the Mouse..78
Chapter 5: Things That Don't Deserve Your Time.....................96
Chapter 5½: How to Ruin the World.......................................105
Chapter 6: Be a Criminal...109
Chapter 7: Don't Lose Days to Rotten People..........................117
Chapter 7½: Write Your Own Damn *Gatsby*..........................129

PART 2: TAKING THE LEAP

Chapter 8: Say Yes...133
Chapter 8½: Concern for Code Monkey...................................145
Chapter 9: Be a Chicken, Not a Pig..147
Chapter 10: You Choose the Finish Line..................................156
Chapter 10½: Five-Year Plans Are Inviting the Universe
　　to Drop a Piano on You..167

Chapter 11: Make Terrible Things................................170
Chapter 11½: Rejection Is Expected, but So Is Persistence.........176
Chapter 12: How Did They Do It?................................178

PART 3: SUPPORT

Chapter 13: Find Your People..................................189
Chapter 14: Put Your Eyes on the Prize.......................199
Chapter 14½: Leave Performative Productivity
    to the Female Lions.......................................209
Chapter 15: Party Often......................................211
Chapter 16: Feed Yourself a Compliment Sandwich.............216
Chapter 17: Know Your Story. Tell Your Story.
    Listen to Your Story.....................................225

PART 4: LIVING THE LIFE

Chapter 18: Creativity Cannot Abide Preciousness............237
Chapter 18½: No Room for Pretty When It Comes
    to Productivity..244
Chapter 19: Make Something into Something...................246
Chapter 20: Don't Be an Asshole.............................252
Chapter 20½: 9 Rules for Making You More Efficient
    with Email and Less of a Jerk Face......................263
Chapter 21: Eat a Lot.......................................265
Chapter 22: Pessimists Die Knowing Only That
    They Were Correct. Optimists Thrive.....................272
Chapter 22½: You Can't Change Unless You Change.............279

Afterword by Matthew Shepard.................................281
Appendix: Chapter-by-Chapter Action Plans...................285
Acknowledgments...311
Notes...313
About the Author..317

Foreword

by Elysha Dicks

Being married to a productivity expert is not always easy. It is, however, my cross to bear. And my husband isn't even just an average productivity expert, like someone who's really organized and whose friends ask them to come over to give advice on how to rearrange their garage. No. My husband is so consistently and admirably productive that he has written a book on this subject. One that you are presumably about to read.

It can be hard not to feel lazy when you're married to a book-writing productivity expert, even when you yourself are fairly productive.

Here's the thing, though: Matt gets a lot of stuff done. He gets it done well and is generally happy doing it. The things he writes about in this book will help you get stuff done, too. He is going to teach you how to make manageable changes so that you can achieve the things you would love to make happen, and he'll show you how to do it without upending your life.

There is no doubt Matt is a hard worker. If you want to be productive and accomplish your goals, it's a given that you will have to work hard. However, you do not need to sacrifice your family time, your fun time, or your health to do it. Matt is going to show you how to maximize the time that you have and get the most out of it.

This is the kind of thing I'm talking about: Matt is always taking the little black holes in time that are so frequent when you have young kids and turning those intervals into productivity nuggets. You know the black holes I mean. The times when you're getting ready to go somewhere, but then you have to wait ten minutes for your son to find his shoes. Or when your kids decide they need to pack snacks and water bottles even though you're just heading out for errands.

Rather than wait by the door and yell for them to hurry up, like I generally do, Matt will just head over to his computer and bang out ten minutes of writing, or he might empty the dishwasher and sweep up the collection of Cheerios that our kids manage to get on the floor every day. It might not be enough time to complete a chapter or clean the whole house, but little by little, it's how he gets things done without adding a lot of burden to his day. It means he's still able to join us on whatever excursion we're taking. He doesn't miss out. But he finds little cracks and fits his work into them. He was even writing book pages in the spaces between my contractions while I was in labor with our daughter (it was fine, I swear!).

At this point, you may be wondering why I stand by the door yelling for the kids and don't also sweep the floor or write a book, and the answer, I think, has to do with a particular drive that Matt possesses and I do not. You have chosen to pick up this book, which likely means you are looking to increase your productivity or maybe you have some creative or life goals that you're trying to figure out how best to achieve. Possibly, you have the same kind of drive that Matt does. Or maybe you long to have that drive and haven't figured out quite how to tap that inner well of motivation.

I am a bit jealous that you're the kind of person who wants to read a book like this. It will definitely help you and will even be an enjoyable read, since Matt is an enjoyable guy and you're about to get to know him better.

I am not that kind of person. I mostly pick up books that present some feminist magical realism and allow my mind to drift while I read by the fire and Matt cleans the kitchen. It's not that I'm not looking to be productive. I'm actually kind of a workaholic perfectionist who tries to fit many things into my day. Matt and I just have different approaches, and it's why we're a good match.

Many years ago, when Matt and I had just gotten married and were teaching together at the same elementary school, I became frustrated because it took me so long to write report cards, and Matt was able to get them done so much more efficiently than me. I mentioned this to our principal, Plato Karafelis. In his usual sage way, he gave me one of the most formative bits of wisdom I've heard in my life: a summation of Matt and of me based on Native American spirituality that has helped me understand our differences and also why we complement each other well. This is what Plato said to me: "Elysha, you are a mouse. You are in the grasses, focusing on what is in front of you and seeing all the details. Matt is an eagle. He flies above and sees the big picture." While this was the truest assessment of both of us that I'd ever heard, I couldn't help but note that in life, the eagle eats the mouse.

Whether you are a mouse or an eagle, this book is going to help you. You're going to learn how to make productivity nuggets out of your black holes, and you're going to learn how to have the mindset of a person who gets things done without having your goals hijack all your free time. In these pages, Matt will become a great adviser to you and will tell you funny stories about how he's accomplished his goals. You will learn to eliminate distractions preventing you from meeting your goals and to spot opportunities you may otherwise have missed and then to use them to their fullest potential. This book will inspire you and give you the tools to turn your inspiration into accomplishment.

I'm so excited for you to get started, and I'm rooting for you from the sidelines.

With love,
Elysha

Elysha Dicks is the cofounder, executive director, and host of Speak Up, a Hartford-based storytelling organization, and the cohost of the *Speak Up Storytelling* podcast. She spends her days teaching kindergarten and her evenings being a mom to her son, daughter, and cats. Elysha likes dark roasts, hates cilantro, and can regularly be found strumming her ukulele or baking a challah.

Prologue

A Boy Finds a Future

It starts with hope.

Andy Dufresne in *The Shawshank Redemption* famously said, "Hope is a good thing, maybe the best of things. And no good thing ever dies." It's a fine sentiment, and it may even be true, but I think this one is even better: "No one ever got off their ass without a little bit of hope in their heart."

That one's mine. It's also true.

It starts with hope because if you're reading this book with an eye to transforming your life, making something great, doing better, being more, you need to have a little hope in your heart that it will work. I need you to believe that this time, it will be different. Or different again. I need you to believe that this is the book that you've been waiting for all your life. I need you to believe that today is the first day of the rest of your life.

Clichéd, I know, but it really is a good way to look at life.

Can you do that?

Can you fill your heart with a little hope?

I hope so.

I've experienced a lot of terrible things in my life. Violence and trauma. Homelessness and jail. A trial for a crime I did not commit. Abandonment by a father. A genetic disease that took my mother's life and may one day take my own. The attempt by a small, anonymous band of coworkers to publicly disgrace me and destroy my career and reputation.

More recently, Tom Brady's departure from the New England Patriots.

But of all the struggles in my life, nothing was ever worse than the absence of hope. The stripping away of a future of possibility. The destruction of my dreams. I can remember each of those moments with frightening clarity.

Lying on a greasy tile floor of a McDonald's restaurant, gun pressed to my head, trigger about to be pulled, knowing that my life was about to end and there was nothing I could do about it.

Homeless, living in my car, believing with all my heart that I would never have a real roof over my head again.

Sitting in a jail cell, arrested for a crime I did not commit, feeling like the entire world had turned against me.

These were moments of abject hopelessness. Moments in my life when the light of possibility had winked out. The worst moments of my life.

But I first experienced real hopelessness as a teenager, spending my senior year of high school knowing that after graduation, I would be kicked out of my childhood home and forced to make it on my own. While my friends and classmates were planning for college, counting down the days left in the school year on the chalkboard in Mr. Fury's chemistry lab, I was worried about where I might live and how I might eat. Each shrinking number brought me closer to despair.

I was so frightened about my future that I went to my vice principal, Stephen Chrabaszcz, during the beginning of my senior year, asking if I could do another year of high school, thinking that if I didn't graduate, my parents — my stepfather, really — might not kick me out. Mr. Chrabaszcz told me that he needed a couple of days to find the answer. "No student in the history of education has ever asked that question," he said with a smirk.

Two days later, he called me back to his office. He had checked with state officials. The answer was no. I would have more than enough credits to graduate at the end of the year — nearly enough credits already — and my grades were excellent. "It's time to move on," he said.

Words that felt like the weight of the world on my shoulders.

I left that office wondering why my life was so hard. Wondering why it needed to be so hard. I walked past classmates in the hallway who worried about prom dates and baseball games and college acceptance letters. I was worried about a roof over my head and food on my plate.

Why can't I be like everyone else? I wondered. *Why can't I go to college?*

I still wonder today why I couldn't. While my friends were meeting with guidance counselors, preparing for SATs, and choosing safety schools, I sat quietly in the classroom, waiting for a turn that never came. No parent, no guidance counselor, and no teacher ever spoke the word *college* to me.

Not once.

Eventually I concluded that I wasn't supposed to go to college. Despite my excellent grades and bounty of extracurricular activities, no one saw me as college material. When the world seems hell-bent on avoiding the subject, you start to believe there is a reason. Kids like me — whatever that meant — needed to find a different path.

It was a sad time in my life. Despite my desire to someday write and teach, I thought that all my dreams were about to die at the end of my senior year of high school. My job as manager of a McDonald's restaurant — I was already working full-time while attending high school — would need to be enough for me. Maybe someday I could train McDonald's managers, I thought. Not exactly teaching kids to read and write, but it would be something.

I had no hope that my dreams would ever come true. I felt like my life was over before it even started. I felt hopelessness for the first time, and it was devastating.

Then something miraculous happened. Tiny but miraculous.

Marc Compopiano — my English teacher — introduced me to satire. It was early November, and I was sitting in a class of college-bound seniors, already worried about housing and food after graduation. Already thinking about how much it would cost me to rent a room, feed myself, make a car payment, and pay for gas. Not the thoughts that any high-school senior should be having.

I was a good student, blessed with a love for reading, an insatiable curiosity, and a competitive drive, but when I didn't care about the subject or the assignment, my effort waned, and understandably so. Absent the possibility of college or someone at home checking my report card, my grades didn't mean all that much to me. Nothing I did at school, I thought, would ever have any impact on my future. When I could avoid work that I considered trivial or pointless, I did.

Case in point: Earlier that year, Mr. Compo assigns us a book report. We march down to the school library to choose a novel. I make a beeline for the highest shelf in the farthest corner of the room. On that shelf, I pull down the dustiest book I can find: *Omoo*, by Herman Melville.

I hand it over to Mr. Compo. "I'd like to read this," I say.

"Great," he says, turning the book over in his hands. "I've never read this one before."

Perfect.

I proceed to write a book report on what I might imagine *Omoo* would be about had I taken the time to read it. Since I'm living in pre-internet days, the only way Mr. Compo can determine the veracity of my book report would be to read the novel himself. There is no way of researching the plot of this lesser-known Melville work online, because online as we now know it doesn't yet exist. Just to be sure that he doesn't decide to read the book, I don't return it until after my book report is scored.

I get a B-.

I still have the book report today. It includes comments like "Concise summary, but a few examples are needed" and "No quotations given? Give examples." Thirty-plus years later, I still haven't read *Omoo*.

This is how I manage to navigate much of high school: I find ways to cut corners. I cheat. I scam. I fake a science-fair project and, thanks to some good storytelling about starving Ethiopian children, end up at the state championship at Worcester Polytechnic Institute. I calculate the numerical impact of ignoring an assignment to determine if a two-or-three-point difference on the one-hundred-point scale of my report card is worth the time required to complete the damn thing.

Even when I'm a teenager, my understanding of the value of time is already acute. I play the game well, ingratiating myself to teachers who matter and cheating those who aren't paying attention. But when Mr. Compo explains satire to us, I get excited.

Satire sounds like fun. It sounds like me. Satire affords me the opportunity to cynically, sarcastically attack institutions of power: politicians, world leaders, my stepfather, religion, the school policy on typing papers, the cafeteria menu, and much more. I have permission to attack, denigrate, disparage, and insult the things I despise with absolute impunity.

I quickly go to work. I read Jonathan Swift, Kurt Vonnegut, and George Orwell. I steep myself in the words of Twain and Voltaire. I create lists of potential targets of my satire. Then I sit down and pen what I believe to be one of the greatest pieces of writing in the English language. An absolute masterpiece in my estimation.

I turn in the assignment on November 29, 1988. Three interminable days later, Mr. Compo places that assignment on my desk. Written in red at the top of the page is the grade: B-. Some of his comments include "Some of this is not satire. It's too obvious," "Not satire," and "Still not satire."

I'm outraged. The school district has hired an impostor of a teacher. A fool. An educator who is incapable of recognizing my obvious brilliance. I'm hurt and angry, but mostly I feel unseen. I feel that no matter what I do, no one is willing to look in my direction, acknowledge my existence, and celebrate my efforts.

I can't allow this to stand.

I rise from my seat and charge to the front of the classroom. I'm going to tell Mr. Compo exactly how I feel. Mr. Compo is a short, balding man. These kinds of men tend to come in one of two types: angry or funny.

On this day, Mr. Compo is the angry version of short and bald. Rightfully so, considering how aggressively I launch into my tirade. In seconds, we are arguing with each other at the front of the class. The room goes silent as we point fingers and raise our voices.

I tell him that he's wrong. He wouldn't know satire if it punched him in the face. He tells me that I'm wrong. I think I'm clever, but I'm not. I still have a lot to learn. The back-and-forth continues until finally he says, "Stop!" Then he offers me a deal: "Read your piece to the class. If they agree that it's satire, your B- will become an A-. But if they agree with me that it's not satire — too obvious — then your B- becomes a C-." My very first teaching lesson: raise the stakes on students.

I agree, of course. I wouldn't normally volunteer to read my work to a room full of peers, but this time it's different. This time I have a chance to prove that I'm right. I'm also proud of what I have written.

I take a position at the head of the classroom, and for the first time in my life, I read something that I think is good — words that really mean something to me — to an audience of my peers. I'm about three sentences into the piece when the girl I've had a crush on since sixth grade laughs. Perhaps the most beautiful sound that I have ever heard.

Then another person begins laughing. Then another. Soon the entire class is laughing as I read. It's exhilarating. An incredible feeling. One of the first best feelings of my life. When I'm finished speaking, Mr. Compo steps forward and asks, "Who thinks what Matt has written is satire?"

Every hand goes up. Including Mr. Compo's.

He explains that on the page, the writing does not sound like satire, but I'm so sarcastic and I perform the piece so well that it sounds exactly like satire. He takes the paper from my hand, crosses out the B-, and above it writes A-. I still have that assignment today.

It's the moment that changed my life forever. Three things happened on that day:

1. I made a girl laugh. I made my audience laugh. More than three decades later, that is still one of the reasons why I write and perform. I want to make people laugh. I want to make my wife laugh.

2. I made a teacher look foolish. Mr. Compo told me that my satire was no good, but I had proved him wrong. For a teenage boy, that was an unforgettable moment. It amounted to speaking truth to power. Taking down the man. Knocking the king off his throne. It felt incredible.

3. But most important, I found my first glimmer of hope. I had transferred thoughts from my brain to a sheet of paper, and in reading them aloud and sharing them with an audience, I had changed my future.

Admittedly, the change was infinitesimal. I had turned a B– into an A–. The new grade probably didn't affect my report-card grade for the semester. But for me, that change was enormous. Life altering.

For a boy with almost nothing to look forward to, I had found a way to change things for the better. I could write. I could speak. I could take an idea from my head and share it with other people, and that could alter my future.

Maybe I could do it again.

The next day I opened my first business: writing term papers for my classmates. Fifty dollars for an untyped paper. One hundred for a typed paper. With the money I earned from doing my classmates' work, I bought my first car: a 1978 Chevy Malibu. The car that would take me on my first post-high-school adventures.

I found hope on that day in Mr. Compo's class. For the first time in a long time, I thought that I had a chance at a better life. I was still poor. Still destined to be kicked out of my home when I graduated. Still frightened about where I would live and how I would survive. Still desperately wishing that I could be like a normal high-school kid, bound for college and a bright future.

I didn't have any of that. Luck would never cross my path. It would take me another six years to make it to college, and a full decade would pass after high school before I would graduate from college with degrees in English and teaching. Along the way, I would end up arrested and tried for a crime I didn't commit, homeless, and the victim of a horrific armed robbery that would lead to a lifetime of debilitating PTSD.

But that moment in Mr. Compo's classroom has never left me. I had found something that I liked to do. Something I could do well, at least once and maybe again someday. I had written something, and as a result, I had found hope.

• • •

This is what I want for you: just a smidgen of hope. You're reading this book for a reason. Presumably you want to change or improve some aspect of your life.

Make stuff.

Make more stuff.

Accomplish more.

Make your dreams come true.

Make your dreams come true again.

I'm not sure if I could've accomplished anything without a little hope. If you're having trouble finding hope as you read these words, know this: You're not special. The strategies and ideas and philosophy that I will present in the coming pages have helped many, many people transform their lives. You're no different from any one of them if you have the desire to do great things.

It's not rocket science. I promise. It's not complicated, nor is it difficult. Anyone can do it. Even you.

So put a little hope in your heart and turn the page. It's time to change your life.

Part 1

TIME

"The cost of a thing is the amount of what I will call life which is required to be exchanged for it."

— HENRY DAVID THOREAU

½ The Worst Word

The title of this book is *Someday Is Today*, yet *someday* might be my least favorite word in the English language. It's the word that prevents so many from trying so much. It's the word that results in lament and regret. *Someday* causes people to live small lives filled with wishes and dreams and delay and inaction.

Someday is the word that allows people to wait until it's too late.

Someday is why two of the greatest regrets expressed by people at the end of life (according to hospice workers) are "I wish I'd taken more risks" and "I wish I'd lived my own dream."

Someday is fool's gold. It's a horizon that will never come. A wish never fulfilled.

Let the title of this book be the only time you use the word *someday*. I'm sure you'll be recommending it often, so you'll need to use the word, of course, but only in the context of this book.

Never your life. Okay?

1 The One-Hundred-Year-Old Plan

"Death is not waiting for us at the end of a long road.
Death is always with us, in the marrow of every passing moment.
She is the secret teacher hiding in plain sight,
helping us to discover what matters most."

— FRANK OSTASESKI

It's the spring of 1993. I'm twenty-two years old and homeless.

Not everyone agrees with this label. The guys I've met on the street tell me that because I'm living in my car, I own a roof, and if you own a roof, then you're not homeless.

They've all been on the streets a lot longer than I have, so I take their word for it. Still, I *feel* homeless, though I know it could be much worse. But my car turns out to be very important because I've also been arrested, and I'm awaiting trial for a crime I didn't commit: grand larceny.

More than $7,000 has gone missing from the McDonald's restaurant that I was managing. Even though I didn't steal the money, and even though my boss doesn't think I stole the money, and even though my boss's boss doesn't think I stole the money, I offer to pay the money back because I was responsible for its security. Nevertheless, while reporting the loss for the insurance company, I meet a police officer who is immediately convinced that I am guilty. So after a week of interrogations, intimidation, and a moment in a closet in the basement of the police station when I nearly confess to something I didn't do, I am finally arrested and charged.

During my arraignment I explain to the judge that I don't have a job anymore because I've been arrested. I also don't have a family to support me or savings of any kind. My roommate is moving out of state next month, so I'm about to lose my apartment, too. I'm in a lot of trouble and will need a court-appointed attorney.

But the judge tells me that I'm not entitled to a court-appointed attorney because my car, a 1992 two-door Toyota Tercel that I've made exactly one payment on, is better than his decade-old Chrysler, so I can certainly afford my own attorney. His words.

So I end up on the streets, living in my car, showering at a community college, working odd jobs on construction sites for cash, until Mary and Gerry Coughlin, an older couple who once worked for me at McDonald's, discover my homelessness and convince me to move in with them. Mary and Gerry are born-again Christians with hearts of gold. They offer me a small room off their kitchen — a former pantry — that I share with a guy named Rick, also a born-again Christian, who speaks in tongues in his sleep, and their indoor pet goat.

It was actually the goat's room first, so technically the goat (named Goat) is sharing his room with Rick and me. Goat will chew my hair into a mash at night, stick his tongue in my ear in the morning, and generally make my life a living hell.

But that's okay because at least I have a roof over my head, and with that roof comes a wall, and with that wall, I finally have access to a phone. At last I can apply for some real work.

I'm hired as a teller at South Shore Bank in Randolph, Massachusetts, because employers — even banks — aren't allowed to ask if you've ever been arrested before. They can only ask if you've been convicted of a crime, but since I haven't been convicted yet, I keep my arrest a secret, and then I go to work for the very bank where that missing $7,000 was supposed to end up.

Different branch, of course. I'm not completely crazy.

Officials from the bank will actually testify against me in my trial, not knowing that I am a bank employee until it's revealed to them in court. Then I go to work for McDonald's in the evening. Though the McDonald's Corporation has fired me, the owner of a McDonald's restaurant in Brockton, Massachusetts — a man named Andy Cheung — knows me well, knows I didn't steal any money, and hires me to manage his closing shift. Between the bank and McDonald's, I work ninety hours a week for more than a year to pay off a $25,000 legal bill.

I barely see the goat.

It's a hard, frightening, seemingly hopeless period in my life, but mostly, it's a time when I become consumed with anger. Anger at my parents, who kicked me out of my childhood home and did nothing to support me. Anger at my teachers and guidance counselors, who never put me on the path to college, even though I graduated in the top 10 percent of my class. Anger at myself for the miserable trajectory of my life.

The hardest thing is that with every passing day, I drift further and further from my dream. I'm actually a very good bank teller — already promoted to a customer service representative — and an outstanding restaurant manager, but I don't want to be either of these things. Ever since I was a little boy, I have wanted to be a writer and a teacher. Now my friends are graduating from college, making their dreams come true, while I sleep in a small room with a goat and await a trial that will likely land me in prison.

I have little hope of my dreams ever coming true. I'm twenty-two years old, and I've already ruined my life.

Then something truly terrible happens.

April 23, 1992. Midnight. We've closed the restaurant for the night. I've locked the doors and turned off the golden arches. My employees are cleaning up and prepping for the morning shift. I'm standing by the open safe in the office, packing money into a bank bag so that one of the daytime managers can bring it to the bank the next morning. Ironically, it's another $7,000. I'm stuffing the money into the bag when I hear the sound of shattering glass and I know what's coming.

Two police officers visited me a week before and told me that a team of three men were robbing fast-food restaurants in the area. They had already robbed the McDonald's on the other side of town a month ago and had robbed the Taco Bell right down the street and killed a person in the process. When I hear the shattering of glass, I know that it's them, and I know they are coming for me, so I make the worst decision of my life. I take that bag of money in my hand, reach into the back of the safe, and drop it down the chute that sends it to a compartment at the bottom of the safe that I can't open.

I do it without thinking.

When the masked men enter the office, they force me and my three employees at gunpoint to lie facedown on the red-tiled floor, and they begin to empty the safe. Quickly they realize that something is wrong. There's not enough money in the safe. They throw the cash drawers across the room and begin to curse. A second later, one of them lifts me by the back of my collar, drags me over to the safe, and orders me to open the bottom compartment.

I tell them I don't have a key. I point to the placard that says as much, but he doesn't believe me. The butt end of a gun collides with the back of my head, filling my field of vision with stars. Then the man holding me releases me. I drop to the floor and they begin kicking me, ordering me: "Open the box!"

I curl into a ball, trying to protect myself from their blows, pleading with them to believe me. Then I feel steel press into the back of my head, forcing my face to the tile. "I'm going to count to three, then I'm going to shoot you in the head if you don't open that box."

I beg for them to believe me as they count: "One."

"Two."

"Three."

Then there's the click. The sound of the trigger firing on an empty chamber. The loudest click in the history of the world.

They laugh. I start to crawl away because it's all I can do, but one of them grabs me by the collar again and drags me back to the open safe, and they start to kick me again. Once more I feel a gun press into the back of my head, forcing my face down into a greasy tile floor. Then I hear a voice say that this gun has a bullet, and he's going to count to three, and this time he's going to shoot me in the head. "You're going to die for McDonald's money, so open the goddamn safe!"

As he begins to count, everything changes. I feel the fear and the anger that I have been holding on to for months roll right over to regret and sadness.

I'm twenty-two. I'm lying on a greasy McDonald's floor, and I know that I'm about to die. I am seconds away from my life winking out forever. All I am left thinking about in those final seconds is everything that I have not done.

All the dreams that will die with this bullet.

Wasted time. A wasted life.

Then I hear the click of the gun again. I can no longer breathe. They kick me. Strike me on the head with the butts of their guns. Then they're gone.

For the next two decades I suffer from post-traumatic stress disorder, until my wife tells me I don't need to wake up every night screaming. She tells me that it's not "just my thing," as I describe it. That I can get better. After a year of hemming and hawing, I finally agree to get some help.

$$\cdots$$

Six months after the robbery, I'm found not guilty in a court of law. Six months after that, I pay off that $25,000 legal fee. Six months after that I move out of Mary and Gerry's house.

I say goodbye to the goat.

Six months after that I enroll in my first class at a community college. Unbelievably, the name of the course is On Death and Dying. It wasn't really my choice of class. It just happened to be available on a convenient night.

Five years later, I graduate from Trinity College in Hartford,

Connecticut, with a degree in creative writing. At the same time I graduate from the University of Saint Joseph in West Hartford, Connecticut, with a degree in elementary education. During those five years, I complete two degree programs while managing a McDonald's restaurant full-time, launching a wedding-DJ business, working part-time in the Trinity College Writing Center, and becoming a columnist for the college newspaper. I'm also elected treasurer of the Student Senate and president of the collegiate honor society.

I barely have time to breathe.

In 1999, I become an elementary-school teacher. I've worked at the same school ever since, and for almost all those years in the same classroom. In 2007 I'm named Teacher of the Year for my school district and am a finalist for Connecticut's Teacher of the Year. More importantly, I meet my wife — one classroom door down — while teaching.

Ten years later, in 2009, I publish my first novel, *Something Missing*, with Doubleday.

Since then, I've published six novels and *Storyworthy*, a nonfiction guide to storytelling. My third novel, *Memoirs of an Imaginary Friend*, became an international bestseller.

I make my dreams come true.

Despite those successes, there are enormous parts of me — maybe all of me — still lying on that greasy tile floor. Three decades on, I have yet to pick myself up off it.

It's no exaggeration to say that every morning I wake up consumed by mortal dread that this might be the last day of my life and that, if so, I may feel the same regret and sadness that I felt in the back of that McDonald's so long ago. It's that fear of regret — of not accomplishing enough, not making something of my life, not making something of every day — that has driven me to achieve what I have today. But that is a terrible way to learn this lesson. I do not wish that on anyone.

What I've done, first for myself and later for others, is to harness all the fear and regret that I continue to feel today to create a simple strategy that has changed my life and perhaps will change yours, too.

I call it the One-Hundred-Year-Old Plan.

When I tell others about this strategy, they like to tell me that it's an example of mindfulness or mindset or it's a Zen way of thinking, but I don't want you to think of it as any of these things. And if you, too, end up thinking of this One-Hundred-Year-Old Plan as just another meditative practice to add to your already-exhaustive list of woo-woo practices, I ask you to please toss those notions aside.

You're doing it wrong. Reread. Rethink. Reconsider what you are about to learn.

I don't like amorphous philosophies. I don't like things that I can't hold on to. I despise complexity. What I'm going to suggest is something that you can begin to do the moment you turn this page, and I promise you that if you do, you will change your life. Doing it has changed mine in ways I could never have imagined.

It's this: Whenever I need to make a decision — monumental or minuscule — I no longer rely upon the current version of myself to make that decision. I have discovered that I am an unreliable, ineffective decision maker in the moment, because I often base my decisions upon my feelings, thoughts, and desires in that moment. I do the thing that makes me happy now — which is sometimes perfectly acceptable and advisable — but is oftentimes shortsighted and counterproductive.

Instead, when I need to make a decision, I try to look to the future. I look to the one-hundred-year-old version of myself. The version of myself near the end of his life. The person who understands what it's like to be on the doorstep of death. I look to the Matthew Dicks who is still lying on that greasy tile floor in a Brockton restaurant, and I ask that version of myself to make the decision for me.

What would the version of me on the doorstep of death want me to do? I rely on the perspective of that person rather than the perspective of the person standing here in the now. If I want to live a productive, fulfilling, meaningful life, I cannot simply base my decisions in the moment. If I were to only do the things that make me happy today, then every day would be filled with cheeseburgers, sex, and the New England Patriots.

Rather, I need to look ahead and ask that version of myself—the one who understands the importance and preciousness of time — how I should spend this hour, this day, or this week. He is my trustworthy narrator. He is the one who knows what is best for me.

So when I'm sitting at my desk, trying to finish a novel, staring down an email from my editor asking why my novel is so late, and my son Charlie, age three, tugs on my shirt and asks to play monster freeze tag, the current version of myself says to finish the damn book. *You have a hundred pages to write and bills to pay and an editor to keep happy.*

But then I look ahead to the one-hundred-year-old version of myself, and he says that bills will somehow get paid and you can always find time to finish a book, but that little boy who wants to play monster freeze tag isn't going to ask to play forever. One day he's going to stop asking. One day he's going to stop asking, and you're going to hate yourself for not saying yes to him. So I shove all my work aside, and as much as I hate monster freeze tag — a truly senseless game — I play, knowing I will be a happier person for it.

When my twelve-year-old daughter Clara, who weighs 102 pounds, asks to be picked up and I have a partially torn rotator cuff, I pick her up every time regardless of what I am doing because the one-hundred-year-old version of myself says that someday this kid is either going to be too big to pick up (she already is) or, even worse, she's going to stop asking, and that will be one of the worst days of my life. So no matter where I am, no matter what I am doing, when Clara says, "Pick me up, Daddy," I pick her up, and when I'm one hundred years old, I'll be happy I did it.

When I'm home alone for the weekend, desperate to binge-watch the latest zeitgeist television show, the one-hundred-year-old version of myself says, *You don't get stretches of time like this to yourself very often. Maybe you should write. Or get the guys together for a poker game. Or finally start learning the piano.* The TV show is supposedly great, but when I'm lying in my deathbed, looking back over my life, will I even remember that show? Probably not.

But will I be happy that I finished that book or spent time with friends or finally learned to play John Lennon's "Imagine"? Yes, I will.

• • •

Asking your future self to make decisions allows you to play the long game.

The problem is that we don't play the long game. We don't plan for the future. We think the future is a day, a week, a month, a year. We think the future is ten years.

The one-hundred-year-old version of yourself will tell you that a decade goes by in the blink of an eye. It's nothing. Making decisions based solely on the next ten years is ludicrous when given the expanse of a lifetime.

Yet we often make decisions as if a day, a week, a month, a year, or even a decade is significant. We do it all the time.

When I ask Shep, my New England Patriots season-ticket seatmate, if he plans on attending a Thursday-night game in early December, he pauses for a moment before saying, "Well, it's going to be pretty cold that night. And it's a two-hour drive to the stadium. The game's going to end at midnight, which means we're getting home at two if we're lucky, so I might be in bed by three, and that's going to make the next workday hell. So no, I'll skip that one and watch from home."

Can you believe it? He actually thinks that the next workday is going to be relevant to the rest of his life. He thinks that a single Friday in December will somehow change anything.

The problem is that Shep isn't asking the one-hundred-year-old version of himself if he should go to that game, because my one-hundred-year-old version says, *Go to the game, you fool. Be with your friends. Enjoy the tailgate. Eat massive amounts of meat. Then sit in a frigid stadium with your best friend and watch what might be history in the making take place before your eyes, because someday you won't be able to climb those stadium stairs. Someday you'll be too old to go to that game. Or someday you will be out of friends willing to go with you.*

So when I get asked to go, I go, regardless of how bleary-eyed I may be the next morning, because I'll never remember the next morning. The next morning will become a forgotten footnote in the history of my life. But that night spent with friends and fans, watching a team that I love? Maybe witnessing history in the making? That will be remembered for a long, long time.

I say yes. Every time. We have to play the long game. Our future selves understand the value of time better than any of us. The version of ourselves looking back over the landscape of our lives, staring down oblivion, knows damn well the importance of time.

We say we value time, then we binge-watch Netflix. We say we value time, but then we sit in a Starbucks drive-through line for twenty-five minutes for a cup of coffee. We say we value time, but then we play a video game on our phone for endless hours. We say we value time, and then we promise ourselves that we'll get to that dream someday. We say we value time, but we toss aside minutes like they are disposable.

When we are facing the last seconds of our lives, minutes become precious. The key is to understand their preciousness *today* when there is still time to make those minutes matter.

Here's the truth: I don't think I'll ever be able to pick myself up off that greasy tile floor. I return to it every single day, more often than you would ever believe. Maybe that's not a bad thing. That terrible, violent night in a Brockton McDonald's has brought me here today, with all the blessings of my life.

My hope is that you don't need to lie on a greasy tile floor with a gun pressed to the back of your head to learn this lesson. All you need to do is to stop living for tomorrow or next week or next month or even next year, because a lifetime absent of regret is a lifetime of happiness.

I promise you there is not a person in the world who is lying on their deathbed, wishing they had watched a little more TV or played a few more video games or waited just a little while longer to make their dreams come true. But that is often what we do when we decide how we will spend our time: we trade momentary pleasure for long-term happiness. Steve Jobs once said, "Remembering that I'll be dead soon is the most important tool I've ever encountered to help me make the big choices in life."

My hope is that people can learn this lesson long before they learn about their imminent demise. So make every decision count by looking ahead at the one-hundred-year-old version of yourself and asking that version of yourself for some wisdom and perspective. Stop making decisions for the current version of yourself, and ask your future self what they want from you.

Listen to your most trustworthy narrator.

If you do, I promise that you will be a happier person. You'll be a more successful person. You'll be the kind of person you have always wanted to be.

2 86,400 Seconds

"Life is not lost by dying; life is lost minute by minute,
day by dragging day, in all the thousand, small, uncaring ways."
— STEPHEN VINCENT BENÉT

I'm sitting in a McDonald's restaurant, speaking to a woman who wants to become a novelist. She asked me for a few minutes of my time to pick my brain, and I agreed. She had proposed a local coffee shop, but I don't drink coffee. I've never even tasted the stuff. So I told her to meet me at the McDonald's on the Turnpike. She sounded a little confused by my choice of location but agreed.

We're sitting on stools at the back of the restaurant. She's asking me about literary agents and editors. Book contracts and international sales. Film rights and royalties. I listen carefully and answer her questions, waiting for the right moment to ask my own. A question far more important than any question she has asked me so far.

Finally, I see my opening. "So," I say, "how's the book coming?"

"Oh," she says, looking a little startled. "I haven't really started it yet."

I was afraid of this answer. I saw it coming from a country mile away. "Really?" I say, feigning surprise. "Why not?"

She tells me that the writing process is complicated for her. She finds that she can only write in two-to-three-hour increments at a time, and she really needs to be in the right space to work. A quiet coffee shop or a park bench. Midmorning. Cappuccino at the ready. She hopes to dedicate a year of her life to writing the book, but she wants to understand the publishing world first before beginning.

I nod. I bite my tongue.

"So what's your writing process like?" she asks me.

I have lots of answers to this question. I'd like to remind her that American soldiers in gas masks were squatting in rain-soaked trenches during World War I, scribbling words on pages as bullets and bombs filled the sky overhead. *Your need for a coffee shop, a cappuccino heated perfectly to 154 degrees, and smooth jazz is a joke.*

But I don't say this.

I'd like to tell her that she doesn't actually want to write. She wants to "have written." She's fond of what she imagines the writing life to be — midmorning visits to the coffee shop to splash a few hundred words on the page before enjoying a late lunch with friends — but she's not prepared to do the actual work required to produce something worthy of people's time and money, nor is she passionate enough to engage in the craft in those less-than-ideal moments. *Writers can't help but write,* I want to tell her. *They don't wait to write. They are compelled to write.*

But I don't say this, either. Instead, I say, "You were seven minutes late arriving today."

She opens her mouth to apologize, but I stop her.

"No, it's fine. You've never been here before. That's not my point."

"Then what's your point?" she asks.

"How did I spend those seven minutes?" I ask.

"I don't know," she says. "How?"

"I wrote nine good sentences." I rotate the laptop on the table toward her and point at the new paragraph I've just written. "I also revised the paragraph above it," I say, pointing to the words directly above the new paragraph. "The average novel is somewhere between five thousand and ten thousand sentences. Every sentence that I write gets me closer to the end. Today I got nine sentences closer."

Realization washes over her face. She understands what I'm saying. It's replaced just as quickly by stubbornness. "That probably works if you're in the middle of a book," she says. "But I haven't even started yet."

"Do you think that I started this novel on a sunny Wednesday morning in a coffee shop?" I ask. "Because I'm sure I didn't."

I explain that my best time of day for writing is also midmorning, and that I, too, like to work in blocks of two or three hours at a time. I also have my favorite places to write. It's not a coffee shop, since I don't drink coffee and can't stand the hushed whispers of coffee-shop conversations, but I definitely have preferred places to work, including the joyous cacophony of a busy fast-food restaurant. Unfortunately, I'm often teaching fifth graders during my ideal writing time, so I started this novel, and every one before it, whenever and wherever I could. As soon as the first minute for writing was available to me.

I tell her about how I started my second novel, *Unexpectedly, Milo*, on a Sunday morning years ago. I was sitting at my dining-room table, writing the last chapter of my first book, *Something Missing*. I wrote the final sentence of the final chapter, sighed, then called my wife on the phone to tell her the good news. "I finished it," I told her. "I actually wrote a book."

She congratulated me. Told me that she'd be home in a couple of hours. "We'll celebrate with lunch and ice cream."

I couldn't believe it. I had finished my novel. I pumped my fist with joy. Blasted Springsteen's "No Surrender." Danced around my apartment in a T-shirt and boxer shorts.

My plan was to take a couple of months off from the grind of writing before starting my next book. Recharge my batteries. Rest my brain cells. Find out how to get the book published. I sat in that dining-room chair, staring at the final page of my first book, watching the cursor blink after the final period.

I still couldn't believe it. I had written a book. A good one, too, I thought. I looked at the clock. Still more than an hour before Elysha would arrive home.

"What the hell?" I said aloud. I moved the mouse to the top left side of the screen and clicked *File* then *New document*. At the top of the page, I wrote "Chapter 1" and began.

The start of my next novel.

• • •

I've written eleven books and published nine over the past dozen years because I don't wait for the right moment to write. I don't waste time on preciousness, pretentiousness, and perfection.

Yes, it's true that in the summers, when I'm not teaching, I have much more time to dedicate to writing, but I don't wait for July and August to get to work. I write all year long. I write in the early-morning hours before my kids tumble down the stairs. I write at lunchtime if I don't have any papers to correct or lessons to plan.

I'm actually writing this very sentence on a Friday during my lunch break. I write while waiting for the water to boil for spaghetti. I write while the mechanic changes my oil at Jiffy Lube. I write in the first few minutes of a meeting that has failed to start on time.

Are these ideal times to write? Of course not. But unless you're blessed with a patron who is willing to support your every earthly desire, you need to make the time to write. Even if blessed with a patron, I still might be writing in these cracks of my life. I'm filled with stories and the desire to share as many of them with the world as possible. Why restrict my creative flow to midmornings? Minutes matter. Every single one of them matters.

The problem is that so many of us discount the value of minutes and overestimate the value of an hour or a day or a weekend. We dither away our minutes as if they were useless, assuming that creativity can only happen in increments of an hour or a day or more. What a bunch of hooey.

The one commodity that we all share in equal amounts is time: 1,440 minutes — 86,400 seconds — per day.

I want you to stop thinking about the length of a day in terms of hours and start thinking in terms of minutes. Minutes matter.

People making things — entrepreneurs, artists, writers, musicians, comedians, sculptors, furniture crafters, potters, knitters, gardeners, video-game designers, YouTube creators, podcasters — must utilize these minutes more effectively, because unless you have a patron or a trust fund, you'll probably need to carve out time among life's many other demands in order to pursue your creative passions. At least for a while.

Most creative people are holding down another job (or two or three) while waiting for their passions to pay off. The tragedy is that creative people (and people who dream of being creative) often use their time less effectively than most, and more often than not, they spend their lives waiting for the right moment instead of making the time.

The trick is to utilize your time effectively. To value every minute of the day equally, regardless of how many other minutes are attached to it. Once you have chosen to value every minute, you can begin to create systems by which those precious minutes can be used.

Everyone's life is different, so everyone's particular system will be different. Your areas of opportunity and systems may be very different from mine, but let me take you through some of the systems that I have created for myself that allow me to make maximal use of my time.

Some may apply to you. Some may not. All should give you a clear sense of how to better prioritize your time.

Rule #1: Include the Element of Time as *a Primary Factor* in All Decision-Making

My friend Steve calls me to ask if I've ever eaten pizza from one of New Haven's world-famous pizza places. He's thinking about driving the hour south to give it a try. "Do you recommend it?"

I tell him that Frank Pepe, in New Haven, Connecticut, serves A+ pizza. Some of the very best pizza I've ever eaten.

"Worth the drive?" he asks.

"It's pizza," I tell him. "Even bad pizza is still a solid B, but there is definitely an A or A– pizza within ten minutes of your home."

So I pose this question. Which would you rather have:

- A+ pizza, or
- A– pizza plus one hundred minutes to do as you please?

He orders from Joey Garlic's down the street. Steve understands the value of time.

My wife has different notions about food. She's more than willing to drive an hour or more to try a new ice-cream place on the opposite side of the state, even though ice cream is the same as pizza. Even bad ice cream is still good ice cream.

So we have a choice:

- Excellent ice cream just five minutes from our home
- Mystery ice cream sixty minutes from our home

In my wife's case, we often drive the 120 minutes round trip for ice cream, but I understand this. Elysha spent her childhood driving to her family's second home in the Berkshires every Friday night. Those ninety-minute rides became a staple of her childhood, complete with roadside stops for dinner, lots of music, and memorable family discussions.

For Elysha, long drives represent precious family time, so she wants to repeat those childhood experiences with our children. We listen to Spotify playlists populated with songs chosen by each member of the family. We talk about life, sing aloud, and stop at interesting locations.

For Elysha, an hour or two in the car is quality family time. It's just as important as the actual ice cream. Maybe even more important. But we are making a cognizant choice, factoring in time and deciding that it's well spent. For Steve, the father of three precocious little boys all under the age of five, family time is fishing, playing football in the backyard, and breaking things. Bringing three small boys on a pilgrimage to New Haven for slightly elevated pizza makes no sense. For Steve, time is better spent in the backyard or down by the pond.

In all decisions, we must consider time as a primary factor. That doesn't mean we should make decisions based solely on efficiency, but far too often, we ignore time as a factor when we make them.

Rule #2: Minimize the Time It Takes to Get Places

Consider your commute to work. For the past twenty-three years, I have worked within ten minutes of the school where I teach, and for the past twelve years, I've lived within five minutes of the school. This was not by accident. When choosing a place to live, Elysha and I opted for apartments and eventually a home that were all a short distance from the school, and the commute was a primary factor in our decision-making. Why?

Time matters.

I have colleagues and friends who drive thirty, forty, and sixty minutes one way to our school every day. Imagine the advantage I have over those people in terms of accomplishing goals, spending quality time with my family, and making my dreams come true.

If your commute is thirty minutes and mine is five, I have fifty minutes per day more than you when I'm not sitting in a car. Nearly an hour per day to do stuff while you do nothing.

That's two hundred fifty minutes per week.

Twelve thousand, five hundred minutes per year. Almost nine extra days.

If your commute is an hour, I have an additional nineteen days per year not spent in my car.

Almost three weeks.

This math works, of course, if I were working 250 days per year, which is what most Americans do. As a teacher, I only work 182 days per year (not counting my many other jobs), which makes the math even better for me. But I'll get to that in a moment.

My school day ends at 3:20. My last student leaves the classroom by 3:25. Now that our monthly after-school faculty meetings have gone virtual, I often leave the building at 3:25 and am home and logging onto our meeting at 3:30.

Why?

When I'm sitting in my office at home, I can watch my kids play in the backyard, open mail, and pet my cats. Want to know what makes a meeting on testing protocols a little less mind-numbing? Add kids and cats to the mix. This wasn't an accident. Twelve years ago, when my wife and I were choosing a home, we chose this one, close to our place of employment, forgoing possibly better homes that were farther away.

Why? Time trumps central air-conditioning. Time spent playing with my kids is more valuable than a guest room. The ability to drive home for lunch with my wife when she was home and caring for our infant children was far more important to me than extra closets.

There are people in this world — maybe you — who choose the longer commute and extra closets. There are people who opt for hours in traffic in exchange for air-conditioning. Their one-hundred-year-old self would punch them in the face for this decision.

I've also met people who tell me that they enjoy their commute. It gives them a chance to decompress. Relax. Process the day. I point out to these delusional lunatics that the same thing could be accomplished via a relaxing walk around the block. Or half an hour at the gym or in a yoga studio. Maybe reading a book on the front porch. Napping beneath a tree.

We don't need a commute to find a way to decompress and relax. There are far better ways. Besides, if teleportation was available today, would these people still choose to spend forty-five minutes in traffic, decompressing, in lieu of instantaneous travel to their patio or veranda or bathtub?

Of course not. Plus, if my commute was somehow necessary to

my mental health, I could simply drive around my block a few times. Take a long, scenic ride home. Hop on the highway if I really needed to. Create my own commute.

Does this mean you should work five minutes from your home? If possible, yes, of course. But that might not be possible for you. What I'm asking you to do is factor in the element of time when choosing your living situation. Make the element of time at least as important as the size of the backyard, the square footage of the house, and your need for a two-car garage.

If you're smart, you will make it even more important than these things.

Rule #3: Consider All the Stuff You Didn't Consider When Choosing (or Changing) a Career

Similarly, consider time when choosing your occupation, too. About ten years ago, I considered leaving the teaching profession to become a lawyer. Had I not chosen to become a teacher or a writer, an attorney was next on my list of life's ambitions. I took the LSAT — not knowing that studying for the test was even an option — and scored in the 94th percentile.

I hate to brag (and Elysha really hates it when I brag), but I kicked that LSAT's ass. I was also Connecticut's collegiate debate champion for two years in a row, so logic, reasoning, and argumentation were all in my wheelhouse. I like to think I would've been an excellent attorney had I chosen the law as my life's pursuit.

Or my next life's pursuit. After scoring well on the LSAT, my next step was to speak to attorneys and their spouses about their lives. Many of my questions centered on time. Specifically:

- What time do you arrive in the office each day?
- When do you typically leave?
- How often do you work from home?
- Do you work on the weekends?
- What kind of vacations do you take?

- How much flexibility do you have with your daily, weekly, and yearly schedule?

Asking the spouses when possible was important. They don't sugarcoat anything.

I quickly realized that if I gave up my teaching career, I'd be earning a much higher salary but paying an enormous cost in terms of time.

As a teacher, I work 182 days a year. I get vacations in February and April, from mid-June through the end of August, and in November and December. While most full-time workers spend about 250 days in the office, I work less than three-quarters of that schedule. I arrive at work around 7:45 a.m. every day and leave work before 4:00 p.m. on most days. I rarely work from home and never on the weekends.

Granted, I'm twenty-three years into my career as I write these words, so I've managed to streamline the job quite a bit for myself. I've also been teaching in the same school for all twenty-three of those years, and in the same grade level for the past thirteen years.

I've even occupied the same classroom for more than two decades, thanks to the installation of a stage, curtaining, lighting, and a sound system, all funded through grants. My new principal entered my classroom on his first day, looked around, and said, "So I guess you don't ever move. Huh?"

Exactly. I play the long game.

Earlier in my career, the job admittedly required more hours of work outside the traditional school day, but most teachers — depending on their department and disposition — reach a point when expertise and routines mitigate the long hours spent working at home.

So not only would I be adding seventy days onto each work year, but I'd almost certainly be adding at least two hours to each workday. Nearly one thousand hours of additional time spent working each year.

During my internal debate over whether to remain a teacher or apply to law school, I heard my then principal, Plato Karafelis, say something important: "Teaching," he said, "is a lifestyle choice." You don't make as much money as many professions with similar credentials. You don't collect bonuses or raises of any significance. But you work less, take vacations with your kids, and spend your summers recharging, all while changing the lives of children and their families for the better.

Add in sick days, personal days, an enormous amount of professional freedom, and a pension, and it's not bad at all.

Becoming an attorney would've increased my salary substantially, and I have no doubt that working in the legal profession would've been something that I enjoyed a great deal. But becoming an attorney would've likely limited my other opportunities. Less time to write books, launch companies, perform onstage, consult with executives, produce musicals, officiate weddings, and more.

Less time to spend with my wife and kids after school, on snow days, during the long holiday breaks, and during the summer.

Am I suggesting that you avoid pursuing a legal career? Of course not. An attorney helped keep me out of prison in 1993 when I was arrested and tried for a crime I didn't commit. The world needs attorneys.

I'm merely asking you to factor in time when making a career choice. Know full well what a career demands in terms of hours per day and days per year before committing to that career.

Think carefully about the kind of life you want to live. Don't make a career choice. Make a lifestyle choice. If you're someone who wants to make things — art, music, artisanal bread, pottery, community theater, haiku, or stone walls — think carefully about the time commitment that your future career may demand. If you're someone who hopes to someday grow a peach orchard, launch a pet-grooming business, write the definitive history of Fire Island, restore Harley-Davidson motorcycles, design affordable jet packs, open a karate dojo, or carve totem poles, consider your career choices carefully.

Time and flexibility are essential for people who want to make things.

A few years ago, I considered making the jump from elementary education to teaching high-school English. After spending summers teaching writing and storytelling to high-school and college students in summer camps and university programs, I wondered if this might be my next great adventure. Needing only two courses to become certified to teach the upper grades, I enrolled in evening classes at a local college but also began interviewing high-school English teachers and their spouses about their lives inside and outside the classroom.

What I discovered was terrifying: high-school English teachers spend an enormous amount of time — often on the weekends — reading and grading essays. In many cases, reading and grading poorly written essays.

I liked teaching older students because of the quality and depth of conversations, their level of commitment to the craft, and their ability and willingness to read and discuss great works of literature. It had not occurred to me that I might also spend my days reading poorly written essays by angsty, hyperbolic teenagers who think they understand the world.

One of the spouses of a high-school English teacher said it best: "My wife works six days a week. Five of them are spent in the classroom with her students. One of them is spent at the dining-room table, telling us to keep it down."

This is why I'm still teaching elementary students today. Before making the leap, I calculated the cost in terms of time. That calculation did not add up for me.

Does this mean you shouldn't teach high-school English? Maybe. It sounds pretty awful. Then again, Mr. Compopiano, my high-school English teacher, changed my life. Patrick Sullivan and Jackie Leblanc, my English professors in college, also changed my life. The poet and educator Hugh Ogden, who passed away several years ago, still serves as a mental role model for me today.

I know English teachers who love their job. They can't imagine doing anything else. If that is the case, absolutely become a high-school English teacher.

Just calculate the cost first. Keep in mind that you have options. I've watched the same fate befall school principals. In education, the only way to climb the career ladder is to become more and more distant from children. As a teacher rises to an administrative role, their contact with students evaporates. Simultaneously, the number of hours of work per week and their level of responsibility increase exponentially.

It's a terrible formula. Yes, their salary also increases, but the dollars per hour that a principal earns compared with a teacher is ultimately atrocious. Should you avoid becoming a principal? It depends.

If you're doing it to climb the career ladder, as I've seen so many do, it might be one of the worst ladders to ever consider climbing. But if you're a visionary leader who wants to design and run an organization that will positively influence the lives of children, teachers, and the community and are more than willing to accept the sacrifices required, then go for it.

Just understand the time required before doing so. Understand the cost in terms of student contact, after-school meetings, late-night phone calls, and long summer days spent in a soulless office somewhere, planning and preparing for teachers and students who are sitting on beaches, relaxing and playing.

Rule #4: Maximize Task Efficiency

Years ago, my wife and I were watching the film *The Founder. The Founder* is the story of Ray Kroc, the man who purchased the first McDonald's restaurant from Richard and Maurice McDonald and created the global brand that we know today. There is a scene in *The Founder* where the McDonald brothers design a kitchen that maximizes productivity by establishing routines for all their employees based upon experimentation, design, and practice. It was a symphony of efficiency, repetition, and cooperation.

In the middle of that scene, Elysha paused the movie, turned to me, and asked, "Is this why you are the way you are?"

It had never occurred to me before. "Maybe," I said.

As I've talked about, I managed McDonald's restaurants from the age of sixteen to twenty-eight, eventually putting myself through college while working for a McDonald's a couple of miles from my school. I learned that same ballet of routines first established by the McDonald brothers years before and internalized the value of establishing routines, avoiding needless steps, and maintaining consistency on a day-to-day basis.

In my heyday, I was the fastest person on the grill, producing more burgers per minute than anyone in the restaurant and competing against employees at other restaurants in company-organized Olympic-style head-to-head competitions. I was the fastest on the grill in my region for two straight years. I'm surprisingly proud of this achievement even though no other person has ever cared at all.

I also developed systems in my restaurant for breakfast that allowed me to double the number of Egg McMuffins I could make in an hour. So yes, perhaps I learned about task maximation at McDonald's.

Elysha sees this process in action every day. For example, I empty the dishwasher about 90 percent of the time in my home. Considering how often I complete this task, I decided years ago to determine the fastest way to empty our dishwater, given its location and the location of cabinets, shelves, hooks, and other areas of storage. The goal was to minimize the amount of time needed to do so.

In this particular case, the minutes saved were instantly tangible. I almost always empty the dishwasher in the morning, just before making my children's breakfast. Prior to this, I'm almost always sitting at my dining-room table, working on a book, a blog post, a musical, a comic book, a letter, or something similarly creative. I only stop working when it's time to empty the dishwasher, feed the kids, and head off to work.

If I could shorten the time required to empty that dishwasher, I could continue writing during those minutes saved. So like the McDonald brothers, I experimented. I emptied the machine from top to bottom. I emptied it from bottom to top. I transferred glasses, cups, and mugs directly to the cabinet, and I transferred them to the countertop first before transferring them all into the cabinet. I experimented with the order of plates, bowls, cooking implements, and more.

Each time I tried something new, I timed myself, searching for the most efficient means of emptying the machine and storing its contents.

I know. This sounds crazy. But I empty that dishwasher about five times per week. That's 260 times per year and 3,120 times in the twelve years we've lived in our home. If I could shave even one minute off the process, I could save more than four hours per year. Two full days over the span of twelve years.

Ultimately I found a way that is about two minutes faster than my original method, saving me almost nine hours per year. Almost five full days since we moved into our home. Those are days that I have spent working at my dining-room table instead of fussing with silverware.

I've worked to maximize other frequently completed chores, including folding the laundry, putting away groceries, preparing breakfast, cooking dinner, mopping, sweeping, and more. I invested time up front to determine the fastest way to complete each of these tasks, thus saving myself precious minutes that quickly add up.

I know. This all makes me sound like a crazy person. Elysha loves me, but she, too, finds all this a bit much. But the one-hundred-year-old version of me — who will have spent fewer hours of his life engaged in mundane chores so that he could spend more time making things, playing with his kids, exercising, playing golf, and reading — won't think it's crazy at all. He'll be thankful that I was the lunatic who used a stopwatch to maximize dishwasher-emptying procedures. He'll be grateful that I reduced the number of steps required to prepare my children's breakfast.

And there is always room for improvement.

I took my children to the beach today for the first time this year. Our family belongs to a lake club called Winding Trails, and we spend many of our summer days on that beach. We swim, boat, read, hike, and more. It is our happy place.

I also spend a lot of time playing with my kids in the water. As my children urged me into the water today, pleading with me to hurry, I instead eased myself in slowly, tentatively. Ten minutes later, I was standing in the water up to my waist, marshaling the courage to take the final plunge, when it occurred to me that I had just wasted ten precious minutes that could've been spent playing with my kids.

If I'm eventually going to dive into the water anyway, why not just dive in right away? Why lose ten minutes of playing with my kids while I allow myself to become accustomed to water?

Never again, I declared. *From now on, I will run into the water with the same reckless abandon that my children do.* They seem to understand the value of time when it comes to swimming.

Rule #5: Relinquish and Reassign Tasks

One of the best ways to be more productive is to stop doing other things.

Simple. Right? The less time you spend on a daily chore, the more time you'll have to paint your mural, invent a more affordable version of Dippin' Dots, or write the great American novel.

So whenever possible, I stop doing things that needlessly occupy my time. I slough off responsibilities and expectations whenever possible. I replace meaningless tasks with meaningful endeavors.

You should, too. I've broken down the strategy of task reassignment into three categories: *pay-for-play*, *delegation*, and *dividing and conquering*.

Pay-for-Play

Two years ago my lawn mower broke down. It had been running poorly for more than a year, so I told my wife that I was going to buy a new one.

"Why don't we hire a landscaping company instead?" she asked.

But I wasn't hiring someone to take care of my lawn. I can mow

my own grass. Mulch my own beds. Trim my own bushes. Rake my own leaves. Hiring a landscaping company is akin to the golfers I know who only play if they can ride in a cart.

Sad, weak, and pathetic.

As I write these words, a man is detailing the interior of my car. Vacuuming and shampooing and whatever else a detailer does. I was going to drive down to the car wash yesterday and take care of it myself, but Elysha suggested that she hire someone so I could spend the time writing this book or riding my bike or watching an episode of *The Simpsons* with Charlie.

I balked for a moment, feeling like washing and vacuuming my car wasn't a big deal, and it wasn't. But to do a good job, plus drive to and from the car wash, would probably cost me an hour.

An hour is a long time. I can cover a dozen miles on my bike in an hour. Listen to my son cackle as we watch a couple of episodes of *The Simpsons*. Probably write about one thousand words depending on my flow.

So I agreed. "Okay," I said. "Please hire someone to clean my car." In less than five minutes, Elysha had found someone who happens to be outside right now. Instead of washing and detailing my car yesterday, I went for a long bike ride. Along the way, I watched a mother deer leading two fawns across a field adjacent to a middle school. I saw a friend on Main Street whom I haven't seen since the pandemic began. I exercised. Spent time outdoors. Explored a neighborhood I'd never been to before.

Time damn well spent. As a man details my car today, I write these words. Get closer to finishing this book. Come closer to putting it into your hands.

Money well spent.

I also finally agreed to hire that landscaping company. I haven't mowed a blade of grass or shoveled a spadeful of mulch in more than two years. Not only have I returned precious hours to my life, but my landscaping has never looked so good. I wasn't always in the position to be able to hire a landscaper, but now that I am, why would I not?

Money can be made. Time cannot.

Delegation

Task reassignment need not only mean hiring people to complete your most cumbersome and time-consuming chores. Thanks to my time spent managing McDonald's restaurants, I am a master delegator. My students, for example, famously run much of my classroom. If a task can be completed by a student, it's assigned to a student, who oftentimes does a better job than I could. Not only does this include some of the more mundane tasks, like managing the classroom library, taking daily attendance, and filing papers, but students are also invited to plan and teach lessons, lead class discussions, design and assemble bulletin boards, and prepare assignments and assessments. Students also routinely create online tools for me like Kahoots (game-based quizzes), Spotify playlists, and Google surveys.

They are paid, of course, for their time, via tickets that can be used for weekly drawings. One student is in charge of payroll. Another is in charge of auditing the payroll.

Checks and balances are important.

A few years ago, I realized that I could even outsource the hiring of students for these jobs by hiring a single student to do the hiring for me. Rather than interviewing for every job in the class (more than twenty-five in all), I simply interview for one job — Human Resources Director — and that person hires my employees and negotiates salaries.

My classroom runs like a well-oiled machine, leaving me time to focus on more important tasks like talking to kids, working with small groups, communicating with parents, designing lessons, and spending my lunch breaks working on things like this book.

Not everyone is good at delegation. In fact, very few are. The desire for things to be "just so" often prevents people from doing important work. I've watched teachers spend hours on creating a bulletin board that is temporary, fleeting, and ultimately meaningless. Oftentimes unnoticed unless it contains a spelling error.

No bulletin board has ever changed a child's life or significantly affected their learning profile, but the desire (and sometimes competitive nature) of teachers to have well-appointed classrooms forces their focus on what one of my corporate clients has coined "ten-cent tasks." Simple, visible task completion that doesn't ultimately move the needle on a company's growth, sales, or innovation. Or in the case of a classroom, learning. These are the kinds of tasks often completed by people who like to check off boxes, avoid deep thinking, dodge hard decisions, and disengage from complex work.

What would ultimately be more educationally beneficial to students: an unattractive bulletin board designed and assembled entirely by students that features their work or a beautiful, color-coordinated bulletin board featuring posters and reference material related to the unit being taught?

Students will feel proud of the former. They will need to collaborate and cooperate with peers to get the job done. They will feel ownership of and pride in their work space once it's complete. They will feel nothing about the latter. They may notice the reference material for a day or an hour or a minute, but then it becomes part of the wallpaper of the classroom, irrelevant and meaningless.

Depending on your specific situation, delegation can increase your productivity immensely. Delegating tasks to employees, students, your own children, an assistant, an intern, or even a friend or neighbor can free up time for your creative life.

In addition to delegating my classroom duties to students, I am currently delegating the following work:

- My friend Andrew has been placed in charge of a February golfing trip to Bermuda to celebrate Plato's birthday and (more importantly) his recent survival from open-heart surgery and Covid-19. Andrew has taken control of every detail of the trip. The rest of us trust his judgment and are simply sending him money when needed. When Andrew asks us to review an itinerary or description of the accommodations, I offer a cursory glance and reply with "Looks great!"

It's his job. He's traveled many times. I trust him to take care of business.

- My friend Tony plans and cooks all meals at our Patriots pregame tailgates. I play no role in the menu, accepting whatever he has to offer and passing over my share of the food cost gladly. When Tony sends an email to the attendees of an upcoming tailgate, asking about a menu option, I simply reply, "Whatever you think is best."

I trust Tony to feed me well.

- A husband-and-wife team have taken over the editorial duties of my daily blog posts, sending me typos, grammatical stumbles, and stupid factual blunders. They do this on a voluntary basis, independently of each other, and I could not be more pleased. Between the two of them, I trust that they will find all my mistakes and correct them for me.

So much time is saved and mental bandwidth preserved by simply letting go of the details and decisions and allowing someone else to be in charge.

The reasons why people cannot or will not delegate are varied and unfortunate, but I believe that they come down to the following:

- They possess an unwavering belief in "one right way."
- They cannot accept less than 100 percent of their expectations being met.
- They lack faith in the capacity of others.
- They fail to understand the importance and necessity of autonomy when delegating responsibilities.
- They fail to recognize the value of an initial investment of time in training for the sake of future productivity.
- They do not plan ahead.
- They do not maintain a to-do list (mental or physical).
- They cannot think open-endedly.
- They are ineffective teachers.

- They value process over results.
- They view a reduction in their workload as a threat to their ego or self-worth.
- They fear failure.
- They are overly attached to habit or routine.
- They do not follow up on the people to whom they have delegated responsibilities in productive and inspiring ways.

When you can delegate tasks and let go of the need for things to be "just so," you find yourself with more time to do the things that are important in your life.

The things that really matter.

Dividing and Conquering

Task reassignment also comes into play in our home. As a rule, Elysha and I very much divide and conquer when it comes to household chores and other responsibilities. This means that not only do we assume the responsibility for each task but, more importantly, we don't burden each other with any aspects of those particular responsibilities.

We do the job, say nothing, and move on.

This means that I manage the money in our home, because this is what Elysha has asked of me. She hates dealing with money, so I am happy to take this chore off her hands, though if she asked to assume responsibility for our finances, I'd be more than happy to pass the responsibility over to her.

Since it's my job, I pay the bills, decide upon an investment strategy, allocate money to college funds and retirement accounts, and prepare the taxes each year. Other than signing the occasional form, Elysha knows nothing about any of this process. If I were to ask her how much money is in any of our accounts at the moment (or how much money we have altogether), she would have no idea. Not only do I take on the responsibility for this job, but I don't steal away any of her bandwidth with talk about money. If we have to make a big decision about our finances or solve a serious problem related to money, I'll consult her, but otherwise, I am in charge.

Elysha handles the maintenance and design of our home. She hires and consults with our handyman, electrician, landscaper, house cleaner, exterminator, and painter. She chooses wall colors, purchases furniture, decides upon window treatments and lighting fixtures, and makes all aesthetic choices. She may ask me to sit in a chair to ensure that I think it's comfortable, but when it comes to negotiating with the arborist to take down a tree or determining the orientation of the living room, she handles it all.

She makes the decisions and moves on.

I take care of all things related to camps and sports. I receive the nineteen emails sent every day by Little League coaches who think that the world revolves around baseball. I schedule the summer camps and the soccer, golf, and swim lessons. I purchase all the equipment required to play these sports, and I ensure that all required medical forms are complete.

Elysha manages all the children's doctor and dentist visits. She schedules physicals, fights with the insurance company when necessary, and ensures that my blind, mole-like children have glasses that accommodate their constantly deteriorating eyesight.

I wash, dry, and fold most of the laundry. She purchases the clothing for the children and rotates out items that are too small or too ragged to remain in circulation.

I drive the car. She controls the music. I sweep the floors and empty the dishwasher. She cooks the majority of the meals. I manage the trash and recycling. She changes the cat litter.

Our rule on making the bed is "Last one in the bed makes the bed." I haven't made the bed in more than a decade.

Not only do we divide and conquer, but we do so in accordance with our strengths and preferences. Elysha has never managed money well, nor does she want to be managing it. While I read about finance and economics and listen to financial podcasts almost daily, Elysha couldn't tell you the difference between a stock and bond. It doesn't interest her. Her method for paying bills before I met her was to pay the ones on the top of the pile.

Similarly, I have no sense of aesthetics or interest in design. I would never choose form over function, making our home look like a Soviet-era bunker if I were in charge. Elysha is also incredibly effective at establishing positive relationships with the people who work in our home. She chats with the electrician. Offers our exterminator a drink and cookies. Speaks to our mail carrier like they are old friends. I have no desire to do any of these things, so she does it all.

I like sports. I played them as a child, still play many as an adult, and understand how to navigate the world of lessons, equipment, and practice schedules.

Elysha knows more doctors and dentists than anyone I know. She can get second, third, and fourth opinions inside of an hour. Years ago, I cracked a wisdom tooth and was in so much pain that I was weeping. An hour later, I was standing in the kitchen of a dentist's home as he wrote me a prescription for painkillers. He was in his pajamas.

Systems like the ones Elysha and I have established afford me the time to make things. While I concern myself with our finances, it's also a topic of interest for me. I like doing it, and my knowledge of the stock market, industry leaders, market strategies, and more has been enormously helpful to me when consulting with corporations. This is a task that makes sense for me to do. I like it, and it's proved very beneficial.

Conversely, I never give a thought to my children's physicals or dentist appointments. I don't worry about haircuts or if Charlie's pants are getting too small. Walls are painted in my home without my knowledge. A new faucet appears in our kitchen sink as if by magic. A patch of burned grass is reseeded without me even noticing that it was needed.

In a perfect world, I would hire someone to do every chore so I could focus on my writing, my performing, my consulting, my comedy, and more.

That is impossible. Perhaps someday when a wealthy patron

chooses to fund my every need, I can sit back and allow other human beings to run my life. Until then, I can ensure that tasks are clearly delineated based upon skill and preference. Elysha and I can avoid burdening each other with the bandwidth required to report on these responsibilities.

We take care of business so we can take care of business.

Rule #6: Choose How to Spend Your Time

During my second year at Manchester Community College, I had to decide if I wanted to accept the position of president of my college's national honor society. I was already taking six classes per semester, while managing a McDonald's restaurant full-time. I was also working in the college's writing center part-time, competing on the debate team, writing a column for the school newspaper, and serving as treasurer of the Student Senate. I had launched my mobile DJ company as well and was working at weddings and anniversary parties nearly every weekend.

My plate was overflowing. I could no longer see my plate.

Unsure about what to do, I found myself wondering what advice my father might offer. My friends often turned to parents in times of uncertainty, but I didn't have that option. My mother was chronically ill, and I didn't know my father, so instead of turning to my real father, I tried to imagine what he might advise me if he were still in my life.

I tried to imagine what I might tell my own son someday. The words came to my mind almost instantly: "People who do great things don't wait until the time is right. They make the time."

I like that a lot. Admittedly the quote originates from me, but it's still pretty good. And my imaginary father was right. At least partially so. None of us can make time, but we can protect and preserve the time we've been given by always treating it as our most precious commodity and ensuring that time is factored into every single decision we make.

I ultimately took the position of president of Phi Theta Kappa honor society. It was a big job with a lot of responsibility. I immediately delegated much of that responsibility to members of the society who were looking to inflate their résumés and lend a hand. Folks with much more room on their plates. They gained valuable experience, and I managed to maintain my GPA and keep my life from falling apart. Eventually my work with Phi Theta Kappa helped me to be named as a *USA Today* Academic All-American in 1996. That honor and the recognition that it brought led to unsolicited scholarship offers from several colleges, including Yale University, Wesleyan University, and Trinity College. I ultimately accepted the offer from Trinity, choosing the school closest to the McDonald's where I worked (because I was factoring in commute time even back then), where I earned my degree in English. For free.

Good advice from a father I never had.

Remember: When you say you don't have enough time, you're actually saying that there are other things more important to you. On your list of priorities, other items were higher on the list than the thing you didn't have time to complete.

"I didn't have enough time" actually means it wasn't important enough to you.

"I didn't have enough time" means it wasn't fun, distracting, profitable, gratifying, pleasurable, or urgent enough to place it at the top of your to-do list.

This isn't necessarily bad. It's perfectly acceptable to say that you don't have enough time to do something, especially if you're prioritizing properly. If spending time with your children or volunteering at an animal shelter or cheering for the New England Patriots is keeping you from making your dreams come true that day, I get it. But if binge-watching Netflix or scrolling social media or shopping in half a dozen grocery stores (topics I will address in just a moment) is keeping you from launching that Etsy store or composing your symphony or writing that screenplay, then "I don't have enough time" is no good.

You have the time for the important things just as soon as you push the less important things down your list of priorities. Remember that time is simply a matter of choice and allocation. Almost everyone is blessed with a certain amount of free time each day. This time should be viewed as the most precious commodity we possess. More important than the money in our bank accounts or the things we own.

Choose how you spend that time more carefully than anything else in your life. It is the most important choice that you make every day. Don't allow things like television and social media or mindless movement to fill the time, as it does for so many.

"I didn't have enough time" often means that you didn't make thoughtful choices about how to spend your time and allowed your nondecisions to determine the course of your life.

Here's another quote that I like:

"You can get a lot done in two hours." — Judy Blume

I agree with Judy Blume. You can accomplish a lot in 120 minutes. In the right hands, with the right attitude, mindset, and plan, two hours is an enormous amount of time.

I'd like to offer a slightly different spin on Judy's quote:

"You can get a lot done in ten minutes." — Matthew Dicks

I'm not kidding. Ten minutes is also an enormous amount of time. I can get a lot done in the stray ten-minute blocks of time that seem to fill my day.

The ten minutes before dinner is ready.

The ten minutes it takes for my son to find his shoes every day.

The ten minutes spent sitting in the drive-through line.

The ten minutes spent waiting for the dryer cycle to finish.

The ten minutes of waiting before it's my turn in the shower.

The ten minutes of a meeting that do not pertain to me.

The ten minutes in the line at the pharmacy.

Little chunks of time that are often assumed to be useless. Precious time wasted and discarded rather than thoughtfully and strategically put to use.

In just ten minutes, I can:

- write eight to ten good sentences.
- empty the dishwasher.
- fold a load of laundry.
- edit a blog post.
- do three sets of push-ups and sit-ups.
- eat a bowl of cereal.
- hug and kiss my wife, tell her I love her, then kiss her again.
- make a cat purr.
- tickle my son.
- stare up into a tree.
- read five to fifteen pages.
- correct twenty spelling tests.
- take a shower and get dressed.
- reply to one to three email messages.
- listen to an episode of *The Memory Palace* or *This Day in Esoteric Political History*.
- write one to two possibly funny jokes.
- do three to five planks.
- listen to two to three songs of a reasonable length or "American Pie."
- pay bills.
- transfer the recycling to the outdoor bin.
- write a letter to a friend, colleague, teacher of my children, or my children.
- fill the bird feeder.
- clean my children's detritus out of the back seat of Elysha's car.

This isn't a joke.

These are all things that I do when I find myself with a stray ten minutes, and all are enormously productive, even though some might not seem so. But listening to music, making a cat purr, and staring into a tree all improve my mood. In fact, it's been scientifically proved that listening to music, spending time with a pet, and staring into a tree substantially reduce stress, yet so often people plod through life, failing to use the time they are given to care for their mental well-being.

Making my cats purr makes me so happy. Listening to Springsteen or Queen or the Beatles fills me with energy and joy. Lying down beneath a tree and looking up into its branches brings me so much peace.

Judy Blume is correct. You can accomplish great things in two hours. But don't discount the ten-minute increments, either. You may not be able to accomplish anything especially great, but pile up enough productive ten-minute bits of time in a day and you can get a hell of a lot done.

Take a moment and make your own list of things you can accomplish in ten minutes. Be sure to include chores, tasks that can move you forward creatively, and things that will make you feel good. Post that list in a few places around your house. Have it ready for the next time you find yourself with ten minutes to kill.

Don't kill the ten minutes. Seize control of them. Make them work for you.

• • •

I hope I've made my point that in addition to these larger lifestyle decisions, there are also a multitude of smaller, more granular decisions that can easily recapture time. The mistake that people make is in failing to recognize the value of smaller quantities of minutes saved, in terms of how these minutes, when combined with others, begin to add up and quickly amount to meaningful chunks of time over the span of weeks, months, and years.

In fact, it's in the small decisions that you can gain your greatest edge. While so many people discount the value of a minute unless it's attached to fifty-nine other minutes, you can be someone who takes advantage of these small decisions to maximize your productivity.

Rule #7: Minimize Time Spent on Routine Tasks and Fruitless Pastimes

Here are some of the places where I recapture time every day. Again, these are decisions that fit my life and my lifestyle. I'm not suggesting that these particular decisions should be your own. Some might be completely adaptable to your life (and I think you should at least consider each one), but there are likely others that fit your lifestyle that I cannot begin to imagine. These are presented as a means of demonstrating the kinds of places where time can be saved but, more importantly, the kind of thinking required to recapture time in your life.

Food

My lunch, almost every single day, is oatmeal. Unless I'm enjoying the occasional meal with a colleague, I choose to eat my lunch in a way that allows me to continue working so I can exit my school shortly after the final bell rings.

Oatmeal is an excellent choice for me because it takes two minutes to cook and about three minutes to eat. I can eat it on the go. It's remarkably filling. Best of all, it may save my life.

Five years ago, my doctor warned me that my cholesterol was slightly elevated. She told me that I might need to begin taking medication to lower it to safer levels. "Or," she said, "you could change your diet." She gave me a list of foods that would lower my cholesterol. Oatmeal was on the list. So I simply shifted my lunch to oatmeal. Every single day for an entire year.

When I returned the following year for my annual physical, my doctor was astounded to discover that I lowered my bad cholesterol by forty points.

"How did you do it?" she asked.

"Oatmeal," I said. "Every day."

I didn't change any other part of my diet, nor did I alter my exercise regime. One small change made the difference.

Not only has oatmeal allowed me to recapture precious minutes in my day, but it will likely keep me off medication and healthier for years to come. Am I telling you to eat oatmeal for lunch every day? Of course not.

If you eat lunch with colleagues and the time spent makes you happy or relieves stress or strengthens and expands your professional network, by all means take an hour for lunch every day. But factor in time when making that decision. Are you a person who never has enough time in your workday? Are you constantly missing your children? Do you value dinner with your spouse? Do you have no room in your day to exercise? Are your creative endeavors stalled because of a lack of time? If so, perhaps that lunch hour could be better spent.

I like my colleagues a lot. Well, some of them, at least. But my one-hundred-year-old self would tell me to work through lunch whenever possible because the additional time spent at home with my wife and children or the time spent working on a novel or writing a musical or building my business is far more important than time spent chatting with coworkers in the lunchroom. In fact, I'm writing these words while sitting at my desk, eating oatmeal.

My general philosophy on food is this: If I'm dining with others, I am more than willing to spend hours of my life on a single meal. Whether I am eating dinner with my family at our dining-room table or enjoying a night out with friends, I believe the time spent sharing a meal is valuable and worth every minute. But if I'm eating alone, which is most of my breakfasts and many of my lunches during the workweek, I try to either spend as little time as possible on the preparation and eating of that meal or do something while eating. If possible, both.

Multitasking has been proved by research to be a misnomer in many instances. Effectively engaging in two or more deep-thinking tasks simultaneously is not possible or, if possible, is entirely inefficient and will produce subpar work. But there are things in which multitasking is legitimately possible and even advisable. Eating is one of these things.

Showering

I like a long, hot shower as much as anyone, but on his deathbed, my one-hundred-year-old self will not be wishing that I'd spent more time in the shower, so I have one of three goals every time I enter the shower:

- Complete it in one hundred seconds.
- Memorize a poem.
- Work on a story.

My most frequent goal is to shower and shave in one hundred seconds or less. When this is the goal, I count aloud and attempt to exit the shower before reaching one hundred. It took a while, but I can now consistently finish in under a hundred seconds.

The CDC says the average American shower lasts eight minutes. Why the Centers for Disease Control is monitoring the shower usage of the average American is beyond me, but if I'm showering for six fewer minutes than the average American, I'm adding an extra six minutes to my day, every day.

That's an extra 36.5 hours over the course of a year. An extra day and a half to accomplish my goals while other people are naked and soapy.

Admittedly I have a lot less hair on the top of my head than someone like my wife (and probably you), and I've never felt the need to shave my legs, but I shave my face, which can be tricky given an unfortunate scar on my chin. But even if the length of your hair and other factors prevent you from getting your shower under one hundred seconds, you can probably reduce the length by half by adopting a greater sense of urgency. Why not recapture that time for more meaningful pursuits?

Besides, nothing good comes from a shower that goes on any longer than necessary. Not only does it waste precious time, but it also costs money, wastes precious natural resources, and contributes to climate change. Also, in the words of my twelve-year-old daughter, "Taking a shower is boring!"

I agree.

On those rare occasions when I decide to relax and spend a few extra minutes in the shower, I get work done as the warm water pours down on me. Oftentimes, I'm memorizing a poem by either reciting one I already know (so the poem is never forgotten) or practicing specific stanzas of one that I am currently working on. Memorizing poetry was something I learned to do in Hugh Ogden's poetry class in college, and I've found the process to be enormously gratifying. Committing a poem to memory is like planting a new seed in your brain that can flower whenever you'd like.

When not memorizing poetry, I'm spending the time working on a story for the stage by speaking it aloud as I shampoo, shave, and soap. As I write these works, I'm working on a solo show that I hope to perform in a year or so. Whenever I step under the water, I either start my solo show from the beginning, pick it up where I left off, or revise.

On the subject of showers and productivity, I also recommend cold showers except before sleep. Or, much more doable, spend the last thirty to sixty seconds of your shower in cold water. The benefits are surprisingly enormous and backed by science, according to Chris Gayomali, writing for *Fast Company* and quoted in a 2016 piece in *Inc.* magazine: "'A 2007 study published by a molecular biologist named Nikolai Shevchuk found evidence that cold showers can help treat depression symptoms, and, if used regularly, might even be more effective than prescription antidepressants,' he writes. How is that possible? In layperson's terms 'cold water can flood the mood-regulating areas of your brain with happy, sparkly neurotransmitters.'"

The experience, disagreeable as may sound, reduces tension and improves mood and memory. And aside from these biological changes, a frigid dip in the morning also has powerful effects on your psychology, according to a *New York Times* piece by Carl Richards praising morning cold showers. Getting into a freezing shower is undeniably hard, he writes, but if you can make yourself do that, what else could possibly daunt you for the rest of the day?

After more than two years of standing in frigid water for a minute or more at a time at the end of every shower, here is what I can say about this practice: I think it works. I step out of every shower with more energy and alertness than ever before. Rather than feeling warm and relaxed, I feel alert and alive. I feel like I've accomplished something. I'm moving faster, and I feel more energized and excited about whatever is next.

This feeling is echoed by Brian Tracy in his book on productivity *Eat that Frog!*: "Starting your morning by tackling challenges head-on will help encourage similar behavior throughout the day. And, it turns out, there's a wealth of research to back up this idea as well. People who do hard things first tend to procrastinate less and get more done."

It's unpleasant, to be sure, but over time, as it becomes a habit, the unpleasantness decreases significantly. By the end of the first month, it was just another thing that I did. And if I've just finished forty-five minutes on the exercise bike, a lukewarm or downright cold shower is just the thing I need to cool down.

If I'm being honest, I can't say whether this practice is increasing my productivity throughout the day. There is no way for me to measure the lasting effects of this cold shower, and since I take some of my showers in the evening, just before bed, I may not be enjoying the full benefit of the practice. But I know that after sixty seconds under the cold water, I exit the shower with a spring in my step and a sharpness of mind, and I like that a lot.

Give it a try.

Incidentally, I also floss in the shower. I began doing this almost twenty years ago when I learned that flossing adds years to your life by preventing gum and heart disease, thus also making it a time-preservation habit. Preserving time at the end of your life is just as important as preserving time now. In an effort to avoid skipping flossing, I transferred this task to the shower, rationalizing that I'd always be more than willing to spend thirty extra seconds in the shower flossing. It worked. I've flossed almost every day for the past two decades.

Years ago, I spent a weekend in Santa Cruz, California, talking about writing, trying like hell to inspire my audience to begin writing. Six months later, I received an email from someone who attended my talk. She wrote: "I'm writing almost every day now, but the real life changer was the tip on flossing in the shower. You mentioned it during the Q&A, and I started doing it that night. I haven't missed a day of flossing since then, and I just had the best dentist appointment of my life."

I went to California to inspire people to write. Somehow I managed to inspire flossing as well.

Speaking of teeth, I also practice balancing while brushing my teeth by standing on one foot for the first minute of brushing and the other foot for the second minute. A reader suggested this to me, pointing out that we never spend enough time practicing and improving our sense of balance, which turns out to be very important as we get older and more fragile. Falls are the second leading cause of unintentional-injury deaths worldwide. My favorite author, Kurt Vonnegut, died from a fall.

After just a week of brushing and balancing, I found myself improving exponentially. Brushing and balancing. More effective multitasking at work.

Shopping

Years ago, I was sitting beside a recent immigrant from Denmark at a storytelling competition in New York. After I finished performing, we struck up a conversation during intermission. I asked her what she liked best about America, and she didn't hesitate in answering: "Stop & Shop."

"The grocery store?" I asked. "Why?"

She explained that in Denmark, grocery shopping was a half-day affair, requiring separate trips to the butcher, the baker, the fishmonger, the greengrocer, and more. "Grocery shopping steals away half your Saturday in Denmark," she said. "You Americans put it all under one roof. It takes me less than an hour to shop for the whole week!"

It's true. In fact, Stop & Shop is the only grocery store where I shop, chosen specifically because it has an enormous selection and is only five minutes from my home. Contrast this to my friends (and sometimes my wife), who purchase their prepared foods at Trader Joe's, their fish at Whole Foods, produce and shelf staples at Stop & Shop, chicken and beef at Stew Leonard's, bulk items at Costco, and more. There are thirty-two grocery stores within a five-mile radius of my home, and it seems as if some of my friends have made it their mission to shop in every single one.

I know people who purchase their olive oil from a shop in town *that only sells olive oil.* I'm sure that the olive oil from the specialty olive-oil store is fantastic, but is it really one-hour-per-month fantastic? More importantly, if I were to conduct a taste test between the olive oil at the specialty olive-oil store and the olive oil sold at Stop & Shop, are you confident that you could tell the difference? Would you bet me a week's paycheck that you could tell the difference?

I'm also sure that the fish at Whole Foods is incredibly fresh, but is it one-hour-per-week fresh? The cuts of meat at our local butcher are probably terrific, but are they twenty-minutes-per-week terrific? Probably not. Not to mention the butcher once hit on Elysha.

All this time adds up. It adds up quickly and profoundly, as my Danish friend knew all too well. I shop for groceries in one store. I know the layout of the store like the back of my hand. I know where every item is located. I know which aisles to skip and which freezer cases to ignore. The average American spends 65.6 minutes per week shopping for food, or about 56 hours per year. More than two full days spent wandering the aisles of grocery stores.

My record time for a full week of shopping is twenty-two minutes. I probably average a little under thirty minutes. If you were to see me shop, you'd notice that I move quickly. I work from a list on my phone — inputted throughout the week via an app and our Amazon Echo — and, as I mentioned, I know where nearly everything I'm purchasing is located.

I don't mess around. I shop only early in the morning when the store is less crowded, thus reducing my time further. Still, I spend about one day per year shopping for food, which is way too much. I only get 365 days every year. Spending one of them shopping for food is a terrible waste of time. In fact, I may eventually switch to delivery if it can save me more time. But I'm still doing better than the average American by more than half. And a hell of a lot better than the Danes.

Apply this philosophy to all your shopping needs. Choose stores that are well stocked and close to home. Set up automatic deliveries whenever possible. Order in bulk whenever possible to reduce the number of trips you need to make. Order online when it makes sense. And seriously ask yourself if the marginal improvement in quality is worth the time required to acquire that marginal improvement.

In a blind taste test, could you even tell the difference? For me, the answer is almost always no.

Price Chasing

My wife's friend extols the virtues of a plant nursery in Southwick, Massachusetts. "Amazing prices," her friend says.

"Maybe we should check it out?" Elysha suggests.

Then I tell my geographically challenged wife that Southwick is nearly an hour from our home. *In another state.* By contrast, there are at least three nurseries less than ten minutes from our house. The prices may be better in Southwick, but are they 120 minutes better? Of course not.

After being educated in the geography of our state and the surrounding regions, Elysha wisely decides that the local nurseries are just fine. But think about it: her friend is driving two hours to a nursery to save some money. Unless she is saving an enormous amount of money and has time to spare, it's almost impossible to justify such a trip.

Yet people do this all the time. Often these are the same people who consistently complain that weekends are too short and there are never enough hours in a day. When you drive two hours to purchase a begonia, I'm not surprised.

The same holds true for gas prices. There is a Citgo station about fifteen minutes from our home that consistently boasts the lowest prices in the state. Always at least ten cents cheaper than any other gas station in the area. As a result, people will drive for miles for the excellent price, frequently creating long lines at the pumps, thus extending the time spent purchasing fuel even more.

But the gas tank of the average American automobile holds twelve gallons, meaning the savings on a full tank of gas between this Citgo station and the other gas stations in the area is about $1.20. Nevertheless, my neighbor will drive past three other gas stations on the way to this particular gas station to save $1.20.

This same person will spend three dollars on a cup of coffee at Starbucks and wait fifteen minutes in the drive-through in order to avoid exiting the car. This is a person who does not value their time appropriately. If you happen to be driving by the cheapest gas in town and have enough room in the tank to warrant a stop, then by all means fill it up. Save a buck. But going out of your way to save less than two dollars? Stupidity.

My wife recently contacted our painter, asking whether we could hire her to assist in hanging our artwork and photographs now that the walls are painted. Not only can she hang these items well, but she also has an eye for design and helps Elysha make good aesthetic decisions. The painter proposed that in lieu of payment, we barter: her services in exchange for my coaching on a story she wants to tell.

Elysha thought this was a great deal. I did not. I explained that I can always earn more money, but I can never find more time. "It's money I have," I told her. "It's time that I need."

Elysha made the faulty assumption that I value money over time. She believed that saving us money by offering a couple of hours of my time was a good idea. But I know the value of time. I value it properly. I'd rather cut the painter a check and continue the pursuit of my dreams.

Similarly, we recently had our broken NordicTrack exercise bike replaced. Truthfully, it's being set up by two NordicTrack employees as I write these words, which is probably why I mention it here. Elysha asked me if the crew setting up the new machine was removing the old one. I wasn't sure. "But I'll pay them a couple hundred dollars to take it away if they're not."

Elysha scoffed at this idea, but the alternative was probably an endless series of phone calls and another two- to four-hour window spent at home, waiting for a truck to arrive. It's worth at least $100 to me if they would take it away. It weighs 350 pounds. I don't own a truck. I wouldn't know where to dispose of it if I did. My time is too valuable to be spent haggling with the NordicTrack company to take away a machine that they should've replaced six months ago.

It turns out a different company is responsible for removing the old bike. Still, I offered the two men setting up the new bike $150 to take away the old one. They declined. They probably value their time as much as I do. With seven more machines to set up today, $150 for disposing of a broken bike didn't make sense.

Does all this mean you should never hunt for a good deal? Of course not. When making big-ticket purchases like homes, cars, furniture, and vacations, price shopping can sometimes save you thousands of dollars. When the savings are large, the time invested makes sense.

You may also need to hunt for the lowest price if money is scarce. When I was kicked out of my childhood home after graduating from high school, my friends and I spent days hunting down secondhand furniture for our apartment. We scoured discount outlets for items like plates, glasses, and silverware. We earned very little from our fast-food and warehouse jobs, so we spent our time clipping coupons, chasing down sale prices, and pinching pennies whenever possible.

When all you have is pennies, pinching is important. Later on in life, when I was homeless, saving every penny became even more important. Just remember: When buying things, time and money are a trade-off. If you're low on money, you should probably spend more time chasing better prices. But if the bills are paid and you're looking to build or create or invent, stop investing your most precious commodity — time — in saving small amounts of money. Chasing the lower price rarely makes sense when you value your time properly, yet people do it routinely.

Don't be one of those people.

Walter Hickey — author of *Numlock News*, a daily newsletter that I read and adore — wrote in June 2021:

> A new survey found that 49 percent of adults would prefer an ad-supported but cheaper version of a streaming platform compared to an ad-free but slightly more expensive version. Meanwhile, 22 percent were able to answer the question correctly and realized that time is the only thing that money cannot buy, [saying] they would prefer the latter. Millennials were the ones who answered the question the least wrong, with a record high of 31 percent of the generation agreeing an ad-free but slightly higher priced offering was preferable to the alternative, compared to 26 percent of Gen Z, 19 percent of Gen X and 14 percent of Boomers.

I loved this. Hickey gets it, too. Time is almost always more valuable than money.

He got me thinking: When I was a kid, before television programs could be streamed or even recorded, I watched thirty-minute sitcoms that contained only twenty-two minutes of actual content, and I watched hour-long dramas that contained only about forty-four minutes of content. Just think of all the time I wasted watching commercials. I'm afraid to even begin adding it up. The number would be staggering.

Some may say that the time wasn't wasted. I probably chatted with family members during commercials. Discussed characters and plot. Used the bathroom. Grabbed a drink. But they are just like those who defend the benefits of a commute. They are justifiers: lunatics who justify their wasteful actions by delusionally claiming that their waste is actually want. But no one is stopping them from pausing their program to chat or pee. They can simulate as many commercial breaks as they'd like.

In all things, it's better to have choice over how you control your time. If you want commercial breaks or commutes, then enjoy. But isn't it better to be able to decide when and how you want those things to happen rather than allowing what's forced on you and beyond your control to dictate your schedule?

Of course it is.

Television

On our first date, Elysha and I were sitting on my uncomfortable futon, deep in meaningful conversation, when she said, "It's six. Do you mind if we watch *The Simpsons*?"

I should've married her right there.

Elysha and I like television a lot. We almost never watch a show independently of each other, and we are strong, vocal supporters of shows like *Buffy the Vampire Slayer*, *Battlestar Galactica*, *Game of Thrones*, and Marvel's latest offerings. As artsy and sophisticated as she may be, Elysha is a bit of a nerd, too. Despite all this love for television, we watch an average of about five hours of TV per week, not because we don't want to watch more, and not because we are television snobs, but because we both know that there are more meaningful endeavors in our lives.

In lieu of watching more television, Elysha practices her ukulele. She reads. She tends to her plants. She cohosts our storytelling podcast. She helps run our storytelling company. She chats on the phone with friends and family. She exercises.

You already know what I do. Despite the fact that we love television and would like to watch more, we know that a life spent in front of the television is not a life well spent.

How much television do you watch in a day?

How much do you watch in a week?

The average American watches *five hours of television per day*. More than thirty-five hours of television per week. In the words of Elysha, "That's like having another full-time job!"

If you're watching thirty-five hours of television per week, and I'm watching just five, is it surprising that I might seem excessively productive to you?

Am I asking you to stop watching television? Of course not. I haven't stopped. Elysha and I are currently rewatching *The Simpsons* with our son Charlie, beginning with season one, episode one. It's almost more entertaining to listen to Charlie cackle than to watch the show itself. I'm currently rewatching *The Office* in order to listen to a podcast hosted by two of the show's stars as they discuss the behind-the-scenes adventures of each episode.

Elysha and I just finished watching Marvel's *Loki*. We're currently watching comedy specials in small chunks. We enjoy television. We purchased a state-of-the-art television and sound system and had them professionally mounted to the wall. We love TV. But what I'm asking is for you to calculate the number of hours per week you spend in front of the television and decide whether that number is right for you.

How would the one-hundred-year-old version of yourself feel about your television habits? Will that future version of yourself be pleased by the amount of time spent watching television? Could you watch less TV and get closer to making your dreams come true?

Many of my friends have insisted that I watch the show *Dexter*. They are sure that I will love it. Apparently the plot of the show resembles that of one of my novels, except my book is less murdery. Another friend desperately wants me to watch *Friday Night Lights*. Knowing my love for football, he's sure I will love this show. Perhaps I'll eventually get to it. But here's what I know: On my deathbed, I will not be lamenting the absence of *Dexter* in my life. I won't be bemoaning my failure to watch *Friday Night Lights*. No one has ever regretted not spending more time watching television.

As Teal Burrell wrote in the *Washington Post* back in 2017: "Americans are obsessed with television, spending an average of five hours a day pointing ourselves at it even as we complain we're busier than ever." Watching television is not only a terrible way to achieve my goals, but too much television is destructive in so many ways. Burrell's *Washington Post* piece also reports: "People who watch more television are generally unhappier, heavier and worse sleepers, and have a higher risk of death over a defined length of time."

Avoiding television is not hard. Simply don't turn the damn thing on. Don't allow it to become the background noise of your life. Don't make it the default means of spending time because you have no other way to fill the hours. Find something else to fill the hours. The list of possibilities is endless. Read a book. Play a board game. Learn to play guitar. Knit. Write letters to friends. Learn to bake. Take a walk. Garden. Paint. Sculpt. Reupholster your couch. Call your grandmother. Start a side hustle. Exercise. Volunteer on a suicide-prevention hotline. Meditate. Breed rabbits. Have more sex. Memorize poetry. Dance naked in your living room.

Live life. Make your dreams come true. Do the things that drew you to this book.

When you're old and decrepit and staring death in the face, I promise you that the evenings spent dancing naked in your living room and hours spent on the phone counseling suicidal teenagers will be more important to you than finishing *The Wire* or finding out if Bad Guy #625 will be sent to jail at the end of *Law & Order*.

Live a richer and more real life than the people you watch on television. Watch television. Love television. Just watch less television.

Social Media

Even worse than television is social media. According to Statista, the average American spent 145 minutes per day on social media in 2019, which amounts to more than a month per year. (That number exploded to 230 minutes per day in 2020, thanks in great part to the pandemic.) Think about it: nearly 10 percent of an average American's year is now spent staring at a phone or computer screen for things other than work, reading, writing, researching, and playing video games.

They are simply scrolling through social media: photos, videos, and the short text-based bursts of other human beings. Where did that time come from? What did we do before social media was born? Weren't we just as busy in 2006 when Facebook, Twitter, Instagram, and TikTok didn't exist for most of us?

If you are using social media on a consistent basis, it has replaced something in your life, and it's probably not a good trade-off.

Is all social media bad? Of course not. I manage to stay connected to friends and family via social media in ways I never could do so before. I've built my readership and my brand through social media. I've made important contacts and honest-to-goodness friends by engaging in social media. My carefully curated Twitter feed provides much of my day-to-day news.

But boy am I careful about how much time I spend on those platforms. I also know this: every moment spent on social media today will be irrelevant and forgotten three days later. Social media is temporary, oftentimes meaningless moments of mild satisfaction that will ultimately yield nothing. Unless you're using social media to earn a living, drive traffic to something more meaningful, build a brand, or effect real change in the world, you should ask yourself what social media is doing for you.

Likes are ultimately worth nothing.

Mentions are meaningless.

Retweets will soon be yesterday's news.

For most people, social media does not yield much by way of real productivity.

I have three friends who do not use social media of any kind. All three are highly successful, exceptionally happy human beings. I mention this because it's possible to not use social media and be a functioning member of society.

Am I suggesting you follow this path? No. But if you're trying to make something of value, launch a business, or expand your creative life, you may want to consider it.

I have. Many times. In the end, social media has value for me, but I limit my use to only those things of value and aggressively limit my time.

You should, too.

Walking

I know it sounds simple and stupid, but if you want to be more productive, walk fast.

I advise this knowing that for some people, walking fast is impossible. My friend Beth has multiple sclerosis and relies on a walker to get around. My friend Ron requires a cane. For four months of my life, my leg was in an ankle-to-hip cast.

This won't work for everyone, but if you're capable of walking quickly, walk quickly. I am often teased by colleagues because I walk down the halls at breakneck speeds. It's assumed by many that I am incredibly busy, and while this may be true, my decision to walk fast is a conscious one that I make in order to recapture time.

I walk fast whenever possible. Parking lots, grocery stores, sidewalks, and malls are great places to walk fast and recapture time, but there are many, many more. If you see me in any of these places, you will probably see me moving faster than the people around me. Not only does the increased speed provide me with an elevated heart rate and a tiny bit of exercise, but I simply get places sooner than everyone else. Almost every day, I park my car and walk past people who are sauntering through the parking lot as if it were adorned with fine art.

As if a parking lot was the place to be.

Do I save much time in the process? Over the course of a day, a week, a month, or a lifetime, the answer is yes. Absolutely. The amount of time I save in each parking lot, hallway, and grocery store is minimal, but it adds up quickly.

Walking fast is not something that comes naturally to me. I must constantly remind myself to walk faster. It's easy to stroll. It's normal to adopt the speed of those around you. It's even a little awkward to be passing people as if we are on a racetrack.

But it saves me time.

It gets me back to the places where I want to be.

It gets me back to the people with whom I want to spend my time.

Five or ten extra minutes with my children are a gift. Don't discount these precious few minutes for the sake of conformity or ease. If you truly understand the value of time, you'll want to preserve every single minute possible.

3 Sleep Correctly

"I'm so good at sleeping that I can do it with my eyes closed."

— Unknown

For years, people who know me well have assumed that I accomplish a lot because I don't sleep very much. Mistakenly, I allowed this belief to take hold. It was an easy answer, and it's true. I don't sleep as much as most people. This was a mistake for three reasons:

1. It's obviously not the only reason I accomplish a lot (the previous chapter hopefully demonstrated this).
2. Sleep is incredibly important to a healthy, creative mind and body, so to imply that sleeping very little is my secret to success is a terrible and inaccurate message to send to the world.
3. Most importantly, perpetuating this myth fails to help people in the pursuit of their dreams.

If you assume that I possess some superhuman ability to sleep fewer hours than most people, then how can you expect to replicate my level of productivity and accomplishment? Either you'll feel defeated before you even begin, or you'll start to sleep less when doing so may be unhealthy and counterproductive to achieving your goals.

So here is the reality: I spend fewer hours in bed than most people, and I may even sleep fewer hours than most people, but far more important than both of these things, I treat sleep seriously and sacredly. I have yet to meet someone who does the same.

This is ironic, because I hate to sleep. Lying down and entering a state of intentional unconsciousness is akin to temporary death for me. Rather than writing a musical, watching Pixar's latest offering, eating a cheeseburger, reading the memoir of a favorite comedian, riding the exercise bike, practicing the piano, or playing *Exploding Kittens* with my children, my stupid body requires me to stop everything at least once per day so I can spend way too much time in a state of nonproductive helplessness.

All the things that make life worth living are left behind so I can close my eyes and cease to exist on a conscious level.

I hate it so much.

That said, I know that sleep is necessary. It's a vital part of a healthy lifestyle and critical to functioning properly both physically and mentally.

It's awful but needed. Kind of like stupid vegetables.

So I treat sleep reverently. Most people do not. I'll venture to say that you probably do not.

This is not to say that some people don't suffer from challenging, debilitating, soul-crushing sleep disorders that make it nearly impossible for them to sleep well. I am certainly not implying that every person on Earth can improve their sleep through some simple but important changes in their habits, but if *you* can (and I believe the vast majority of people can), just imagine the benefits.

I go to bed sometime between 11:00 and 11:30 p.m. and awake sometime between 4:00 and 4:30 a.m. I average about 5.5 hours of sleep per night. The average American averages almost 7.5 hours of sleep per night. This means that I am gaining two hours every day on the average American. More than half a day over the course of a week. More than thirty days over the course of a year. One month of additional time per year when I am awake and the average American is asleep.

The advantage is enormous.

Please understand: I'm not proposing that you sleep 5.5 hours per night. For me, this is enough sleep. Anyone who knows me well would tell you that I almost never appear sleepy, sluggish, or worn-out. I am energetic until the moment I go to bed, and I pop out of bed with the same energy and enthusiasm. Part of this may be genetics. My brother and sister are also famously short sleepers.

But if you can shorten the time you spend in bed every night by even fifteen minutes, that would result in more than ninety additional hours spent every year awake.

Nearly four days.

Again, I'm not asking you to simply start sleeping less. But I'll bet that if you begin treating sleep as sacredly as it deserves to be treated, you can likely recapture fifteen minutes or more every night. My proposal is that you begin by increasing your efficiency of sleep. If you're forced to lie down and render yourself unconscious at least once every day, you should try to do it in the shortest, most restful way possible.

Of course, you may love sleep. The thought of spending fewer minutes in bed may sound like blasphemy to you. You may think of sleep in the same way I think about golf or sex or cheeseburgers. If that's the case, by all means, sleep. Enjoy your lengthy period of unconsciousness. As long as you have sufficient time to paint your canvas, invent the better mousetrap, compose your rap album, or harvest your new apple varietal, sleep as much as you'd like.

But also ask yourself if that is what your one-hundred-year-old self wants you to do. If you think that end-of-your-life version of yourself is pleased with the amount of time you're spending in bed, good for you. Sleep all you want.

But I suspect that the one-hundred-year-old version of yourself — the one preparing for an eternal dirt nap — might want you to do more with the time you have left. Don't you?

If you're looking for more time in your day to do your thing, make your stuff, invent your doodad, and be creative, then efficiency of sleep is often the place to find it.

At least some of it.

So let's talk about sleep and, more specifically, what you need to do in order to improve its quality and shorten its duration.

What Is Sleep?

It seems like a silly question, but the truth is this: most people confuse the amount of sleep they require with the amount of time they spend in bed, when these two numbers almost never correlate.

In order to understand the difference between these two numbers, answer these questions:

- How much time passes between the moment you lie down in bed and the moment you fall asleep?
- Do you read, watch television, use your phone, or do anything else in bed prior to going to sleep?
- Do you fall asleep quickly, or do you toss and turn?
- Do you wake up in the middle of the night with any regularity?
- When you awaken in the morning, how long do you linger in bed in a state of wakefulness or partial wakefulness before starting your day?

I recently asked a client these questions in order to determine her attitude and habits toward sleep. She informed me that she needs at least eight hours of sleep every night to feel healthy and refreshed. I had no qualms about this number if this were the truth, but here's the thing: it wasn't.

My client's reported eight hours of sleep actually represented the amount of time she spent in bed every night. These eight hours included:

- at least twenty to thirty minutes of reading or watching television in bed before turning out the lights. Sometimes much more.
- fifteen to twenty minutes of tossing and turning before falling asleep.
- at least fifteen minutes every morning spent lying in bed after the alarm had awoken her.

By this math, my client only needs about seven hours of actual sleep every night, and she might need even less if she treated sleep sacredly, which she most decidedly does not.

Save an hour a night, and you'll save 365 hours over the course of the year. More than fifteen days of your life suddenly recaptured.

So how much sleep are you actually getting every night? Is there a difference between the amount of time you spend in bed and the amount of time you spend sleeping? If so, how much sleep do you really need? Have you been counting time spent in bed but not sleeping as required sleep time?

If so, your math, like my client's math, is way off.

The goal of sleep is to sleep. Not to spend time in bed fiddling around before and after sleep. Efficiency of sleep attempts to minimize the amount of time spent in bed when you are not sleeping. This is time easily recaptured for better use.

Treating Sleep Sacredly

The steps to improving your sleep are simple and critical, but they will likely demand a change of routine.

None should be skipped. This should not be treated like a buffet of strategies. Every one of them is critical.

Adopt a Sleep Schedule

Go to bed and wake up at approximately the same time every day without exception. It is critical to establishing a permanent bedtime and wake-up time.

Weekends, vacations, and holidays should not cause drastic changes in your sleep schedule. You should be going to sleep and rising from bed at approximately the same time every day, 365 days a year, regardless of the circumstances.

Sadly, most people don't maintain regular sleep schedules. The time when they go to bed and the time when they wake up vary widely on a day-to-day basis. They'll extend their bedtime by an hour or more to watch one more episode of the TV show they are currently bingeing or go to bed an hour earlier than normal because they are feeling sluggish when what they probably could've used was a little exercise instead. Most people also alter their sleep schedule on the weekends, either shifting their sleep in order to go to bed and wake up later than normal or simply sleeping in on Saturday and Sunday mornings.

None of this is good. In fact, it's enormously detrimental to your sleep and is harmful to your long-term health.

Get yourself on a regular sleep schedule.

The goal of a consistent sleep schedule is for your body to learn when it's time to sleep and when it's time to wake up. You can't train your body to be aware of your sleeping and waking times if you're constantly altering your sleep schedule.

I've just begun my summer vacation from teaching. Two glorious months when I need not leave for school every morning, yet I am still awakening sometime between 4:30 and 4:45 a.m. because this is how I have trained my body. To alter my sleep schedule on weekends or while I'm on summer vacation would be a terrible mistake.

This is because your body needs to know when to begin the physical process of falling asleep, which ideally starts about two hours before actual sleep begins when melatonin is released into your bloodstream, making you begin to feel drowsy. If you assign your body two different sleep schedules — a workweek and a weekend schedule — then you have no sleep schedule. Your body is perpetually confused.

There is a saying in football that if your team has two quarterbacks, it doesn't have a quarterback. Same rule applies to sleep schedules.

One or none.

I am so rigorous in my sleep schedule that if I'm performing in New York City or officiating a wedding or attending a performance of *The Rocky Horror Picture Show* that keeps me out until midnight or later, I will still get out of bed the next morning before 5:00. I'd rather be tired the next day than be confusing my body any more than necessary.

My schedule is so consistent that when my daughter was four years old, she asked me why mommies need to sleep but daddies do not, because she had never seen me in bed. I was always awake before she ever opened her eyes and always in bed well after she was asleep.

The benefits of a consistent sleep schedule are huge:

- You will fall asleep faster by training your body to prepare for sleep at the same time every day. I fall asleep less than one minute after my head hits the pillow every single night without exaggeration or exception, and while there are many reasons for this that I will discuss, one of them is that my body expects to fall asleep sometime between 11:00 and 11:30 every night and is well prepared for sleep when I crawl under the covers.

- You will begin to awaken naturally every morning, oftentimes without the assistance of an alarm clock. I set an alarm for 4:45 every morning just in case I don't wake up before then, but as I write these words, I've now gone thirty-two consecutive days where I've awakened naturally before the alarm has fired off. This morning I awoke at 4:44.

Why is this important?

Awakening naturally is a much healthier and far better start to your day. Rather than being shocked out of sleep by an alarm, I awaken slowly, the way my body was designed to awaken. By the time I open my eyes to begin my day, I feel well rested and ready to go.

Truthfully, I feel great.

When was the last time you awoke naturally at the time you wanted to awaken? For me, it happens about 85 percent of the time. If my alarm does go off, I am almost always in the process of awakening, so even then, I feel well rested and ready to go.

Most people awaken bleary-eyed and half-asleep because their brains have not been trained to release the chemicals necessary to stimulate the mind and body and begin the physical processes required to awaken naturally. Their bodies are often fully engaged in sleep when their alarm startles them awake, making the process confusing, unnatural, and unappealing.

Most people hate waking up in the morning. This is often simply because of the way they wake up. These are the same people who don't understand how I can possess the energy and focus to write before the sun has risen.

I can do so because my body and brain are primed to go. I am awake, alert, energetic, and feeling good. I don't drink coffee (as I said earlier, I've never even tasted it) and don't require caffeine or any other stimulant to achieve a greater state of alertness. I simply adhere to a sleep schedule that takes advantage of the way my body and brain naturally operate.

You can, too.

Remember That the Purpose of a Bed Is Sleep

If you are reading, watching television, looking at your phone, or doing anything else in bed prior to sleep, stop now. Doing so is a perfect way to ruin sleep.

You're essentially sabotaging your sleep.

Just like we train our bodies and brains to sleep on a schedule, we must also train our bodies and brains to know that when we lie down in bed, there is but one purpose: sleep.

As soon as you introduce a book, the television, or the phone to your bed, you've now trained your brain that sleep is one of several things you do while in bed. This is not good. It is likely to prevent you from falling asleep and entering deep sleep as quickly, and it will almost certainly increase the amount of time spent in bed.

Eliminate all these things from your bedtime ritual immediately. Common complaints:

"But I love reading before bed. It makes me sleepy." First, establish a regular sleep schedule. That, too, will make you sleepy and will do so naturally, absent the need for complex subplots and realistic dialogue.

Also, read before bed if you'd like. No problem at all. Not on an electronic device, of course — the light from an iPad, laptop, or phone will wreak havoc on your ability to quickly fall asleep and sleep well, so make sure that you're reading an actual book or an e-reader without a backlight — but read in a cozy chair or on the sofa. In a bean-bag chair. On a kitchen stool. On a park bench. Under the dining-room table.

Just never in bed.

"But I can't sleep without the television on in the background." Once again, establish a regular sleep schedule. That will help you fall asleep naturally absent the unnaturally attractive actors and multitude of commercials for erectile-dysfunction cures and personal-injury attorneys.

Also, your belief that you can't sleep without the television in the background is silly nonsense. Are you telling me that when the power goes out in a storm, you don't sleep? Are you telling me that if you go camping in a tent, you won't sleep?

Back in October 2011, Connecticut was struck by a winter storm when many of the leaves were still on the trees. The weight of the snow on those leaves brought thousands of trees and limbs crashing to the ground, dragging power lines with them. Most of the residents in the Hartford area were without power for ten days or more. In fact, Elysha and I were some of the only people in the area who still had power, so our home became a hub for laundry, device charging, and food preparation for those in need.

Did those "I must watch TV in order to fall asleep" folks go ten days without sleep?

Of course not.

Watching television in bed trains your brain to think of your bed as a sofa, which is why you can't fall asleep without the TV in the first place. You simply fell into an unhealthy habit at some point that requires correction in order to vastly improve your sleep. Train your body and brain to think of your bed as only a bed, and the need for the television will evaporate and more restful sleep will take its place.

Play White Noise

If you're not using white noise while you sleep, you're not even trying. Even if you sleep well, you should give white noise a try. Elysha and I play white noise via our Amazon Echo, but white-noise machines can be purchased, too.

White noise serves two important functions:

1. **Providing a unique auditory cue to trigger the brain to fall asleep.** Just like you can train your body to fall asleep at a consistent time, you can also train it to do so upon hearing a specific sound. For me, that sound is actual white noise: the hissing of gentle, consistent static. But sounds like ocean surf, a babbling brook, wind through a sea of grass, or anything else gentle and consistent will work.

2. **Increasing your chances of sleeping through the night by masking any sounds that might awaken you.** If you frequently awaken in the middle of the night, there is a reason. Perhaps you need to pee (and therefore need to drink less before bed). You may be between the two cycles that characterize the sleep of most people. Or maybe a neighborhood dog barked. A helicopter flew over your house. Your partner coughed. Your house creaked. You often won't know what has awakened you, but it likely was a sound. And white

noise drowns out most sounds, allowing you to remain asleep and thus increasing your sleep efficiency.

Relax

Anxiety and stress are sleep killers. They will keep you tossing and turning all night long. My wife loves to talk about the stresses of the day just as my head hits the pillow. Unfortunately for her, I am always asleep less than a minute later, leaving her to toss and turn on her own.

The ability to relax before bed is critical to falling asleep quickly. If your mind is plagued with worries and concerns or your body is filled with tension, sleep will be difficult. But there are ways to relax both your mind and body prior to sleep that will greatly assist your ability to fall asleep quickly.

They include:

Meditation. I've spent the past ten years practicing meditation every morning for ten to fifteen minutes.

This statement itself is astounding. I am not a spiritual person. I am not earthy-crunchy in any way. I don't practice yoga because there is no scoring. No winners or losers. I love cheeseburgers, confrontation, and contact sports. I miss my childhood days of fistfights, rock fights, and an old-fashioned game of slapsies or knuckles.

Meditation does not fit my brand.

As a result, I initially thought meditation was nonsense, but someone I know and trust insisted that I give it a fair shake, and I'm so happy I did. Within a year, I was able to clear my mind of all worries and concerns and enter a state of empty bliss. I've gotten so good at meditation that I can now meditate at almost any time, which also allows me to take a refreshing ten-minute nap in the middle of the day if the need arises. I accomplished all this without the benefit of the many meditation apps available today.

The message here: If I can do this, you can, too. And you should.

I have met so many people — my wife included — who tell me that they can't sleep at night because of the worries and stresses of the day. But there is a solution. It's not a magic pill or a mystical bracelet. It's meditation. It will take time and practice, but the benefits, both for sleeping and for the rest of your life, are amazing.

Relieving tension. I struggled with sleep when I was young. The worries and fears associated with a childhood absent of parental support caused me to feel constant stress as a kid. I was oftentimes hungry, had to bum rides from other adults, and was desperately trying to keep my brothers and sisters out of trouble.

I mentioned this to my music teacher, Russ Arnold, one day when he said that I looked tense during a flute lesson. He told me to locate the places in my body where I held my stress so I could relax those places before sleep — also to practice before the next flute lesson. It turned out that I hold my stress in my jaw and my hands. When I relaxed those parts of my body, it not only helped me sleep but made me a slightly better flute player, too.

So every night, as I place my head on the pillow, I purposefully release the tension in my jaw and hands, where it still resides today. Once that tension is released and my mind is emptied thanks to meditation, sleep comes almost instantly.

Find the places where you hold your stress by starting at your toes and moving up your body, relaxing each part slowly and deliberately. Eventually you will find a place where it's either difficult to relax or incredibly relieving when you do so. Release the tension from these places and sleep will likely come sooner.

Warm water. I'm not suggesting you take a bath, because I'm fundamentally opposed to baths. They consume an enormous amount of time, and to paraphrase Cosmo Kramer, a bath is disgusting. You sit in a tepid pool of your own filth.

I suggest a warm shower before bed if you're struggling to sleep, but if you prefer a bath, go right ahead.

The point is this: Water temperature has an impact on your state of alertness. Warm water relaxes the body and brain, which makes a hot shower a terrible way to start your day but a great way to end it.

Exercise

I know it sounds strange, but exercise will vastly improve your sleep. Even a brisk walk at some point during the day will improve the efficiency of your sleep. Research has repeatedly shown that moderate-to-vigorous exercise can increase sleep quality for adults by reducing the time to onset of sleep. Exercise is also an outstanding reliever of stress — which, as you know, will help you sleep better.

There are few things in life that can improve the quality of your life more than exercise. Skipping it is a dreadful mistake.

Forgo the Snooze Alarm

Never use a snooze alarm. The snooze alarm is one of the worst things ever invented and should be eliminated from this earth immediately after nuclear weapons and green-bean casserole.

My friend Jeff recently told me that he unintentionally fell back asleep one morning for fifteen minutes and never felt right for the rest of the day. This is because he allowed his body to enter a new sleep cycle, then abruptly interrupted that cycle to start his day.

This is terrible for your brain and body.

The snooze button operates on the idiotic belief that startling yourself awake twice in a ten-to-fifteen-minute period is a good idea.

It's not.

The snooze button operates on the idiotic belief that an extra ten minutes spent in bed after being awakened is somehow useful.

It's also not.

End the use of the snooze button immediately. When your alarm fires off or, even better, when you awaken naturally, leap out of bed. Get your ass moving. Start your day with vim and vigor.

I'm not sure what "vim" is, but you get the point.

Set an Optimal Room Temperature

Sleep in a cool room, with a temperature of 65°F if possible. Oddly enough, there are scientific reasons why a room temperature of around 65°F is optimal for sleep. This relates to your body's internal temperature regulation.

Your body's internal temperature shifts throughout the day. This is known as your circadian rhythm. Your body begins to lower its internal temperature around the time you go to bed and continues to cool down until reaching its low point near daybreak.

Your body accomplishes this cooling process by expanding the blood vessels in your skin. When your temperature starts to drop at night, you may notice that your hands and feet get warmer. This is because your body is letting heat escape through them to reduce your core temperature.

If the temperature in your sleeping environment is too hot or cold, this can affect the drop in your body's internal temperature and cause you to have disrupted sleep.

Look at Your Lighting

Sleep in a dark room, especially if the sun will rise before you plan to wake. Install blackout curtains if necessary. You don't want your last hour or two of sleep to be spent in a loungy, less-than-restful snooze because the sun is peeking into your bedroom.

Sleep or don't sleep. Nothing in between.

If you're using your laptop or device after the sun has set, install an app called f.lux on your machines. Free and compatible with Mac and PC, f.lux makes the color of your computer's display adapt to the time of day, mimicking a warm, indoor light at night and sunlight during the day. Tell f.lux what kind of lighting you have, where you live, and your typical sleep pattern, and it will do the rest.

Elysha complains that my screen looks like a yellow-brown smudge by the end of the night. True, but I never complain about struggling to fall asleep. Which is more important?

Sadly, f.lux also has a "sleep in on weekends" setting for people who don't understand how to treat sleep appropriately. Never use this inane feature.

Can You Sleep Less?

A few years ago, my friend and colleague Erica came to me looking for advice. She had recently given birth to her third daughter — all three are named after US presidents (I'll let you guess which presidents, but two were assassinated and one was shot) — and was struggling to find time for herself. She wasn't accomplishing all that she wanted in life. She was aware of my level of productivity and asked if I could offer some suggestions.

My first was this: "Try waking up one hour earlier."

She balked, insisting that she needed that sleep.

"Maybe," I said. "But why not just give it a try?" I suggested that she try using the extra hour to exercise or read or meditate or whatever else she needed to do. Just try. I told her that I believe in the importance of adequate sleep and take it very seriously, so if waking up an hour early doesn't work, that's fine. "At least you gave it a shot."

Three weeks later, she popped her head into my classroom to tell me that the extra hour she had been spending in the morning by herself — exercising, eating breakfast, and generally taking care of herself — had changed her life. After a couple of weeks, she had discovered that an hour of exercise and self-care was more important than an hour of sleep. She felt better sleeping a little less and doing a little more.

Am I suggesting that you simply shave an hour of sleep off your day? No. I think you should first implement all the strategies I've outlined above. Treat sleep sacredly. Increase your sleep efficiency in order to shorten the amount of time spent in bed and promote more deep and restful sleep.

But after all that, maybe you can experiment with sleep, too. Maybe shave off thirty minutes or an hour of sleep every day and see what happens. If you convert that lost sleep into exercise, a healthier diet, meditation, or the pursuit of your creative endeavors, you might discover what Erica did: maybe you don't need to sleep quite as much as you once thought.

While writing this book, I asked Erica if she was still rising an hour earlier than before. She texted this back:

> *Since I started working out at home, that is when I work out. So yes. The ripple effect is that it gives me more time with my family after work because I am not going to the gym from 4:00 to 5:00 and not getting home until 5:30 every day. Also, it gives me time if I need to catch up on work. I can stay at school and do the work instead of bringing it home, because I am not rushing to the 4:00 class at the gym.*

Ripple effect. I like that phrase a lot.

See how one hour can quite literally change a life?

Erica, a CrossFit enthusiast, recently launched her own creative endeavor: a personal coaching business, helping people manage their diet, exercise regime, and mental health. It's something she's been working on for a while, and now it's finally happening for her.

That extra hour is probably paying dividends in that regard, too.

My friend Bill recently quoted something that I apparently say often enough to be quoted: "You can sleep eight hours a night and not write a book, or you can sleep seven hours a night and become an author." It's true. If you wake up one hour earlier than you currently do and spend that time writing, you'll have yourself a book in a year or two.

Sleep less?

Maybe.

Sleep correctly? Sleep efficiently?

Absolutely.

• • •

Here's the craziest thing about my recent colonoscopy: I could not stay awake for it.

After climbing onto the gurney and being covered by a warm blanket, I was left alone for about ten minutes. When the nurse arrived to administer an IV and ask me lots of questions, I was asleep. She awoke me, and we proceeded with her questionnaire.

When she left, I was alone again for another ten minutes. When the anesthesiologist arrived to review my medical history, I was asleep again. He had to wake me up before proceeding with the review.

When he left, I was alone for about half an hour before a nurse arrived to roll me into the room where the procedure would take place. She found me asleep, too. She awoke me, and we were off.

In the room where the procedure was to take place, I fell asleep *again* while waiting for final preparations to be made. A nurse had to awaken me so she could put me back to sleep. She commented that she never had to awaken a patient before administering the medicine that would put the patient back to sleep.

"You really like to sleep," one of the nurses said. "Huh?"

"No," I said. "I actually hate sleep."

I've simply spent years training my body and mind to fall asleep in bed almost instantly. I do this at home. I do this in hotels. I can do this almost anywhere when I want to take a ten-minute nap.

My persistent sleepwalking is admittedly less than ideal, but this problem has plagued me since childhood and doesn't seem to be going away anytime soon. I often awaken in places other than my bed, and many times I awaken to find myself eating a bowl of cereal, engaged in a conversation with Elysha, getting dressed for work, or sitting on the couch watching a blank TV screen.

I once approved emergency spinal surgery on my dog when my vet called in the middle of the night. Though Elysha and I had a short but serious discussion about the thousands of dollars we would spend on an uncertain outcome, I have no recollection of that conversation, nor the decision, because I was still asleep. Thankfully the surgery was a success, and my dog went on to live for many years.

I once wrote five hundred words of a novel while I was sleeping, and they were good enough to leave in the book. Multitasking at its best.

But other than these occasional nocturnal adventures, sleep is something I can do with ease. It's something I treat sacredly. It's something I strive to do efficiently. It's something that my body falls into without much effort. Even in the midst of a colonoscopy.

I want the same for you.

4 The Eagle and the Mouse

"People are frugal in guarding their personal property;
but as soon as it comes to squandering time they are most
wasteful of the one thing in which it is right to be stingy."

— SENECA

Years ago, before children, life insurance, and window treatments, Elysha and I worked in the same school. It's where we met and fell in love.

Actually, I fell in love first. It took Elysha a lot longer to come around. Eventually, we began dating and were married. Then one day during the first year of our marriage, Elysha stopped our principal, Plato Karafelis, in the hallway to complain about me.

No joke.

Her complaint was this: The previous evening, she and I had sat down together to work on report cards. In less than two hours, I had completed all twenty-one of my report cards while simultaneously winning $400 in online poker (back when that was legal in the United States) and listening to an audiobook. In that same amount of time, Elysha had completed just two report cards and had accomplished nothing more.

"It's really annoying," she told Plato. "I don't know how to live with him." This was her complaint, about her newlywed husband, lodged with our boss.

Plato's advice was this: The traditional Native American spirit wheel is inhabited by four animals, including the eagle and the mouse. At their core, Plato explained, the eagle soars above the fray, seeing the larger picture and totality of the terrain. The mouse, by contrast, is close to the ground, hidden in the weeds, seeing the tiny but important aspects of life.

Neither position on the spirit wheel is good or bad. Neither is better than the other. The purpose of life is to ultimately inhabit all parts of this spirit wheel. Be an eagle when seeing the larger picture is advantageous, and be a mouse when the details matter most.

"Matt is an eagle," Plato explained to Elysha. "He flies above and sees the big picture. He knows where his effort is best directed. He gets things done by knowing what needs to be done and what can be avoided. You, by contrast, are the mouse. You see every little detail. You care about every detail. You invest yourself in every little detail, and details are also important."

Elysha listened, pondered, and then said, "But eagles eat mice!"

The advice didn't exactly change anything in our relationship, and thankfully, it didn't damage my career in any way, but it helped Elysha understand me better, and when she told me about the conversation, it helped me understand Elysha better.

While Elysha suffered over word choice, sentence construction, and just the right examples to include on her students' report cards (as most teachers do), I knew that these choices don't mean a lot in the grand scheme of things. Parents aren't concerned about the quality of the writing on a report card. They aren't upset over an easily corrected typo. They wouldn't be judging me on my proper use of commas and semicolons.

I've never actually used a semicolon in my life. I don't have time for that nonsense.

Parents just want to know that I love their child. They want to know that I see their child clearly. They want to be sure that I understand their child's strengths and weaknesses. Parents want to hear that I will encourage and cajole and push their child to their highest academic achievement possible while also trying like hell to make them laugh along the way. I need not worry about writing exceptionally well or providing assessment data when a slightly less articulate version of the same report card would do the job.

Elysha strove for perfection. I was aiming to be just good enough. In the end, we both accomplished the same goal. I just managed to win some money and listen to a book in the process. In the case of report cards, the eagle understood what to do without doing too much. The mouse did it all.

In truth, I have a lot of mouse in me, too. You can't write novels, minister weddings, perform onstage, manage investments, and own and operate multiple businesses without attention to detail. For a maker of things, details are immensely important.

Sometimes. But not always.

But Plato was absolutely correct. In many ways, I am the eagle. I see the big picture. I know where to direct my attention and where it will not serve me well.

Unfortunately, most makers of things have too much mouse in them. They obsess over the details and worry about every little thing. This makes sense. If you're going to make anything of any value, you must spend time on the details. Novelists, painters, chefs, inventors, choreographers, sculptors, bonsai artists, fireworks designers, and entrepreneurs must always sweat the small stuff. Attention to detail will often determine success or failure.

But without embracing the power of the eagle, too, creators can become lost in the weeds, unable to carve out the time, focus, and resources needed to do the work that must be done. They invest time in things that do not matter, treating everything with the same level of attention and thus prioritizing poorly.

If you're looking to make something, you must harness the strengths of the eagle in order to succeed. The eagle teaches you to prioritize those things that will advance your career and overall happiness while letting go of those that do not.

Curiosity Kills Productivity:
Cultivate Deliberate Incuriosity

I recently received a royalty check from my Korean publisher. Along with the check came a report on the number of books sold in various formats in South Korea. My father-in-law, who was sitting at the table as I was signing the back of the check, asked me how many of my novels had sold in Korea.

"I don't know," I said. "I threw out the sales statement."

"Didn't you look at it?" he asked.

"Why bother?" I asked. "I got my check. Knowing how many books actually sold doesn't change anything. It's not like I can market my books half a world away in a language I can't speak."

He thought I was crazy. He thought I was tragically incurious.

He was right about my lack of curiosity. But it's not tragic. It's strategic.

Minutes count. I could spend them trying to figure out how to read a Korean sales statement to determine how many copies of a translation of one of my books sold, or I could get closer to finishing the next book.

I chose the next book.

The eagle knows not to invest your most precious resource in things that are ultimately irrelevant. Don't waste time on things that will mean nothing to you hours or days later. Don't spend a minute on something that you will forget in an hour. Don't even think about things over which you have no control.

Limit Decision-Making

We have only so much bandwidth at any given moment and only so much mental capacity on any given day. The more information we process and the greater the number of decisions we make, the less capacity we will have when it's time to be creative and productive.

If I concern myself with the number of books I have sold in South Korea, I will have less capacity when it comes time to revise a chapter or rehearse a speech or write a column or draft a letter asking for a local hotel to sponsor our storytelling show. Science has shown us again and again that the more information we process in a day and the more decisions we must make, the less effective we are as the day proceeds. Decisions wear us down. Eagles know to limit them whenever possible.

This is why Steve Jobs wore the same outfit every day, including a turtleneck designed by Issey Miyake, purchased in bulk so that he had "enough to last for the rest of my life."

It's why President Obama limited himself to the choice of one of two suit colors. "You need to remove from your life the day-to-day problems that absorb most people for meaningful parts of their day," Obama said. "You'll see I wear only gray or blue suits. I'm trying to pare down decisions. I don't want to make decisions about what I'm eating or wearing. Because I have too many other decisions to make." Obama also mentioned research that shows the simple act of making decisions degrades one's ability to make further decisions.

Facebook CEO Mark Zuckerberg said that he owns about twenty identical gray T-shirts. "I mean, I wear the same thing every day, right? I mean, it's literally, if you could see my closet at home. It's just easier that way."

It's why Einstein purchased several identical gray suits so that he would never need to decide what to wear again.

It's why Matthew Dicks always wears blue jeans, a black T-shirt, a pair of sneakers, and a hat whenever he performs onstage. It's why his choice of clothing on any given day often comes down to "What's on top of the pile?"

I may be a little crazy, but I'm in damn good company. Productive company, too.

One of my students recently said to me, "You don't dress badly, but you definitely don't dress to impress. You sort of dress haphazardly."

Exactly. Also, *haphazardly* was one of our weekly vocabulary words, so she was killing it.

Why would I dress to impress when my clients are ten-year-old children who are often speckled with bits of their own breakfast and hand-drawn tattoos? If my choice of clothing somehow influenced the trajectory of my career or contributed to the writing of a book or the growth of my company, then I would be more judicious about my choices. But given that the opinions of ten-year-old children mean nothing to me when it comes to fashion and style, my student was correct: I do not dress to impress. I dress quickly so that I can move on.

One might argue that I should be dressing to impress my administrators. The saying goes, "Dress for the job you want, not the job you have." But I want to be a teacher. I seek no further advancement in the teaching realm. To climb the ladder in education would mean spending less time with children and more time with adults. This is not why I became a teacher. It's not why I remain a teacher.

I dress for the job that I want. That job also happens to be the job I currently have. And in that position, the clothing I choose to wear (which is to say, the clothing I happen to be wearing) is irrelevant to my success with fifth graders.

I don't make decisions about anything that is ultimately irrelevant, because decision-making is taxing on the brain, and I have more important things to worry about than shirts and pants. The eagle understands when fashion is relevant and when it is not.

And yes, I am also incredibly and deliberately incurious about any decision that I cannot control or does not advance my cause. I keep the big picture in mind at all times in order to have the time, energy, and bandwidth available to focus on the stuff that matters.

Every August, for example, an email is sent to teachers with a list of schedules for the coming year. Recess duties. Art and music and physical-education classes. The schedules are balanced in that they each afford teachers the same amount of planning and duty time each week, but the actual day-to-day schedule is different. One might have art on Tuesday and music on Thursday, and another might reverse the two. One schedule might require a teacher to monitor recess on Monday, while another might assign the teacher to Thursday's recess. So begins the battle of the preferred schedule.

The negotiation for the ideal assemblage of responsibilities and planning time.

I do not participate in this negotiation. I simply tell my colleagues to assign me whatever schedule is left over. It's because the schedule doesn't really matter. Never in my twenty-three-year teaching career has the placement of my music class or the day of my recess duty had a bearing on my teaching, my business, or my creative life. In truth, I don't even look at the schedule until the first day back from the summer. I am strategically incurious about anything related to school before the first day, because to do otherwise is foolish.

By the end of the school year, I will not look back and think that the four days I spent during the summer planning, maneuvering, and negotiating my schedule were productive in any way. So I don't do it.

Focus on What Really Matters ... Today and Tomorrow

The vision of the eagle says this: *If this won't matter in an hour, a day, a week, or even a year, why should I allow it to matter now?*

Case in point: During the pandemic, I stocked up the freezer in our basement with hundreds of dollars of meat and prepared foods, worried that food might be hard to come by for a while. In some cases, this was true. Once supply chains stabilized and grocery-store shelves were stocked again, Elysha and I vowed to spend the summer eating through our stores of frozen food.

Then one day Clara took a Popsicle out of the freezer and failed to close the door. Three days passed before Elysha went to the basement and discovered that the entire contents of the freezer had defrosted. All the stockpiled meat and prepared foods were sitting in tepid puddles of water.

Elysha was upset. She stared at the mess and the waste, mentally calculating the loss in time and dollars. I allowed her a moment of distress, which was entirely understandable and reasonable, but then I said, "Listen, in three days, none of this will matter to us. Before we know it, this is going to turn into an amusing anecdote about the most expensive Popsicle ever. So let's just pretend that's already happened and not let this ruin our day."

To her credit, my mouse-visioned wife embraced this eagle-like philosophy and let go of her anger and frustration. Mostly.

The eagle calculates the future value of decisions and actions taken in the moment to determine whether they are worth our time. The eagle says things like:

If it won't matter tomorrow, don't let it matter today.

If I'm the only one who will notice, it ain't worth doing.

Procrastinate on stupid, menial tasks. You could be killed by a crashing airplane in five minutes. Do you want to spend the last five minutes of your life on a meaningless task that could've been accomplished next week?

Organization for organization's sake is a fool's errand, perpetrated by people who don't value their time appropriately and forget how soon they will be dead. If color-coding papers in a folder costs you ten minutes in labor but saves only thirty seconds of effort, then don't do it.

Be Organized When It Saves Time

This is not to say that staying organized isn't important. It's enormously important.

The eagle knows that if you spend twenty minutes every week looking for your keys because you haven't assigned an "every time place" for them, you're wasting enormous amounts of time. Instead, invest in establishing a location and a routine for your keys.

The eagle knows that if it takes you hours to collect tax documents every April because you failed to file receipts and statements throughout the year, you are costing yourself precious time and energy. Instead, invest in a system to document and collect information throughout the year so that you're not scrambling at tax time.

The eagle knows that if you spend an hour every week cleaning off your desk instead of avoiding the mess altogether by staying organized, you are dithering your life away.

The eagle knows that you cannot fall behind. This seems exceptionally obvious, but it's also extremely important and often overlooked.

Almost always overlooked.

Grading assignments is a good example of this that I see a lot. If a teacher allows themselves to fall behind on a week or two of correcting, the mountain of uncorrected papers transforms (in many people's minds) into a long-term project that will require a specifically assigned period of time — a Saturday afternoon, a Tuesday night, or an entire Sunday — to complete.

As a result of this unfortunate mindset, if that same teacher finds themselves with five or ten free minutes in their day (which happens a lot), it is far less likely that they will attempt to use that free time to put a tiny dent in their enormous pile, since the progress made will feel meaningless. Rather than working for five or ten minutes, the teacher will likely waste those small slivers of time, which add up quickly, as I keep emphasizing.

I once worked with a teacher who had to take a sick day before writing her report cards because the mountain of grading that she had accumulated required a full day of work. But if you don't fall behind on your correcting and the pile of ungraded papers remains manageable, then the few extra minutes found during the day can truly be productive, and it's far more likely that you will use these few extra minutes for productive purposes.

The same can be said about so many tasks. Laundry is another good example. If you don't allow dirty clothing to collect in enormous piles, and if you don't allow folded clothing to fill numerous laundry baskets, then you will be in a better position to tackle a small load or put your clothes away when you find yourself with a few minutes to kill. I put most of my folded clothing away while waiting for my wife to get ready for bed. This would otherwise be unproductive time, but because the amount of my clothing in the laundry basket is never overwhelming, I can complete enough of the job to make the time feel well spent.

This also applies to tasks like cleaning the garage or a closet, cleaning out your car, or organizing a pantry. If you never allow any of these areas to go to hell, then you can use a few minutes here and a few minutes there to tidy a corner and make marginal progress but still feel like you've made a difference.

When you feel like you are able to make a difference, you are more likely to use that time productively. But once your garage or closet or car or pantry reaches the point that it will require hours to clean, you are far less likely to utilize the slivers of time between life to make progress.

This is not to say that you can't or won't. Writing a book is an enormous, unwieldy, yearslong process, but if I find myself with ten free minutes, I will sit down and attempt to write four good sentences. This type of productive vigilance is difficult to achieve. But much less so if you haven't fallen behind. Much less so if you are organized with respect to your time, your space, and your materials.

The eagle knows that if you keep the job small and manageable, you are far more likely to use the slivers of free time throughout your day more productively, and these few moments will add up.

The eagle also knows the value of organization. The eagle understands that maintaining a certain level of organization in your life is critical to success.

Sometimes.

But if you're color-coordinating your sock drawer because you like the way it looks, stop it. If you're labeling your silverware drawer to avoid the occasional spoon mixing in with the forks, knock it off. If you're re-creating a document so that the font and formatting matches the font and formatting of the documents alongside it, you need to reassess your priorities.

I once watched a teacher — the mother of three small children — cut the image of a giraffe out of a spelling workbook page and replace it with a different image of a giraffe that she liked better. The image was irrelevant to the assignment. The word *giraffe* was included in the week's spelling list, but the assignment didn't rely upon the image in any way whatsoever. It was purely decorative.

Yet this teacher spent time swapping out giraffes. Why?

There are a few possibilities:

- She assumed that she would live forever, so time was meaningless to her.
- She did not value time well spent with her husband and children, probably because they are monsters.
- She was so incredibly mouselike and fixated on needless detail that she couldn't prioritize the simplest of tasks.
- She had such a small, empty, unambitious life that it had somehow made swapping out meaningless giraffe images a worthy, well-lived activity.

In cases like these, the eagle should eat you. You deserve to be eaten for wasting time like this.

In the words of Pulitzer Prize–winning writer Stephen Vincent Benét, whom I quoted at the beginning of chapter 2, "Life is not lost by dying; life is lost minute by minute, day by dragging day, in all the thousand, small, uncaring ways."

Well said.

Also, for the record, that was Benét's semicolon. Not my own.

Those "thousand, small, uncaring ways" include replacement giraffes, color-coordinated sock drawers, endless discussions about font sizes, restaurant choices, or paint colors, and a seventy-five-minute marketing meeting wherein attendees debated the use of "communication" versus "collaboration" in a PowerPoint deck containing two dozen slides.

That last one is a true story. Thankfully, I was paid well to listen intently, while rolling my eyes.

You're Not the Center of the Universe, So Stop Acting Like You Are: The Spotlight Effect

That endless argument over the choice of "communication" or "collaboration" is an excellent example of the spotlight effect: a phenomenon in which people tend to believe they are being noticed more than they really are. This comes into play most often when you've chosen to do something atypical, but it also applies to physical appearance, conversation, and many other aspects of life.

Simply put, people think that other people are paying way more attention to them than they really are. The misconception makes sense: you are the center of your own universe, so it's only natural to think that you are the center of other people's universe, too.

Or at least in the vicinity of the center of their universe.

Fortunately, this is not true. Eagles understand this is not true. No one will notice and absolutely no one will remember if you chose to use "communication" or "collaboration" in your slide deck. Ten minutes after your presentation, you won't care, either.

Yet for some reason, a certain group of marketing executives thought everyone listening to their presentation would notice, when the truth is that no one would.

Eagles understand this.

Eagles understand that the small things that often consume other people are irrelevant because no one is paying much attention to you.

The spotlight effect is real.

Here is the truth: Nearly every good hair day that you experience is only experienced by you. No one will notice, let alone remember, the coffee stain on your shirt. No one will remember when you misspoke during your sales pitch. No one knows that you put on or took off ten pounds. Once you embrace this truth, life becomes much easier, as the routines, rituals, and endless concern for meaningless minutiae fall away.

Eagles do not suffer the "thousand, small, uncaring ways." The eagle ignores, discards, disregards, and plows through the small, un-caring ways, striving instead to put the power of the mouse to only the most pertinent, productive pursuits.

I ran into a friend at the grocery store on Saturday morning. After exchanging pleasantries, he said, "I admire you. I could never leave the house like that."

"Like that" consisted of sweatpants, an old T-shirt, and a base-ball cap. I had just come from the gym, though I could've just as easily been dressed this way regardless. "I look *that bad*?" I asked.

"No," he said, immediately backtracking. "I'm just saying ... I need to make myself look more presentable before I leave the house. You know?"

I do. I also know that he is not alone in his need to make himself presentable before leaving the house. Sadly for my friend, he doesn't realize that no one cares if he's presentable. No one remembers, and hardly anyone even notices.

This need to look presentable in most, if not all, public circum-stances is highly unproductive. While I'm not saying that you need to look like a slob in order to be productive, I also don't think that you should be too worried about your appearance if your destination is a grocery store, retail outlet, or similar location, especially if it will delay your trip.

The store where I was shopping — Stop & Shop, of course — opens at 6:00 a.m. I like to be there early because the checkout lines can become unreasonably long on a weekend. I also wanted to stop at the gym on the way.

I explained all this to my friend. He said that he just couldn't do that. "It might save time, but I just couldn't go shopping looking like that. I would need to work out at the gym, go home, take a shower, get dressed, and then go out shopping."

This poor guy actually thinks that people care what he looks like while shopping on a Saturday morning. He thinks they will remem-ber a day later what he looked like.

He's not alone, of course.

But the less you care about your physical appearance, the more productive you can be. And caring less is a good idea in many, many cases. Perhaps not when you are meeting with a client or making a presentation or attending your cousin's wedding, but in your day-to-day existence, caring less is good, because no one ever cares as much as you think.

I attended a wedding a while back. I no longer wear ties, and a friend pointed out to me that I was the only man at the entire wedding not wearing a tie. "Doesn't that make you uncomfortable?" she asked.

It didn't. That wedding was more than a year ago. How many of the guests at that wedding still remember that I was not wearing a tie? How many even noticed the absence of a tie that evening? How many noticed and thought poorly of me?

The answer to all these questions is none or almost none.

No one cares what you look like.

In a test of the spotlight effect, students were asked to wear bright yellow oversize Barry Manilow T-shirts to a large introductory psychology class. Researchers then had them estimate how many people in the class had noticed their shirt.

Students estimated that 50 percent of their classmates noticed their shirt. In reality almost no one did.

Not only do people not care what you look like, but they are rarely paying attention. When you can embrace this belief, you will be more productive. You'll spend less time getting ready to go out. You'll be more willing to jump in the car in pajama pants and a T-shirt to run an errand. You'll be more likely to dress sensibly rather than stylishly.

Just imagine how much life you could recapture if you spent less time in front of a mirror every day. Or less time choosing an outfit. Or less time worrying about how you look.

Think back on how my friend would've handled his morning differently had he understood the reality of the spotlight effect. He would've made less effort to "look presentable," absolutely saving time in the process.

By going from the gym to the store and then home, without

showering in between, I saved a needless trip. My route guaranteed that I would be at the store when it opened, allowing me to avoid the checkout lines. My way was much faster and therefore more productive, and I promise you, I used the time I gained wisely.

I am not saying to look like a slob. I am not saying that you should ignore your physical appearance entirely. I'm suggesting that you probably spend too much time worrying about your appearance and, as a result, too much time making yourself presentable.

I'm suggesting that you could probably shave precious minutes off your morning routine while not changing anyone's opinion of you or your appearance whatsoever.

At the same time, you can eliminate the needless stress and worry that come with concern over appearance. With a limited amount of bandwidth at all times, the last thing you want to be worried about is your self-perceived bad hair day or ill-fitting jeans or which pair of shoes to wear on a given day. The creators of things have enough to worry about already without concerning themselves about their appearance while running errands, especially when no one else is concerned.

• • •

Maybe eliminating shoe selection is impossible for you. Perhaps the color palette of your feet is too important for you to abandon this daily decision. But are there other decisions that you could eliminate from your life instead?

I don't carry an umbrella or wear sunglasses, a watch, or jewelry of any kind for similar reasons. I opt for an uncomplicated, streamlined existence. I believe that eliminating these items from my life saves me time and frees my mind.

Except for days when I am going to spend hours outdoors in the frigid weather, I wear the same coat, hat, and gloves. The coat is admittedly only a sweatshirt, but it's thick and warm, and I tend to be a person who doesn't get cold easily. My students claim that they have never seen me wear a coat, but that's because they don't recognize the warmth of a well-made hoodie. Besides, I try to dress for where I am going to be and not the one to three minutes that I will spend between my car and that space.

If not the shoes, perhaps you could eliminate some other choices and layers of accoutrement from your life instead.

Andy Anderson, a 104-year-old great-grandfather, offered this piece of advice to his great-granddaughter writer Macy Cate Williams: "Everyone has too many clothes. Wear what you have and quit buying more."

I know many people who, if given the chance, would spend every weekend buying clothing. Many people.

I also know too many people who *actually* spend every weekend buying clothing.

A friend once told me that she couldn't ever spend a day in New York City with me because if she was ever in possession of that much time away from her children, she would want to spend it at the outlets. I thought she was kidding. She wasn't.

While speaking in Chicago recently, I was asked for some tips on productivity from an audience member. My response: "Try owning one belt."

I explained that when I opened up my suitcase in my hotel room, I thought I'd forgotten to pack my belt, which would've forced me to purchase a new belt and thus double my current supply of belts. "Happily," I said, "I found the belt, rolled into the toe of my shoes. So I still own one belt. It's black on one side and brown on the other. It's all that I have ever needed."

I know a person who owns fourteen belts. I know another who owns eleven. According to at least one fashion-industry poll, the average American owns "more than five" belts.

Knowing nothing except the number of belts a person owns, who would you expect to have more time in the day to be productive? The person who owns one belt or the person who owns double-digit belts? Does anyone even notice those double-digit belts? The spotlight effect says probably not.

I say no, too.

When it comes to productivity, less is more. The fewer decisions you have to make and the fewer items you need to constantly inventory, the more time you will have and the better decisions you will make.

Numlock News reported:

A new study published in *Nature* found that when subjects were set to the task of trying to fix something, they favored adding stuff rather than removing things in order to try to get it to work the right way. When asked to fix a travel itinerary, just 28 percent removed something. When asked to improve an essay, word counts shrank in only 17 percent of edits. When asked to make a pattern out of squares just 20 percent removed squares to create a pattern. When asked how to improve a university, just 11 percent wanted to drop something.

When consulting with clients about productivity and efficiency, I find this to be entirely true. So many individuals and organizations attempt to solve a problem by creating a form, establishing a new procedure, developing a new sequence, or outlining a new list of rules or regulations. This frequently leads to frustration, wasted time, squandered energy, and less meaningful work. Also, the problem is oftentimes not entirely solved by the added work.

So much of what we are asked to do or what we ask of ourselves can be eliminated.

There are forms I must complete at work that often ask me to indicate my "position." I'm supposed to enter "teacher," but for the past twenty-three years, I have entered my position as "upright," and no one has ever said a word. As I suspected, the question is unnecessary and a waste of time.

Even if the giraffe-swapping teacher had no goals in life other than improving worksheets for students, replacing this giraffe was still incredibly stupid, because she most assuredly complains from time to time about not having enough time to do things, and she's right. None of us have enough time.

I opened the first chapter with this quote from Buddhist teacher and hospice-care expert Frank Ostaseski, but it really can't be said enough: "Death is not waiting for us at the end of a long road. Death is always with us, in the marrow of every passing moment. She is the secret teacher hiding in plain sight, helping us to discover what matters most."

I agree with the first part of his quote. Death is with us at all times. As we swap out giraffes, we continue our endless march toward death, but we invalidate the steps we take. We render them meaningless. The problem is that unless we have the vision of the eagle, we never discover what matters most. We waste our steps on nothing. We dishonor the time we have in this world. We remain blind to the preciousness of the minute.

The eagle reminds us to clear our march of needless things. Spend as little time, energy, and bandwidth as possible on the nonsense of life so that we can spend more time on the things we wish to see, do, build, make, and learn.

5 Things That Don't Deserve Your Time

I'm admittedly hyperfocused on productivity. *How can I do more in less time?* has been a flashing beacon in my mind for a long, long time. As far back as I can remember. Along those same lines has been this question: *What is the most productive way to spend my time?*

More important: *What is the least productive way to spend my time?*

Even more important: *What things don't matter?*

The second and third questions came into focus when I was about twelve years old. My friend Jeff had a paper route in his neighborhood, and one day he asked me to walk along with him. I agreed. He delivered the afternoon edition of the Woonsocket *Call* Monday through Friday plus the Sunday-morning edition. We had fun, walking from house to house as he introduced me to the idiosyncrasies of each of his customers, recounting the events on payday:

- The old lady who gave him one stale Oreo cookie every Friday.

- The woman who once answered the door not realizing that she was topless.
- The guy who always answered his door in a robe and slippers while smoking a cigar.
- The customers he had never seen before. "They just leave money in an envelope under the mat for me, like they did for the last paperboy."
- The endless string of angry dogs.

Back then, paper routes were precious. In order to secure one, you had to purchase it from a retiring paperboy for a considerable amount of money. As I walked with Jeff, I wondered if my paperboy might be retiring soon. Maybe I could be a paperboy and finally have some money in my pocket. I walked the paper route with Jeff several times until one day, he and I walked together on Friday.

Payday. That was when I saw how much money Jeff made per week. I couldn't believe it. As poor as I was, and as much as I wanted to have money in my pocket, a quick calculation in my head determined that this must be the least productive job on the planet. The pay was atrocious. It was minuscule. It was not worth his time.

Not only was the pay pathetic, but taking on the job as a paperboy meant committing every afternoon to your route without exception. No after-school sports. No visits with friends. Just straight home to deliver the papers. And it didn't matter if it was raining or snowing. It didn't matter if it was ten degrees or one hundred degrees. It didn't matter if you were sick or hurt. A paperboy was outside, delivering papers, every day, no matter what.

He was the damn Pony Express without the pony.

That was the moment I realized that as poor as I may be, some jobs are simply not worth the compensation or my time. My time, I came to understand, is exceptionally valuable, and simply having more money than I had before should never be the reason to take a job. It was the moment I realized that my time was worth a certain amount of money and, perhaps more importantly, should result in something that I am proud to do, so my goal was to find work that balanced the equation between my time and effort and the money and benefits being offered in return.

A few months later I would be hired for my first job: laborer on a local farm owned by a man named Jesse Deacon. I hooked and flung bales of hay off tractor trailers. Hung barbed wire. Sunk fence posts. Mucked stalls. Cleared brush. Fed and exercised horses. I worked six hours every Saturday morning and made more money than Jeff made in a week.

Still not great money, but $10 per hour in 1984, when the minimum wage in Massachusetts was $3.35, was more than worth my Saturday morning.

Sadly, I never saw any of that money. I handed every paycheck for more than two years to my stepfather, who told me that he was depositing it into a savings account for me. When I was old enough to need money, he told me that it had been used for more important things. My nest egg of nearly $5,000 was gone. To a seventeen-year-old looking for gas money, I had lost a fortune. Later, when I totaled my mother's car — a 1978 Datsun B-210 — and nearly died in the process, that same man would require me to take out a loan of $8,000 to pay for the car. A worthless car more than a decade old. This loan burdened me for years. Not a great start to my financial life.

But despite the loss of wages, I learned that time is money. More importantly, my time is valuable. If I'm going to trade it in the form of labor or anything else, I had better ensure that the money and benefits offered in return match the time being given.

The job of farm laborer wasn't exactly changing the world. The difference between it and newspaper carrier may seem marginal at best, but to me, the work on the farm meant something important. The posts that I sunk and the barbed wire that I strung were meaningful, physical signs of the work that I had accomplished. A loft loaded with hay and horses well fed mattered a great deal to me.

Maybe Jeff felt the same way about delivering newspapers. Perhaps he took great pride in bringing the news of the world to the doorsteps in his neighborhood. Based upon the way he treated the job, I don't think so, but it's possible. If he did, then perhaps he spent his time wisely after all, despite his meager wages.

More than three decades later, I still drive by Jesse Deacon's farm when I return to my hometown, and I can still see the fence posts that I sunk into the ground as a boy. The barn where I once loaded hay and mucked stalls. As I drive by the farm, I feel like it still possesses a tiny piece of me. I left my mark on a place, and evidence of that mark remains.

As I said, it's work that meant something to me. I'm the son of an actual cowboy who left my life when I was just seven years old. The work that I did on that farm made me feel connected to the boy I once was and the roots of a family that fell apart far too soon in my life.

Your time can be accounted for in dollars, but the way you spend your time should also mean something to you. Ideally, it should be something that will always mean something to you, even decades later.

Far too often, I watch people take on additional work, new assignments, and side jobs that are simply not worth the time invested and will ultimately be meaningless in the long run. While I understand the inclination to say yes to any additional income, you must keep the big picture in mind: time is the most valuable commodity on the planet, and you have just as much of it as the wealthiest people alive. Value it accordingly. Never waste it away. Find the additional work and side jobs that price your time according to its worth. Take the time to find the right fit. Invest in yourself and your skills so you can ultimately earn what you deserve. Demand of every employer that your compensation be commensurate with your ability.

The Stupidity of Bragging Rights

Here's another criminally negligent time waster.

California fast-food chain In-N-Out Burger opened its first two Colorado locations back in 2018, in Aurora and Colorado Springs.

Lines in Aurora reportedly reached two miles long according to police, who struggled to control traffic all day, with some customers waiting fourteen hours to be served.

Fourteen hours is more than half a day. Fourteen hours is longer than it took to complete the initial landings on Omaha Beach on D-Day.

Fourteen hours spent waiting for a cheeseburger is like murdering time. These are people who are quite literally wasting their life away. The odds of a human being existing are infinitesimal. One tiny sperm cell must outrace hundreds of millions of other tiny sperm cells in order to fertilize an egg to create a human life. Then that human spends fourteen hours of that precious, unlikely life waiting for a cheeseburger.

Harsh, I know. I try not to judge, but this In-N-Out Burger situation was too much for me. I know that I place a premium (and perhaps too high a premium) on productivity, efficiency, and the calculated, decisive, strategic use of one's time. Maybe I could benefit from a little less intensity and a little more relaxation. But fourteen hours for a cheeseburger strikes me as lunacy. A complete and total disregard for all that could have been accomplished or enjoyed in that time. An overvaluing of an experience that could just as easily be had a week later for a tiny fraction of the time.

Years ago, a Krispy Kreme opened in my town. For three weeks, traffic around the doughnut shop was a nightmare. It stretched for more than a mile. The local news reported on the long lines for a week. Wait times on the first day exceeded six hours.

Three weeks after the grand opening, I strolled into the shop and purchased a doughnut in less than five minutes. Same doughnut. Same experience. Except that it cost me five minutes instead of three hundred sixty minutes. Also, it was just a doughnut. Not that great, either. Today that Krispy Kreme location is a bank. Never believe the hype.

When people waste time in proportions like those in Aurora in 2018, I cannot help but feel incensed about their complete and total disregard for the most precious commodity on this planet: time. A person would never spend fourteen hours' worth of their paycheck on a cheeseburger. They would never toil away at their job for nearly two days in order to purchase cow meat on bread. They treat their money like it has great value but toss away their time like it is meaningless. It makes no sense. Why do they do it?

So they can eat an In-N-Out burger on the first day. Take a photo of themselves receiving their burger for Instagram. Tell their friends that they were one of the first people in Colorado to try the famed Double-Double. They do it because they think that waiting for hours for an In-N-Out burger means something. They get to say that they ate one of the first In-N-Out burgers in Colorado. One of the first Krispy Kreme doughnuts in Connecticut.

Here's the thing about bragging rights: no one cares.

There have been only twenty-three perfect games in Major League Baseball. More than 200,000 games have been played in all of Major League history, but only twenty-three have been perfect — a game by a pitcher (or combination of pitchers) that lasts nine or more innings in which no opposing batter advances to first base via hit, walk, or error.

I was in attendance for two of them. I have personally attended fewer than a hundred Major League games in my lifetime, yet I have also witnessed the rarest occurrence in all of baseball. Twice.

Talk about bragging rights. But do you care? I suspect not.

It means something to me, but it means little to anyone else. It probably means a little more to you than the feather in the cap of the person who ate the first In-N-Out burger in Colorado or the first Krispy Kreme doughnut in Connecticut, but probably only a little bit more. Photos on social media are ephemeral at best. Claims of being first are forgotten minutes after the claim is uttered. None of it means anything, yet for some people, they think it will mean something.

It doesn't.

I try not to judge, but in this case, I judge. It's foolishness. Stupidity. In the words of my wife, when I told her about the fourteen-hour wait: "It's the dumbest thing ever."

The Black Hole of Addictive Games

Dong Nguyen, the creator of *Flappy Bird* (which overtook *Angry Birds* in terms of popularity in 2014 to become the most downloaded free game in Apple's App Store) unexpectedly removed his game from the iOS and Android app stores on February 10, 2014, despite its popularity. Nguyen tweeted about the removal of *Flappy Bird*, claiming that despite the $50,000 that he was earning daily from the game, it was "ruining" his life and the lives of users over what he considered to be its overly addictive nature and overuse.

I cheered the end of *Flappy Bird*. I'd never played the game. I'd never even seen the game played. But what I have seen is the shockingly addictive power of these games and the vast amounts of time that are wasted by the people who are playing them. *Flappy Bird* may have been ruining Dong Nguyen's life, but games like *Flappy Bird* continue to ruin the lives of people who stare at their phones every day and play them.

Candy Crush is the game that I see played most often in my circles. I see this game played a lot. Every time I do, I can't help but think about the time being wasted and lost. Time that can never be recovered.

Don't get me wrong: I love video games. I spent untold numbers of hours playing video games, both at home and in arcades, as a child. Even as an adult, I have spent entire weekends playing video games with friends. But the difference between the video games that I have played and games like *Candy Crush* and *Flappy Bird* is that when I play video games, they are played socially. My friends and I bring our laptops together or gather around my friend's Wii, and we spend a weekend attempting to conquer a game or each other.

When I am playing video games, I am spending time with friends. I am talking, taunting, scheming, laughing, reminiscing, fighting, competing, and cajoling. The people I watch play games like *Candy Crush* (and presumably *Flappy Bird*) are lost in their cellphone screens, present in body but absent from the world and the people around them, accomplishing little more than momentary, mind-numbing, purposeless pleasure.

This is not to say you will never see me with my head buried in my phone. You will. Too often, in fact. But when I am staring at a screen, I like to think that I am at least being productive. Most likely, I am reading. I am scrolling through my carefully curated Twitter stream for news or reading a web page, a PDF of a company's earnings report or the latest educational theory, or a book. Or I am working on a project in Notion (which has recently replaced Evernote). I am either gathering information, reading for pleasure, or moving something forward.

This may cause me to sound like a productivity lunatic. I probably sound as fun as a dish towel. I may appear to be someone who doesn't know how to turn off and relax. All these things may be true, but here is what will not happen to me: I will not be lying on my deathbed someday, hating myself for the precious hours spent playing *Candy Crush*. When I am an old man, I will not be hating the younger version of myself for all the time I spent playing *Flappy Bird*.

Nor is this to say that I would not love to play a game like *Candy Crush* or *Flappy Bird*. Knowing my addictive, obsessive personality and my natural inclination toward video games, I think I would crush *Candy Crush*. I would flap the hell out of *Flappy Bird*.

This is why I never download any games onto my phone. I do not allow myself to begin playing these games. To do so would surely lead down the *Candy Crush* path to certain doom.

My advice: Remove all the games from your phone immediately. Find a more productive use of the time you spend with your face in your phone.

My suggestions: Load a book onto your phone. Find news sources that appeal to you. Use the time spent on your phone to make a grocery list, respond to an email, review your bank statement, or answer a question that you have always been curious about.

I am currently reading about the Teapot Dome scandal via the Wikipedia app on my phone. It's something that I've always been vaguely aware of but never really understood. By the end of today or tomorrow, I will. Next, I plan on reading about Elvis Presley. I've been listening to the song "Suspicious Minds," and it's got me think-ing about him a lot. I don't know much about his life, but by the end of the week, I will. Fleetwood Mac is next.

A free app called Duolingo will teach you a foreign language and is designed to be played like a game. It's fantastic. It's compet-itive, challenging, and full of the levels, rewards, and markers that make games like *Candy Crush* so addictive. I'm not ready to shift the reading that I do on my phone over to a pursuit like this, but there may come a time when I do. But if you're sitting in a meeting or a waiting room playing *Candy Crush*, why not play a game that will result in the ability to speak Spanish or French or German instead?

There are millions of uses of your cell phone. New apps are being developed and added to the app stores. For the sake of your aged, infirm future self, make the time spent with your head in your phone more useful and productive.

How to Ruin the World

"People who enjoy meetings should not be in charge of anything."
— THOMAS SOWELL

In the book *Simple Sabotage: A Modern Field Manual for Detecting and Rooting Out Everyday Behaviors That Undermine Your Workplace*, Robert M. Galford, Bob Frisch, and Cary Greene examine the "Simple Sabotage Field Manual," a guide published by the OSS (the predecessor of the CIA) in 1944 to assist European spies in undermining the Axis powers from within. Galford, Frisch, and Greene examine eight techniques outlined in the field manual that are eerily similar to what often goes on in workplaces today.

Here are the eight tactics the OSS recommended for tripping up an Axis agency from the inside:

1. Insist on doing everything through channels. Never permit short-cuts to be taken to expedite decisions.
2. Make speeches. Talk as frequently as possible and at great length. Illustrate your "points" by long anecdotes and accounts of personal experiences.
3. When possible, refer all matters to committees, for "further study and consideration." Attempt to make the committees as large as possible — never less than five.

4. Bring up irrelevant issues as frequently as possible.
5. Haggle over precise wordings of communications, minutes, and resolutions.
6. Refer back to a matter decided upon at the last meeting and attempt to re-open the question of the advisability of that decision.
7. Advocate "caution." Be "reasonable" and urge your fellow conferees to be "reasonable" and avoid haste which might result in embarrassments or difficulties later on.
8. Be worried about the propriety of any decision. Raise the question of whether [it] lies within the jurisdiction of the group or whether it might conflict with the policy of some higher echelon.

In my nearly three decades of work in a variety of fields, I have seen these strategies deployed with frightening regularity. My own additions to the list would include:

- Run meetings and training sessions with PowerPoint decks consisting of dozens of text-filled slides. If possible, read directly from your slides.
- Assemble meeting agendas in reverse order of importance, thus placing the most important item last and ensuring that if the meeting is running late, the agenda cannot be cut short.
- At the beginning of every meeting, require grown adults to review (and if possible read aloud) a set of norms — a list of ways that reasonable adults behave decently — thus treating your meeting attendees like poorly behaved children.
- Assign seats in meetings and training sessions, thus reinforcing the idea that you view your meeting attendees like poorly behaved children. Infantilizing your subordinates is a highly effective means of generating discord. Do so whenever possible.

- Open meetings with meaningless "getting to know you" activities. Activities that include sticking Post-it Notes onto colleagues' backs, tossing playground balls to one another, and scavenger hunts are especially destructive to both productivity and morale.
- In email correspondence, use "reply all" and add unnecessary people to distribution lists whenever possible.
- Before sending an email to subordinates, ask yourself: *Could I include this relatively simple piece of information on the agenda of my next meeting, thus prolonging that meeting?* If the answer is yes — and it almost always is — delete the email and add the information as an agenda item.
- Never allow a string of emails to end. Always reply — regardless of the finality of the last email — with anodyne phrases like "Thank you" and "Sounds good" and "I understand." Every additional email sent amounts to productivity lost.

Friend and storyteller Anne McGrath, who once consulted with nonprofit groups and now does organizational assessments, offered these additions to the list that I thought were well worth sharing:

- Assume no one has ever attempted to do what you're trying to do, and start from scratch.
- Hide mistakes along the way and don't bother collecting or sharing ideas for your best-practices or lessons-learned folder.
- Spend no time identifying and recruiting effective partners or participants for your project. Just invite anyone and everyone, regardless of what they'd bring to the table.
- Have murky or never-discussed visions, goals, purposes, and values. Assume everyone has the same identical end goal in mind.

- Don't evaluate leadership capacity. Just use the leader you've always used for every project.
- Don't engage the people you are trying to help. For example, if in a school, leave students out of the equation regarding all decisions that will have direct impact on their lives.
- End meetings with no clear action plan for things to accomplish and bring back for the next meeting. This helps create meetings that go on forever with nothing changing.

6 Be a Criminal

"Life is short. Break the rules."

— MARK TWAIN

Years ago my principal of fourteen years, the great Plato Karafelis, retired. One of the very worst days of my professional career.

In his place arrived a crocodile who proceeded to chew up the scenery, upend every applecart, and make a mess of all that was once good.

So began three miserable years until we finally managed to expel the crocodile from our school.

Part of this misery was the endless series of faculty meetings and professional-development sessions, which were decidedly less inspiring, informative, relevant, and respectful than what I was accustomed to under our previous administration. Terrible content presented terribly by a terrible person.

Finding myself in these time-wasting, mind-numbing, meaningless exercises in self-promotion and relentless narcissism, I needed a way to make my time more useful and more productive. In the words of my friend Steve, who joined our faculty during the crocodile years, I decided to "Matt Dicks" these meetings, meaning I always came armed with something more meaningful to do.

My first task was to become a notary. My friend's mother was a notary, and as a result, she could often help friends, family, and neighbors who needed something notarized quickly. Always looking for another job to add to my already sizable pile of jobs, I decided to do the same.

The process involved reading a fifty-eight-page PDF and completing a long application that required handwritten, paragraph-length answers. Rather than giving over four hours of my life to the reading and application process, I came to every meeting and training session armed with my notary folder, prepared to complete a little bit each time. It took almost two years to get through the application, but just recently my friend's son, who was renting his first apartment in New York City, needed something notarized immediately lest he lose the apartment to someone else. It being a Sunday, notaries were hard to come by, but knowing that I'm a notary, he and his mother stopped by my house and took care of business in a couple of minutes.

When I tell people that I am productive in the cracks of my life, this is what I mean. A few minutes here and there over the course of two years turned me into a notary without dedicating any real time to the process. Was this the right and proper way to spend time in a faculty meeting or a professional-development session? Of course not. But sometimes we need to think like criminals. We need to break rules, cut corners, and violate norms in order to allow our creative pursuits to flourish.

Even better, I wrote almost an entire novel during those dreadful meetings, too. At one of those early soul-crushing faculty meetings, I looked up to see that my tablemates and friends weren't doing well. They looked sad. Downtrodden. Uninspired by the reptilian administrator who couldn't stop talking about himself. Perhaps worried about the future of our school.

I know I was.

So I took the notebook in front of me and quickly wrote a list: *Stupid Things Stupid Administrators Do in Faculty Meetings.*

It was a combination of reality and hyperbole. Amusing observations and real-life awfulness. After finishing the list, I passed the notebook around to my tablemates and watched as each read the list and smiled. One even laughed. When the notebook returned to me, I started another list: *Why Meetings Suck*. Again, I passed the list around and made my friends smile.

This process of list writing continued meeting after meeting until something odd began to happen: the protagonist writing these lists ceased being me. Instead of lists of things that I thought and believed, they became the lists of someone entirely unlike myself. Someone decidedly less confident. Less stable and optimistic. More financially fraught. A character was born in my mind, and he quickly became as real as any protagonist in one of my novels.

Also, the lists began to tell a story.

By the time I mentioned this collection of lists to my literary agent, more than half of the book had been completed. A book written entirely in lists. A story told entirely in list form. A book written entirely in meetings that otherwise wasted my time. Eventually my editor wanted to publish this unfinished book, so I put aside my other writing projects and completed it.

A little more than a year later, that book, *Twenty-One Truths about Love*, hit bookstore shelves. I wrote nearly an entire book and became a notary while a crocodile facilitated his self-centered, navel-gazing versions of meetings. This is what I mean when I say, "Be a criminal." Not only should you be looking to bend or break a rule to steal a little time, but as a creative maker of things, you must also take care of your soul. You must find ways to nurture your spirit and creativity at all costs. Being a criminal means recognizing that the world was not formulated for your needs, so sometimes, you need to bend or break some parts of it for your own good. It's not always easy, but there are times in life when you must decide that the rules do not apply to you. That your time is more valuable than expectations, policies, or conformity. That preservation of your creative soul must be placed ahead of other needs.

Here's the truth: Rule followers have taller, steeper hills to climb. More gatekeepers to get past. More demands on their time and energy. People endeavoring to lead a more productive, more creative, more fulfilling life can't always afford to battle these additional challenges, so rules must be broken so that they can succeed. This can mean everything from stealing time when needed to cutting corners in order to achieve success.

The Misconceptions of Rule Followers

Earlier this summer, I took my family to Yawgoog Scout Reservation for Alumni Day. I spent my childhood summers at this camp and wanted my own children to see the places that had generated so many of my memories and so many dinner-table stories. When we arrived at the waterfront, it was closed. The campers and lifeguards were off at lunch, so no one was on duty. I took my kids around to the watchtower, where I once spent many a summer day staring out at the lake and peeking through the mounted binoculars.

I wanted my kids to see the view that captivated me for so much of my youth. And I wanted to see the view again.

But when we arrived at the stairs to the tower, a rope cord was stretched across the entrance, indicating that the tower was closed. I unhooked the rope, dropped it aside, and began to mount the steps.

"Wait," my son said. "It's closed."

"I know," I said. "But c'mon. What's the worst that can happen?"

My son and daughter balked until I ordered them up the steps. My kids are rule followers of the greatest order, and it makes me crazy as a parent. Always afraid to get in trouble, always worried about stepping outside the expected norms, they are trapped within the confines of needless rules, unnecessary laws, and short lengths of rope preventing them from climbing stairs to glorious views.

Once they reached the top, they were so glad they had listened to me. The view was spectacular, and the stories I told were endless in number. Even so, they were constantly worried that a lifeguard might return and what? Tell us to get down? A simple rope would've denied them an incredible view and a bounty of stories. This happens to people all the time. They allow small, unnecessary, arbitrary barriers to stop them from doing what is right for them.

Even worse, they fail to take into consideration the consequences of breaking the rules, which are oftentimes infinitesimal or non-existent. When there is no bite to the bark, the bark is rendered meaningless. Act accordingly.

As a teacher, I work almost exclusively with rule followers. Teachers tend to be formerly excellent, obedient students who decided to become teachers. They have never experienced any real trouble before, so they perceive authority figures as having far more power than they really do. They perceive "trouble" as being told by a superior to stop doing something or to do something correctly.

This is not trouble, of course. This is simply feedback. "Trouble" occurs when real, life-altering consequences follow the feedback: Loss of job, privileges, position, or pay. Delayed or permanently stunted career advancement. Tragically, most teachers (and rule followers in general) never see things this way. They follow rules because that is what they have been told to do for all their lives. They don't want to disappoint authority figures. They don't want to be perceived by others as a bad seed.

They fail to realize their dreams because they are too busy worrying about meaningless consequences and the perceptions of others.

By contrast, I was a poorly behaved student in school — setting the record for most consecutive hours of detention — and I was also arrested, as I shared in chapter 1, and tried for a crime I did not commit. I spent time in jail. I understand what real trouble is. I've learned that short lengths of rope should never hold you back.

It's why I teach my fifth graders, and previously my third and second graders, Shakespeare every year. We read novelizations of the plays, then we study the original text. As I mentioned, I built a stage in my classroom, complete with lighting welded onto the support beams, a sound system, and curtains. At the end of the year, we perform a full Shakespearean production for parents.

Here's the thing: Shakespeare isn't a part of our curriculum. I simply decided, with the support of my former principal, to teach Shakespeare.

Teachers have asked me over the years: "How do you get away with teaching something not in the curriculum?" My answer is always the same: My students love it. Parents are happy. My standardized-test scores are always good. Who wants to be the person to stop Shakespeare in my classroom? Truthfully, the crocodile tried, but I fought back and won.

I break the rules and get away with it because the results warrant my criminal behavior. Kids fall in love with *Macbeth* and *Hamlet*. They perform *Romeo and Juliet*. They do things that few elementary students ever do.

Breaking the rules allowed me to install enormous rocks as seating outside my classroom without telling anyone, because had I informed the proper authorities, then paperwork, approvals, and other nonsense would've prevented their installation. Instead, the stone company simply showed up one day and dropped them in a semicircle before anyone even noticed. The custodian wasn't happy, complaining about mowing the grass around the stones. My principal wasn't happy about a large-scale installation taking place without his knowledge. But by the time anyone was complaining, the rocks were installed and kids were sitting on them, reading and writing under a tree.

Who was going to force me to remove them?

If we want to make things happen, we sometimes need to be criminals. We sometimes need to break the rules, dodge regulation, defy the norms, and be daring.

At work, I like to pilot the "I'm not going to do this — let's see what happens" plan. When a task seems arbitrary, meaningless, or purely bureaucratic, I try to avoid it at all costs, knowing that failure to execute it will almost certainly result in no trouble at all. Years ago, the teachers in my district were asked to enter testing data into a spreadsheet that I knew no one would ever use, so I skipped the assignment.

Nothing happened.

I skipped it the next year. Nothing happened again.

Four years went by like this until a new principal took over. He's the mousiest mouse I've ever met. He's the type of person who labels your faculty-meeting folder (which was never a thing until I met him) with your name, then gets upset if you doodle on the folder before you hand it back in to be refilled for the next meeting.

He also color-codes everything, plans eighteen months in advance, insists on the final design decisions for all school-wide documents, and dresses impeccably every single day of his life. He's an incredible leader, but his heart will likely give out before he reaches retirement age. He worries about everything rather than trying to worry about only the important things.

Being a mouse, he followed up on the database-entry task, not to utilize the data (I had already proved after four years that no one was utilizing the data) but to ensure that the pointless, meaningless, soul-crushing task was completed. He popped into my room one day when my students were outside at recess.

"Matt, you didn't enter your testing data in the online spreadsheet."

"I know," I said. "I never enter that data, and no one cares."

"You *what*?" He had to grab on to a desk lest my words knock him off his feet.

"Four years ago, I piloted the 'I'm not going to do this — let's see what happens' plan, and nothing happened. So I don't do that silly task."

My principal is a kind, gentle man, but somewhere deep inside him, his own personal Chernobyl nuclear reactor exploded. He told me to enter the data. I told him I would. I subvert rules whenever possible, but I'm never intentionally insubordinate.

Except when the crocodile was in charge.

But just think of all the time I saved, and how much of it undoubtedly transferred into more positive outcomes for my students and me.

Be a criminal.

Someone Else's Rules Need Not Be Your Own

My wife thinks that I do a terrible job of emptying the dishwasher. I put plates that are still wet into cabinets rather than drying them with a towel or leaving them out to dry. I'm intentionally avoiding that needless step. I argue that my way of emptying the dishwasher is faster, and while she concurs, she argues that it is also incorrect.

Weird. Right?

She thinks there is a Platonic ideal when it comes to emptying a dishwasher. She thinks that there is a right and wrong way to accomplish this chore. She seems to believe that there is an International Commission on the Appropriate Use of Dishwashers that has decided on the only correct way that this chore should be done.

This, I told her, is the perfect distillation of my argument: She is willing to trade drops of water on a clean dinner plate for time. I am not.

So often in life, people assume that there is a correct way of doing things, when in truth, we are more often simply saddled by norms, tradition, the way our parents did something, or societal expectations.

When you relieve yourself of these unnecessary, unwieldy, illogical norms, time is saved. Bandwidth is preserved.

Be a criminal.

I often "invent" parking spots in lots and garages that are supposedly full. Elysha and I recently pretended to be hotel guests in order to use a restroom in New York City.

In order to land a speaking spot in a TEDx conference, I bypassed the required application process, lied to an administrative assistant to get the phone number of the conference organizer, and gave her a call.

Be a criminal.

If you are creating or building or inventing, you need every second that you can get. You cannot allow the avoidable to stop you.

I'm not proposing that you break any serious laws or hurt someone in pursuit of your dreams. I'm merely asking you to keep a weather eye on the world for opportunities when you can bend, break, or bypass the self-imposed or even legally imposed rules of others.

Don't allow a short length of rope to stop you from ascending to greatness.

Don't Lose Days to Rotten People

"Stupid people are dangerous."

— Suzanne Collins

A few years ago, I was teaching an all-day storytelling workshop to about a dozen people. It was a beginner-level workshop, designed to allow attendees to sit and say nothing.

"Be a mushroom," I will typically say at the beginning. "No need to speak your truth today. Just learn." It's a workshop specifically aiming to get participants to dip their toes into the storytelling waters without making them feel self-conscious about not sharing.

Three hours into the workshop, one of the attendees emailed Elysha, who was visiting her sister that weekend in New Jersey with the kids. She wanted Elysha to know how this workshop — with more than three hours still to go — had already transformed her life. For three long paragraphs, written during our lunch break, she sang my praises.

Three hours later, as the workshop was wrapping up, she sent a second email to my wife, telling her that I was wasting her time. Ruining her life. Stealing money from her pocket. She told Elysha that if she had a hammer in her purse, she would've used it on my skull.

She also sent an email to the Connecticut Historical Society — my partner in this endeavor — demanding her money back.

All this was done while I was still teaching her.

The woman's problem was that she hadn't been given a chance to tell a story, even though the description of the event clearly stated that this was a workshop designed to create a stakes-free environment where students could learn without the pressure of performance. I teach many workshops in which students tell stories. Just not this one.

I had no idea that these emails were flying (and was unaware of the threat of violence) as I finished teaching the workshop. It wasn't until I arrived home that Elysha called me to tell me about this attendee's bizarre flip-flop over the course of the day. An hour later, my contact at the historical society called to tell me about the woman's email and their decision to issue her a refund.

I was home alone that weekend. I had to perform the next day, so my plan was to spend the weekend writing, performing, and playing golf with friends. Instead, as I sat at my desk, staring at my laptop screen, I allowed this woman's criticism to consume me.

Had I made a mistake by not allowing her to tell her story? Were other students in the class equally upset but afraid to speak up? Maybe I wasn't the teacher I had envisioned myself to be at the beginning of the day?

For the rest of the evening and much of the following morning, I was overcome by doubt and uncertainty. I was upset with myself and unsure whether my methods were any good. It wasn't until I spoke to Elysha again on the phone and admitted my feelings that she told me what I needed to hear: I've been teaching storytelling for years. I'd taught thousands of students. Worked with dozens of companies and nonprofits. Priests and ministers and rabbis. Adults and kids.

This was my first complaint. Ever.

The woman, in short, was irrational and mean. She expressed the desire to bash in my skull with a hammer. She was not someone who should be occupying even a tiny bit of my mind.

Elysha was right. Sadly, I lost nearly a day of my life figuring that out.

• • •

I remember that weekend well because I don't often allow negative people to affect me in this way. I often brush them off with ease.

Back in the spring of 2007, a small number of anonymous cowards excerpted five years of my blog posts, taking sentences entirely out of context, in order to cast me in a very negative light. They compared me to a mass murderer, declared me unfit to teach small children, and demanded that I be fired from my teaching position, along with my wife and my principal, Plato. They sent this content, thirty-seven pages in all, to the board of education and the council in the town where I teach. School officials investigated the allegations, found them to be untrue, scurrilous, and deliberately misleading, and did nothing.

In response, the same collection of cowards sent the thirty-seven-page packet to three hundred families in my school district. Everyone in my community had been told that I was a violent, dangerous man who should not be trusted with children.

Somehow that negativity did not affect me as profoundly as that woman in my workshop did. Perhaps it was the support of friends and colleagues. Maybe it was the amateurish attempt to undermine my credibility. Maybe it was the warlike footing that I assumed during that time.

Most likely, I knew that their claims were untrue. I knew that I was a good teacher. I had no doubt about my skill or integrity. Confidence, resilience, and self-awareness served as a shield against their attacks. As a result, I rebounded quickly.

But I wasn't as confident when the woman who wanted to cave in my skull filed her complaint. For some reason, I was less assured of my ability to teach storytelling at the time. I was probably still fighting off impostor syndrome.

I suspect that a lot of people react to negativity in the way I responded to that woman. Self-doubt, fear, and uncertainty can creep into the mind and ruin a day, a week, a month, or more. Negative people can destroy our spirit. Strip us of our enthusiasm, excitement, and motivation. These are critical components to creativity. They are the lifeblood of anyone trying to make something.

We cannot afford to allow anyone to do damage to these precious commodities. If anything, we need to find a way to surround ourselves with more positive, productive people. A 2017 study found that working near people who are good at their job makes you more effective at yours. Sitting within twenty-five feet of a high performer at work improved a given worker's performance by 15 percent, while sitting within twenty-five feet of a low performer hurt their performance by 30 percent.

Role models, it would appear, are very important. What does this mean for me?

I'm a man who spends his workday within twenty-five feet of two dozen fifth graders at almost all times. Two dozen ten-year-old children who can sometimes perform at a high level but can also spend enormous amounts of time staring out windows, watching pencils roll down their desks, and doodling the image of a pig's head hundreds of times on dozens of Post-it Notes.

These are kids who jam important papers into the far reaches of their desks never to be seen again, who somehow lose library books during the fifty-foot walk from library to classroom, and who can struggle getting water from the drinking fountain to their mouths without somehow making a puddle on the floor. Even when they're performing at their highest level, it's not like our optimal levels are commensurate in any way. I deserve hazard pay.

For all their faults, children are generally joyous human beings. They find wonder in the smallest of things. Laugh at the simplest of things. Become excited over a candy bar in their lunch box, a field trip to a water-treatment plant, or pajama day. They have been a constant source of inspiration for me over the years. While I may have colleagues who have turned complaining into a pastime and can find fault with just about anything, they are quickly made irrelevant by the positive energy of my students.

Several years ago, the aforementioned fellow teacher Steve transferred into our school after his wife was promoted to principal in his school. Up until the moment I met Steve, I considered myself the most positive person in my life. My wife described me as "oppressively optimistic." Also "relentlessly positive."

Neither was meant as a compliment.

Steve, it turns out, is even more positive than me. He is an everlasting source of optimism. He is someone who believes that hard work, determination, and grit can achieve miracles. The result? I became even more positive than before. I raised my game. I found a role model who offered me a view of a level of positivity I never knew existed. I felt inspired to be better and obligated to be an equally positive force in Steve's life.

A high performer in proximity to me improved my performance.

• • •

Negative people will bring you down. Positive people will lift you up.

This isn't to say that we are not sometimes saddled with negative individuals in our lives. We are sometimes forced to deal with people who whine, complain, criticize, gossip, and even do us wrong. Unintentionally or deliberately attempt to hurt us.

For these people, we must take action. Not dealing with these people in purposeful and strategic ways steals away from our psychic energy. They wear us down. Knock us off our game. Make life more difficult than it needs to be. We spend time worrying and fretting about them, and it robs us of our ability to be creative, make things, and be productive.

The last thing you want while harvesting your strawberries or writing that aria or inventing a better paper-towel dispenser is to be thinking about how Sarah wronged you or how Alan played unfairly or how Bonnie and Linda tried to destroy your career.

These may or may not be actual examples from my life.

Either way, these are not productive thoughts, nor are they conducive to creativity.

I have four strategies for dealing with these people who continue to plague our psyches. The people in our lives today who cause us grief as well as the ones from our past who might still bother us.

The high-school bully.

The ex-spouse.

The evil stepfather.

The toxic frenemy.

The miserable boss.

The selfish aunt.

You can't allow these people to continue to rule your mind. You can't permit them to consume your thoughts or influence your mood. My suggestion is to use one of the following four strategies to bring an end to the festering: *forgiveness*, *empathy*, *elimination*, or an *enemies list*.

Forgiveness

This is perhaps the hardest strategy to employ, but it's also the one that wipes the slate entirely clean. When you can find a way to forgive the negative person who plagues your thoughts and feelings, you can find true freedom.

Forgiveness is for *you*.

My mother was not the most effective parent. I spent much of my childhood feeling ignored and forgotten. My parents never spoke to me about my future and never helped me plan for life after school. Instead, they kicked me out after high-school graduation, feeling like their job was complete. I've been on my own ever since.

For a long time, I was angry with my mother for not doing more. I thought she should've been a much better parent. I was upset that I'd not been given the childhood I thought every child deserved. I loved my mother. I just didn't understand why she didn't love me more.

Then one day, while speaking about my mother to a friend, Elysha said, "Matt, you realize that your mother was depressed for most of her life. Right?"

This thought had never occurred to me, but as soon as Elysha spoke those words aloud, I knew with certainty that it was true, and almost instantly, I found forgiveness for my mother for the first time in my life. All her failings as a parent were washed away with the understanding that my mother suffered from untreated depression for most, if not all, of her adult life.

Oftentimes forgiveness requires some kind of understanding. You can't forgive until something about the transgressor or their transgression makes sense to you. Seeking understanding is often the first step toward forgiveness.

But not always.

A person with whom I work once treated me poorly. She failed to support me in a way that would have been simple for her but could have meant the world to me. Though my wife is still upset about it to this day and has not forgiven this person, I have. I decided that her transgression wasn't worth my time or my mental energy. Continuing to be angry with her would have consumed unnecessary thought and focus. I have more important things to accomplish, and I need my focus and energy directed at those things. Also, I need to work with her on a daily basis. Remaining angry would make the workday more challenging than necessary. Besides, I'm doing quite well both personally and professionally. Though her unwillingness to support me didn't help my career, she didn't torpedo it, either. Her slight has become irrelevant. No less cruel or selfish, but trivial and meaningless.

I forgave her, because it was convenient and helpful to do so, even if Elysha's blood still boils.

Forgiveness is hard, but when it becomes possible, it is the best way to stop the festering and eliminate the negativity from your life. Maya Angelou once said, "It's one of your greatest gifts you can give yourself, to forgive. Forgive everybody."

If you can forgive everybody, more power to you. For the rest of us, you may need a different strategy sometimes....

Empathy

Empathy is different from forgiveness because empathy simply allows you to understand your transgressor without extending yourself in any way. Empathy allows you to say, "He's going through a tough time right now. His divorce was ugly, and the fact that his ex-wife married his younger brother must make Christmas awkward. The meteor that landed in his coat closet was unbelievably unfortunate. And that damn third nipple can't be easy now that he's dating again. He did great harm to my career through no fault of my own, and he doesn't have a positive bone in his body, but I understand why. I can't forgive him for being a monster, but I understand why he is a monster."

Empathy doesn't heal a relationship, but it reduces its toxicity. It prevents you from wasting time and bandwidth on wondering the how and why. Empathy has allowed me to ignore the negativity of neighbors who believe that Covid-19 vaccines contain tracking chips and mask mandates violate their freedom, because I know they're trapped inside bubbles of misinformation, partisanship, and deliberate deceit. These are people who were born into these beliefs. Taught these beliefs at an early age. Constantly surrounded by these beliefs. Reinforced every day for supporting these beliefs.

I don't forgive them for endangering my life and the lives of my wife and children, but I can at least understand why their beliefs are so ingrained. I'm still mad as hell at what they are doing to our country, but I understand their misunderstanding and confusion.

It's not intentional. It's simply unavoidable.

If I was trapped in the bubble of family, friends, and a community who believed this nonsense, I might struggle to trust science, too. I might also be thinking that human beings and dinosaurs occupied the planet at the same time.

I don't forgive, mostly because I can't. Thus far it's been beyond my capacity. But I can at least understand, which allows me to push the negativity aside a bit and move on with my life. Maybe not all the negativity, but enough to make the relationships easier to manage.

Ask yourself why someone in your life is acting so poorly. Seek the source of their negativity. Try to understand the reason behind their stupidity and cruelty. When you can empathize with their struggle, you may find yourself better equipped to brush that negativity aside, recapture some of that necessary bandwidth, and get on with the stuff that matters.

Elimination

This strategy is simple: eliminate the negative person from your life, or at the very least, minimize the time spent with this person.

This, of course, is much harder than it sounds, but sometimes the best way to remove a cancer is to simply cut it out.

It hurts, but it's effective.

My friends and I used to play golf with someone who often lost his temper on the golf course. He would pound his club into the ground, stomp around the green, and act like a toddler when things weren't going his way. Eventually, his temper tantrums began to ruin our fun, so we simply stopped inviting him to play. He never asked why we stopped calling, but had he inquired, I would've been honest. A difficult conversation, of course, but a lifetime of more enjoyable rounds of golf as a result.

When you can't eliminate contact, sometimes minimizing contact can make a big difference. Wishing to minimize time spent with a particularly negative person, one of my colleagues began locking her door during lunch, hoping that it might deter this person from eating lunch with her. Unable to eliminate a colleague entirely from her life, she instead took care of herself by establishing boundaries. In this case, a wooden boundary with an actual lock.

Years ago, my principal announced a new, yearlong curriculum initiative. Teams composed of teachers from each grade level would work together for the year, designing a new reading framework. In an effort to avoid working with negative people, I met with the principal immediately after the meeting and asked if I could assemble my own team. He agreed.

While some of my colleagues found this act unfair and rage inducing, my principal saw it as someone willing to take the initiative. I saw it as the ability to avoid the kinds of people who would consider this unfair. I eliminated negativity from my life by surrounding myself with as many positive people as possible.

When I was managing McDonald's restaurants, I would manipulate the schedule to avoid working shifts with awful people. When I was attending college, I would quietly identify the classes that a certain student was taking each semester and avoid those classes whenever possible. When I was being interviewed by couples who were considering hiring me to DJ their wedding, I would also be interviewing them, determining if they were the kind of people I wanted to spend time with. If they weren't, I was suddenly unavailable on their wedding day.

Rotten people abound in this world. They grow like weeds. We can't eliminate all contact with the worst of the worst, but when we can, we must. Time, bandwidth, and our emotional well-being are all at stake.

One specific note on eliminating negativity from your life: If you are dating someone whom the majority of your friends do not like, stop dating that person immediately. In the history of human civilization, there has never been a boyfriend or girlfriend whom someone's closest friends initially hated or did not trust whom they eventually experienced a change of heart about and came to love.

When it comes to romantic relationships, group consensus is always correct.

Enemies List

Stay with me on this one. I know it sounds a little Nixonian, but maintaining an enemies list is a reasonable, viable strategy for eliminating rotten people from your life. There are times when a person has treated you so egregiously that forgiveness or empathy is simply impossible. Even when you eliminate this person from your life, their past behavior still plagues you on a regular basis. Even if the person is no longer around you, the thought of their existence or the reminder of the wrongdoing occupies your mind.

In these cases, an enemies list may help you.

An enemies list is a place where the name of the offending

person, business, or organization can be placed until forgiveness, empathy, or revenge can be achieved. It's essentially an opportunity to put these forces of darkness away for a while, trusting that the list is ready and waiting whenever needed.

It sounds odd, I know, but it's proved highly effective for me, and two therapists I know support the practice, acknowledging that sometimes the best thing we can do with anger is box it up for another day.

This is what my enemies list does for me. Puts these rotten people aside for a time so I can move on with the business of life.

There are currently eight names on my enemies list: Two are elementary-school principals or former principals who wronged either me, my colleagues, or someone I love. Two are relatives or former relatives by marriage who have wronged my loved ones. One is a former elected official whom I have already successfully sued once, but I am not satisfied with that single victory. One is a nonprofit that did me wrong. One is a corporation that did me wrong. One is an anonymous group of cowards who tried to do me wrong.

I'm legitimately enraged by all these entities, but by placing their names on my enemies list, I am suddenly free from obsessing over my revenge. I can let those feelings go, trusting that they will eventually be addressed through action, empathy, forgiveness, or some combination of the three.

Mostly through revenge, I suspect, though if a couple were magnanimous enough to acknowledge their awfulness, ask for forgiveness, and perhaps make efforts to correct their wrongdoing, that might be enough. For the rest, it's probably revenge. Not the "hiring a contract killer" or "publishing surreptitious photos of someone's third nipple" kind of revenge. More like achieving remarkable success or someday exposing them for their awfulness.

The "Yeah, but" Monster

One more rotten person I'd like you to avoid at all costs: the "Yeah, but" monster. These people are the worst. These two words are the worst.

It's not that I don't say these two words myself from time to time, but whenever I catch myself saying them, I despise myself. I remind myself of how stupid and defeatist I sound. I'll even apologize for them if the moment is right.

"Yeah, but" is never good. It's a disingenuous agreement. An artificial attempt to move on and discount all that was possible a moment before. It's an attempt to discredit or ignore what was said but to do so under the guise of acceptance, only to move right past it into the land of negativity.

"Yeah, but" is the language of those who cry over spilled milk. People who perseverate over past injustices. Individuals who are incapable of putting the unchangeable and implacable behind them and moving on.

It's also the language of the unaccountable. The complainers. The blamers. The finger pointers. Those who cannot give credit where credit is due. Those who are unable to acknowledge the wisdom or success of others. It's the blunted, ineffectual weapon of the jealous, the envious, and the small-minded.

It's spoken by people who don't believe in the future.

"Yeah, but" is also often a leap into an illogical argument. An unreasoned appeal. An emotion-riddled mess of verbal detritus. No one likes the "Yeah, but" monster. These are the whiners of the world. They are the people who bring moments of genuine productivity to a grinding halt. Remove the "Yeah, buts" from your own conversations whenever possible. Despise them as much as I do.

Make the world a better place.

7½ Write Your Own Damn *Gatsby*

Author Hunter S. Thompson once retyped *The Great Gatsby* just to feel what it was like to write a great novel. This fact is often lauded as a demonstration of his commitment to the craft and his desire for excellence.

I can't imagine a stupider way to spend your time.

Want to write a great novel? Try writing one. Then try again and again and again.

Thompson did this, of course (and with great success, in my opinion), but perhaps if he hadn't spent so much time doing what amounted to a popular form of punishment from my childhood (copying definitions from the dictionary), he would've had time to write one more story. Or spent a little more time polishing one of his manuscripts.

I have far too many stories to tell to spend a moment retyping someone else's story. Frankly, I doubt that Thompson even did this ridiculous exercise. It's the kind of story that a great writer like Thompson would make up, knowing its inherent appeal to the general public.

I hope he made it up. Wasted time — even when it's wasted by someone else — pains me.

Part 2

TAKING THE LEAP

"To begin, begin."
— WILLIAM WORDSWORTH

8 Say Yes

"Everything in the world began with a yes.
One molecule said yes to another molecule and life was born."

— Clarice Lispector

It's the fall of 1997. I'm sitting at my desk, writing an essay on obscure sixteenth-century poet martyrs, when my phone rings. It's my best friend Bengi. Before he even says hello, he asks me the question that's going to change my life forever: "Do you want to be a wedding DJ?"

This is a crazy question for many reasons. In the decade that I've known Bengi, I've never once mentioned the desire to be a wedding DJ. Nor has he until this very moment. Also, I don't want to own and operate my own business. I've never even considered going to work for myself. Frankly, it sounds dreadful. Fraught with stress and responsibility. I want to be a teacher and a writer. Not a music man.

Add to this that in my entire life I've only attended two weddings, and one of them was Bengi's two months ago. Not only do I know nothing about being a wedding DJ, but I know nothing about weddings.

But this is why he's calling. He hated his wedding DJ and is convinced that we could do a better job.

I am convinced that we cannot do a better job. We are also the least-equipped people for the job. We know nothing about the industry. We know nothing about music outside of our own rock and heavy-metal favorites. I didn't even realize that there was a wedding industry.

Even if I wanted to be a wedding DJ, which I don't, I am currently attending Trinity College in Hartford, Connecticut, full-time, working on a degree in English, hence the poet martyrs. At the same time, I'm attending the University of Saint Joseph, studying for a degree in elementary education. Also full-time.

I'm *also* working full-time at a McDonald's restaurant as a manager and part-time as a writing tutor in Trinity's writing center. I'm also married to a woman who I will soon discover is the wrong woman for me. I'm helping to raise her daughter.

This is the busiest I have ever been in my life. So, when Bengi asks me "Do you want to be a wedding DJ?" my answer is simple.

I say yes.

I say yes, because that is what life has taught me to do. I say yes, because that one-hundred-year-old version of me says, "No one's going to ever ask you this question again. This opportunity will never come your way again."

Truthfully, I say, "Yes, but let me finish this essay on Anne Askew, then we can talk."

The result of that simple yes is remarkable. That yes results in a possibility tree — the branching of new opportunities — of enormous proportions. The growth that comes from that simple yes is astounding. First, I become a wedding DJ. This involves the purchasing of equipment and music, endless hours of practice, creating a database of songs, and hosting a party for friends at a local Veterans of Foreign Wars hall as a sort of trial run.

It doesn't go well.

Still, less than six months after that phone call, we are working at our first wedding. Three months later, we book three dozen weddings for the following year at our first bridal show. Off we go.

In our twenty-five years in business, Bengi and I have entertained guests at 454 weddings. That's 454 couples — 907 people — who have us working for them on one of the most important days of their lives.

I know what you're thinking: 454 × 2 = 908. But my number is 907 because years ago a guy named Doug hired us for his wedding, then he got divorced, and then he got remarried and hired us again. He changed his wife, but he did not change his DJ.

In addition to Doug, I meet an enormous number of people through the years. Many pass through my life briefly without leaving much of a mark, but some of them are categorically unforgettable. Like the bride who disappears from her reception for more than an hour. When I finally find her, she is sitting behind the car, smoking a cigarette and crying because no one in her entire life knows that she is a smoker, including her newly minted husband. Her plan had been to quit on her wedding day, but now she knows she can't, and she doesn't know how she is going to tell her husband. And so I sit down with her and make a plan about how, when, and where she is going to tell her husband that she's a smoker and needs help quitting.

Once the plan is made, she and I return to the reception, where she dances the night away. I told that story a decade later for a Moth GrandSLAM championship and won.

Then there is Scott, who asks me if I could minister at his wedding in addition to being the DJ. I point out to Scott that I am a reluctant atheist — someone who would like to believe in a higher power but simply cannot — but he says he doesn't care. "I want you to be my minister. Get ordained online."

And so I do. Despite never wanting to be a minister and not really knowing what the job entails, I say yes. We plan a ceremony that includes small references to the Dallas Cowboys — Scott's favorite team — which makes his father-in-law crazy but results in a beautiful occasion.

So then I become the DJ who could officiate your wedding. Soon I'm performing ceremonies for all kinds of couples. I officiate a wedding for a woman who has to cut her wrists and bleed on the ground where she will be married an hour before we perform the ceremony, which sounds bizarre but is also beautiful.

Then these couples start having babies and ask me to baptize their children, so I begin performing baptisms and baby-naming ceremonies. Remember: I'm a person who doesn't actually believe in God, baptizing children in backyards.

All because I said yes.

Then one day the minister of a Unitarian Universalist church calls and asks if I might be willing to lead the Sunday service while she's on vacation. When I point out to her that I was ordained online and don't really believe in God, she says that doesn't matter. When I tell her that I don't know how to run an actual church service, she says that she'll teach me. When I tell her that I don't know what to say during the sermon, she says, "Just tell stories. They'll like that, and it will make them think."

So I agree. I say yes. Three years later, I'm working as the substitute minister at half a dozen services for three different churches. I even get to ring the church bells.

And then there is Matthew Shepard, author of the afterword of this book, who we call Shep because two Matts is one too many. He marries Kelly in 2002. The marriage doesn't last, but our friendship does. And if the only thing I've ever gotten out of being a wedding DJ were Shep, that would be enough. He becomes one of my closest friends. But Shep introduces me to Tony, his cousin, who has two extra season tickets to the New England Patriots and needs to sell them. Being lifelong fans of the Patriots, Shep and I buy them during the season when Tom Brady takes over the team and leads them to their first Super Bowl championship. Ever since that season, Shep and I have sat side by side in section 331 at Gillette Stadium, in the wind and the cold and the rain and the occasional sun. We scream and cheer. Fight with Jets and Ravens fans. Hug strange men when our team scores a touchdown. Weep during epic comebacks. Swear at referees. Witness a record seven AFC championship games.

It's not an exaggeration to say that some of my best moments in the past two decades have been in section 331 of Gillette Stadium.

In the fall of 2021, I'm called by Shep's ex-wife Kelly. She's getting remarried and wants me to officiate the wedding. Once her DJ, I now become her minister.

But Shep does something even bigger for me. One day he calls me and asks me if I want to start playing Dungeons & Dragons with him. I don't have a girlfriend at the time, so I say "No," because I'd like to find a girlfriend someday, and I don't think Dungeons & Dragons will help in that mission. Also, I played Dungeons & Dragons as a kid. I liked the game back then, but it's far less appealing to me today.

Shep calls back the next day. "Okay," he says. "Why don't you write the adventures for us?"

"That sounds worse than actually playing Dungeons & Dragons," I say.

Then Shep's tone changes. He sounds serious but also aggressive. He says, "Didn't you tell me that you want to be a writer someday? Because as far as I can tell, you're not writing anything, so why not write this?"

Shep is right. Since graduating college, I have tried to write several novels, but every attempt was worse than the last. So I have sort of given up on that dream, deciding that maybe writing isn't for me. Fiction, at least. That dream of becoming a novelist is nearly dead. Shep has called me on it. We all need people like Shep in our lives.

So I say yes. For more than a year, I write Dungeons & Dragons adventures for my friends. For the first time in a long time, people are reading my work. I start to think of myself as a writer again.

Then one day in the spring of 2004, I call Shep and I say, "I'm not writing Dungeons & Dragons anymore. I'm going to try to write a novel." Shep says that I should do both. I decline. Shep offers to be my first reader. He remains my first reader to this day.

In 2007 I complete my novel. In 2008 my agent Taryn and I sell it to Doubleday, and in 2009 it's published. I publish books in 2010, 2013, 2017, 2018, 2019, and 2021. My novels are translated into more than twenty-five languages around the world. My third novel becomes an international bestseller, as I've mentioned. Four of them are optioned for film.

But it's not finished. As I publish novels (and because I'm publishing novels), my friend Andy, a musician, comes to me with an idea for a rock opera and a few songs.

I hate opera.

I listen to his songs. I don't like them.

He tells me the idea for his story. I hate it. "Will you write it with me?"

I say yes. Even though I really shouldn't, I say yes. Two years later, we produce that rock opera at our local playhouse. I sit in the front row and listen to professional actors speak and sing the words and story that I envisioned in my mind. It's incredible.

At the end of that production, Andy says, "I want to write a musical for tweens and early teens, ages twelve to fourteen."

I hate kids ages twelve to fourteen. That's why I teach elementary school. But I say yes. So far we've written and produced three musicals for summer camps. I love each one better than the last.

Today I'm writing a musical in which I will star alongside my writing partner. I will sing even though I can't sing. Why?

My writing partner Kaia said she would help me, so I said yes.

But something even better happens back in 2009. My family celebrates the publication of my first novel with a party at my cousin's house. I'm signing a book for my aunt when my father steps through the gate into the backyard.

I haven't seen my father in twenty years. He has come to the book party because I wrote my book. We agree to write letters to each other. We still write those letters today.

Don't forget. All this started by me saying yes to Bengi.

Ask Yourself Hard Questions

What if you don't have a Bengi in your life asking you to become a wedding DJ? What if you don't have people asking you to step outside your comfort zone? What if you're not blessed with a Bengi or a Shep or a Kaia? In that case, you have to ask yourself these questions, too. You can't wait for others to ask of you. Sometimes you have to ask of yourself.

In 2009, I start listening to a podcast from an organization called

The Moth, which produces shows featuring true stories told live in front of an audience without notes. I like the podcast. I really like the stories being told on stages in New York, Chicago, Boston, and around the world. I ask myself, *Could I do that someday? Could I be one of those storytellers?*

I mention it to Elysha and friends, proposing that maybe someday I could be a Moth storyteller.

"Yes," they say. "You should give it a try."

Two years later, I finally say yes to the question I first asked myself in 2009. I go to a Moth StorySLAM in New York City with Elysha. An open-mic storytelling competition. I drop my name in the hat filled with the names of hopeful storytellers. The plan is to tell one story. One and done.

Truthfully, the moment I drop my name in the hat, I begin to hope that it's never pulled. There are more than twenty names in the hat that night. Only ten will be drawn. Maybe I can turn this yes into an "Oh well…"

My name is drawn tenth. I can't believe it. At first I remain quiet and still. No one besides my wife knows me in this room. If I don't move, they'll eventually assume that Matthew Dicks has gone home and will draw another name.

Elysha kicks me under the table. "Get on the stage and tell your story."

I tell a story about pole-vaulting in high school. By some miracle of miracles I win. I become a storyteller. Except it's not really a miracle. I've been training for this moment for a long, long time without ever knowing it.

My training began when Bengi asked me to be a wedding DJ, and for a decade, I would stand in front of hundreds of wedding guests at a time, speaking extemporaneously, gaining confidence with public speaking, learning to speak without notes.

It continued as I wrote my books, immersing myself in the nuance of effective storytelling. Practicing the craft on the page before I took it to the stage.

Did I know any of this when I said yes to Bengi years ago? Of course not. That is why we say yes: we never know where a yes may lead.

But a no? A no always leads to one place: nowhere.

Since winning that first Moth StorySLAM in 2011 I've won more than fifty slams in all, plus seven GrandSLAM champions. I've become the winningest storyteller in Moth history. I've told stories all over the world. My stories have appeared on *The Moth Radio Hour*, and millions of people in America have heard them.

But that's just the tip of the iceberg of that yes. Editors see me perform onstage and begin asking me to write for them. I publish pieces in *Parents* and *Slate* magazines. A comic-book publisher asks me to begin writing for them, even though I don't like comics and don't read comics.

I say yes. As a result, I am a comic-book writer today.

Two years later, Elysha and I launch Speak Up, a storytelling business of our own. We begin producing shows in Connecticut and throughout New England. Eventually audience members ask me to teach them what I'm doing onstage. I don't want to at first. I teach children all day long. The last thing I want to do is teach adults. But instead, I say yes. I don't want to teach storytelling, but I'll try it once and see what I think.

It turns out that I love helping people tell their stories. That workshop, taught in a small room of a public library, is the first step toward a career in teaching, coaching, and consulting. Today, I work with Fortune 500 corporations, advertising firms, universities, hospitals, Olympic athletes, world-class mountaineers, comedians, the clergy, Santa Clauses, the Mohawk tribe of Canada, and many, many more. I work with them on storytelling, marketing, strategy, advertising, sales, and more. Though I am still an elementary-school teacher to this day, I do that job because I love the kids. My financial advisers insist that I quit. My storytelling opportunities have become far more profitable than teaching will ever be. But I really like the kids.

Storytelling has led me to writing screenplays, pitching television shows to streaming networks, and collaborating with TV writers and documentary directors. Storytelling landed me a contract for *Storyworthy: Engage, Teach, Persuade, and Change Your Life through the Power of Storytelling*, my first book of nonfiction. That book's success led to my publisher purchasing the book you're reading now.

Sometimes we have to ask ourselves the hard questions. When others aren't daring us to exit our comfort zone, we have to be willing to step into that discomfort ourselves. We must demand it of ourselves.

The Gift of Yes

Just before the start of the pandemic, I wondered if I could ever perform stand-up comedy. The thought of it terrified me, which made me feel like I should probably give it a try. A difficult yes is often the best yes. Over the course of a year, I began performing at open mics in Hartford, New York, Boston, and Michigan. I was even paid to perform three times before the coronavirus brought a pause to my career in comedy. For now, it is on hold as I wait for this pandemic to subside, but once I feel it's safe again, I will return to the comedy stage, even though doing so still frightens the hell out of me.

It's become popular for coaches, gurus, thought leaders, and the like to encourage people to say no more often. Protect and preserve your time by not allowing others to infringe upon it more than necessary. Focus your time and energy.

"Be willing to say no" is a mantra often preached today.

It's nonsense. Frankly, it's what people want to hear, and what you want to hear and what you need to hear are often two very different things. Remember: a yes can always easily become a no if needed. Had I decided that a career as a wedding DJ wasn't for me, I could've switched my yes to a no at any time. Had I decided that musicals or ministering were a waste of my time, I could've easily stopped and moved on to something else.

Yes is not a permanent state of being. It's a willingness to try something new, even if that thing strikes you as ridiculous, unappealing, time-consuming, or foolhardy. It's the acknowledgment that being asked to try something new is a gift. It's the realization that there will come a day when people stop asking you to say yes, and when that day comes, the one-hundred-year-old version of yourself will be enraged by your unwillingness to say yes now and try something new.

I thought golf was a stupid, elitist, boring sport when my friends bought me a $10 set of clubs at a yard sale and asked me to play. But I said, "Yes, I'll give it a try." Today it's one of my favorite things in the world.

When second grader Elizabeth Donoghue, in my very first class, asked if we could put on a Shakespearean play after I told the students the story of *Julius Caesar*, I thought the notion of seven-year-old children performing Shakespeare was ridiculous. But I said yes.

Two decades later, I am the teacher who teaches Shakespeare to his students and produces full-length plays at the end of every year. As I've mentioned, I've since installed a stage, lighting, a sound system, and curtains in my classroom. I have stacks of bins, filled with costumes, swords, daggers, and other props. I've become nationally known as a teacher of theater in the classroom.

When Elysha told me that Steely Dan was a much better band than I thought, I said yes. "I'll give them a try."

Turns out I was correct about that one. That yes quickly became a no.

But far more often, my willingness to say yes has led me down unexpected and improbable forks in the road. When you say yes, your life is in a constant state of change. Enormous, blessed change.

My mother died in February 2007. Since she passed away, I've become an author, a storyteller, a comic, a columnist, a consultant, a golfer, and a playwright. She is never going to know any of those things about me. These are some of the most important things about me today, and it breaks my heart that she never got to read one of my books, listen to one of my stories, or watch one of my musicals. She never even met my children.

But I also know it's the reality of yes. When you say yes, doors are constantly opening, and your life changes in profound and un-predictable ways.

When our daughter Clara was born back in 2009, I thought we were done with children. I pointed out to my wife that we could send one child to Yale or two children to the University of Connecticut. "You make the call."

I thought I was a genius. Two years later, she started talking about having another child. She wanted a sibling for Clara, but I wasn't so sure.

Then one day, I was sitting on my couch, petting a cat, when it occurred to me that Elysha's question "Do you want to be a father again?" was no different from "Do you want to be a DJ?"

So I said yes. A year later, we got Charlie. I can't imagine a world without him.

Just Start

One of the primary stumbling blocks for most of the creative and entrepreneurial people I meet is the inability to actually launch their endeavor. Rather than saying yes and leaping into the abyss, people wait, calculate, ponder, and prepare. There is always a better time. The right time. Conditions that must be met in order to achieve the perfect time.

They also tend to cling to their original vision, unable to see divergent paths and new opportunities. They have dreamed of a single thing for a long time, and as a result, they cannot reconfigure, reimagine, or pivot to something new. They can't say yes to a new possibility because they remain locked on their original dream.

But instead of waiting, you must say yes. You must launch, re-gardless of your state of preparation or accumulation of resources. Perfection is insidious. The desire for perfection is nothing more than fear masquerading as something else. You must remain nimble, open-minded, and adaptable. You must embrace imperfection, con-fusion, and evolution.

Slack, a company for which I consult, began as the internal communication system for a failing video-game start-up. When the video-game industry was unkind to them, the company pivoted into an industry-leading business communication and collaboration platform today.

I am a marketing and communications consultant for Slack today because a long time ago, I said yes to becoming a wedding DJ and continued to say yes when opportunities arose. Like Slack, I remained open-minded and altered course when a new and more interesting path presented itself. I dove in, oftentimes unskilled, ill-informed, and unprepared for the next step on my journey.

Start something new. Forget about the perfect launch or the right equipment or the ideal partner.

Just start.

If you find yourself a slave to perfection, remember these three things:

1. More than likely your need for perfection is simply a symptom of your fear of failure or your tendency to procrastinate.
2. Almost no one is doing anything perfectly. Join the crowd.
3. Just starting something, as imperfect as it may be, already makes you better than the vast majority of people, who never start anything.

Be better than everyone else. Start something terribly imperfect today. Or be like everyone else and go nowhere. Harsh, I know. But it's what I say to myself almost every day, and it works.

8½   Concern for Code Monkey

I first heard Jonathan Coulton's song "Code Monkey" about ten years ago. It's a song about a lovelorn computer programmer who is pining for an office receptionist. After offering a soda to the receptionist and being told that she is too busy to chat, Code Monkey slinks back to his cubicle, "not feeling so great."

The final set of lyrics before the chorus go like this:

Code Monkey think someday he have everything
Even pretty girl like you
Code Monkey just waiting for now
Code Monkey say someday, somehow

Tragic. Right? Code Monkey is waiting for "someday, somehow."

How many people in this world spend their whole lives waiting for "someday, somehow"? Ever since I first heard this song, my heart has ached for Code Monkey. Coulton's song has trapped him in this moment of yearning, dreaming, and loss.

Does Code Monkey ever escape the mindless drudgery of his job? The disregard by his superiors? Does he find the creativity that he desires so badly? Does he ever get his pretty girl?

It's stupid and ridiculous and a little embarrassing, but I feel a pang every time I hear this song, not for the Code Monkey of the song but for the Code Monkey beyond the song. The future Code Monkey.

Does he make his dreams come true? I want to know. I need to know. *Someday, somehow* are words that haunt me.

Here's the truth: I don't think he does. I don't think Code Monkey gets everything. So few people do.

And it breaks my heart. Every single time. I think most people walk through life like Code Monkey, saying that someday, somehow, they will make their dreams come true. Then life escapes them, and they die, filled with regret for what they might have done.

Don't suffer the fate of Code Monkey. Turn "someday, somehow" into "today, now."

9 Be a Chicken, Not a Pig

"Do not feel lonely, the entire universe is inside you.
Stop acting so small. You are the universe in ecstatic motion.
Set your life on fire. Seek those who fan your flames."

— RUMI

A famous entrepreneur in Silicon Valley used to demand that people joining his company be a pig. Not a chicken. This idea comes from a famous fable.

Pig and Chicken are walking down the road. Chicken says, "Hey, Pig, I was thinking we should open a restaurant!"

"Maybe," says Pig. "What would we call it?"

"How about Ham-'n'-Eggs?"

Pig thinks for a moment, then says, "No, thanks. I'd be committed, but you'd only be involved."

Sometimes the story is instead presented as a riddle.

Question: In a bacon-and-egg breakfast, what's the difference between the chicken and the pig?

Answer: The chicken is involved, but the pig commits.

When it comes to a bacon-and-egg breakfast, the Silicon Valley entrepreneur argued, the pig is all in. There is no ambiguity. It's all or nothing for the pig. But the chicken leaves itself with options. It contributes to the meal while maintaining flexibility. The chicken can always change its mind. It has the opportunity to approach tomorrow in an entirely different way.

The chicken is never all in.

This particular entrepreneur believed that pigs rule the world. Like Cortés scuttling his ships upon arriving in the New World so that his crew was forced to fight in order to survive, the best of the best are fully committed to the single task at hand.

Here's the thing: Cortés was a murderous asshole. And that Silicon Valley entrepreneur? In addition to running his company, he was also designing software on the side that could steer his yacht around the world remotely while he was dreaming up his next new company. Not exactly committed to the task at hand as fully as he might want you to think. He was a chicken in pig's clothing.

Unless you plan on being Harper Lee and make one great thing and nothing more, you need to be a chicken who lays a lot of eggs. Simply put, creativity flourishes, productivity increases, and opportunities expand when the mind is permitted to wander, the maker of things is free to tinker, and the creative spirit is allowed to dip its toes into many waters.

Single-mindedness is not a useful trait for most creative people, yet it's quite often the perception that people have when they embark on their creative journey. They focus on a single project, just like they were probably taught in high school and college, instead of allowing their disparate, divergent, incongruous interests to seize control of them.

This is a mistake. I believe in the power of chickens. I believe in the possibilities connected to laying many eggs. I believe that your best chance of making something great is by making many possibly great things.

Stuff Begets Stuff

I also believe in the power of cross-pollination: Allowing one area of interest to inform another. Creating a space for the convergence of many ideas.

This is where the unexpected occurs. This is where real creation can take place.

One of the questions I get asked most often as a novelist is "How do you avoid writer's block?" My response: "I've never had writer's block. If you're suffering from writer's block, you're suffering from a lack of things to write. Write different stuff."

The problem is this: as students, we're often advised by people who teach writing but don't actually write themselves that we must finish one project before moving on to another.

Complete that essay.

Finish that poem.

Wrap up that story.

You must reach the finish line before finding a new starting line.

This, of course, is bunk. Utter nonsense. The words of the non-writer.

I don't suffer from writer's block because when one project isn't moving forward, I simply switch to another. At the moment, I'm writing this book. I'm also working on my next novel. I'm revising a middle-grade novel. I'm writing columns for two different magazines. I write a blog post every day. I'm writing a memoir. I'm working on a comic.

If all that fails (and it never has), I try to write one hundred letters every year. Physical letters stuffed inside envelopes with stamps. This week I've written letters to two authors I adore, two former students, the founder of Norton AntiVirus (to compliment him on his Martha's Vineyard home), the Harborside Inn (to compliment Celine, who made our stay absolute perfection), and my aunt.

How could I possibly be blocked on all those projects?

I couldn't, and the same should hold true for all creative people. It's perfectly fine to have one primary project that you are working on most often, but you should have other side projects in various stages of completion, too.

Remember that the Silicon Valley entrepreneur was designing software for his yacht and planning his next business venture while running his company. He understood the power of multiple projects. A chicken laying many eggs.

More importantly, creative people — the makers of things — benefit from expanding their horizons, taking on new challenges, and placing many irons in the fire. Creativity and productivity are spurred by allowing novel disciplines, new learning, constant experimentation, and varied interests to mix. The blending of original ideas and new learning often culminates in something impossible to foresee or even imagine.

Stuff begets stuff. Not the loveliest sentence I've ever written, but true nonetheless.

I am a better writer because I tell stories onstage. I am a better marketing consultant because I do stand-up. I am a better playwright because I write comics. I am a better storyteller because I officiate weddings. I am a better elementary-school teacher because I am a parent. I am a better public speaker because I am a wedding DJ. I am a better leadership coach because I am an investor.

Oddly enough, I'm also a much better teacher — perhaps an immensely better teacher — because I managed McDonald's restaurants for a decade. The skills and strategies I learned while working under the golden arches were probably more valuable to me than any class in college ever was.

I'm also a much better teacher — perhaps an immensely better teacher — because I agreed to give golf a try more than a decade ago. Engaging in something new, difficult, frustrating, oftentimes inexplicable, and endlessly expansive has helped me understand students like never before.

Golf is akin to long division. Initially impenetrable and absolutely infuriating. When a student is struggling, I remind myself of how I felt about golf in those early years, and how I sometimes still feel today.

Stuff begets stuff.

Stuff begetting stuff happens a lot less often for pigs. Pigs get stuck making breakfast every day. Day after day after day. If they're lucky, they might eventually make the best ham-and-egg sandwich anyone has ever tasted. A noble achievement, but being the best at one thing is hard, and it presumes that there aren't even more thrilling pursuits awaiting you around the corner. The pig presumes that he can see into tomorrow. He assumes that breakfast will always be his jam. He believes that he can and should do only one thing.

Chickens make breakfast, too, but then they have time to also plant a tulip garden. Make a sculpture from paper clips. Build the world's first two-stringed banjo. Write sketch comedy. Create a new pasta shape. Design a new wedding dress / bathing suit. Maybe make breakfast for dinner.

The chicken knows that an expanding array of knowledge, skills, interests, and pursuits often leads to unexpected and sometimes re-markable results. The chicken does not pretend that tomorrow is knowable. The chicken doesn't assume that today's passion will be tomorrow's passion.

I took a stage back in July 2011 with the intention of telling one story. One and done. A decade later, I make my living consulting on storytelling, communication strategies, marketing plans, and more.

Imagine if I had decided to be a pig in 2011 and focus solely on my teaching or my writing. I would have missed out on so many extraordinary opportunities. Everything that flowed from that first story on that first stage has also made me a better teacher and writer today.

Chickens know that knowing many things makes everything better. Chickens know that a diverse set of experiences opens up a host of unpredictable possibilities.

Leave the Juggling to Jugglers

A few years ago, a journalist asked me how I juggle so many balls at one time. I laughed. "There is no juggling," I said. "There are simply many different balls of many sizes sitting in front of me. I pick up a ball — the novel I'm writing, let's say — then I work with it for a while. Write a few pages. Revise a few paragraphs. Then I put it down. Now it's time for the teaching ball. For the next seven or eight hours, I toss around that ball. Focus on students, curriculum, and pedagogy. At lunch, I might put the teaching ball down for an hour and pick up my playwriting ball. Much smaller than my teaching or novel-writing balls, but still something I'm working on from time to time. After lunch, it's back to the teaching ball."

No one can juggle multiple projects. You can't be making different things at the same time. But in the same day? The same week? Can you work as a tattoo artist by day and soundscape designer by night? Can you spend your weekends carving ice sculptures for weddings? Build boats in the summer? Write the great American novel on the side?

I think you can.

Not only do I think you can do all those things, but I think that each would inform and improve the others. You'll be a more creative tattoo artist because you're also ice sculpting. You'll design better soundscapes by spending hours on the shoreline, listening to the wind and surf while building boats. You'll write a better novel because the creative parts of your brain will be engaged in auditory, visual, and kinesthetic ways. You may even include a tattoo artist in your great American novel or, better yet, a character who deeply regrets their tattoo. Maybe the tattoo fractures a relationship. Reveals a secret. Contains a hidden code.

We don't juggle our passions. We engage with them, one at a time, over the course of time. We divide our interests and divide our time in pursuit of those interests, knowing that one may very well inform another.

Stuff begets stuff.

The Idea File

I've been writing a blog since I took a class on blogging at Trinity College back in February 2003, when blogging was actually a popular and viable means of finding an audience. I have not missed a day since I began, as I've talked about before, even when others attempted to derail my teaching career by blatantly mischaracterizing what I had written and tried to portray me as some crazed lunatic.

But I'm still teaching and writing, and they are still hiding in some cave, wrapped in their cloak of cowardly anonymity. I hope they are still reading today.

In my two decades spent blogging, I've shifted to three different platforms and changed the name of the blog each time, but I also migrated the content from each of those sites onto my current blog, where I have been writing since 2008. Just about everything that I've written for the past twenty years can still be found online today. The first blog, which was taken down because of the loser cowards, was called *Perpetual Perpetuity*. The second was *Conform Me Not*. The current blog is *Grin and Bare It*.

I'm often asked: "How could you possibly have something to say every day for twenty years?" Six thousand, eight hundred thirty days and counting as I write these words. Part of the answer is there are many days when my post consists of a photo with three sentences essentially saying, "Hey! Look at this! I think it's cool!"

Not everything I write is profound or transformational.

But the truth is that I'm a chicken. Rather than single-mindedly focusing on one subject, I am enormously interested in an enormous number of things. Like the number of projects I am working on, I am also constantly expanding my horizons in terms of subject matter, always looking for the next interesting thing.

This past week is a good example of the secret sauce of idea collection. In my blogging software, I currently have 128 half-written, partially written, or almost entirely unwritten drafts. Some are single sentences representing a thought I want to explore someday. Others are links to news reports and stories that have triggered an idea or an opinion. Still others are photos, graphs, or images that will ultimately inspire writing and lead to a post.

The oldest of these drafts dates back to 2015. A thought from seven years ago, just waiting for me to finally expand upon it.

A look at this week's posts is a good example of how an open, curious mind can lead to content. How a chicken can always find something to say about something.

Yesterday, Wednesday, I wrote about a visit to my former Boy Scout camp and the realization that some of the first, most important lessons of my life were learned on the grounds of that Scout reservation. I'd thought that my first stage was the Nuyorican Poets Cafe back in July 2011 at a Moth StorySLAM. Upon stepping into the dining hall at Camp Sandy Beach and seeing the stage, unchanged after almost forty years, I was suddenly reminded that I spent an enormous amount of time on it when I was a boy, telling stories, cracking jokes, leading sing-alongs, and more. I'd forgotten all this until I visited the camp with my family earlier this summer.

On Tuesday, I wrote about a sentence I'd heard on an NPR report about a recent spate of thunderstorms in Connecticut. I didn't like the construction of the sentence and wrote a post explaining why.

On Monday, I wrote about a ridiculous letter that Governor Cox of Utah received admonishing him for his obscene last name. Having a similarly obscene surname, I wrote an amusing post about the letter and an incident involving my own last name.

On Sunday, I wrote about an inspirational speech delivered to the Alabama football team by sportscaster Ernie Johnson.

On Saturday, I wrote about how much I despise the phrase "God will never give you more than you can handle." It was an idea that had been lingering in my draft file for more than two years until I heard a man at the recent Sturgis motorcycle rally say it about the pandemic and his willingness to remain unvaccinated. Finally I had a portal into the post.

On Friday, I wrote about the importance of reminding yourself of your own good deeds, giving yourself credit for doing well, and telling yourself the right stories, all tied into the joy I feel about our two rescue cats. The idea had actually been on the list for six years, but a recent photo of our cats triggered the idea again and gave me a way of writing about it.

On Thursday, I wrote about Charlie's unique way of scoring his golf round. Rather than using numbers, he uses faces. Smiley faces for holes played well. Less enthusiastic faces for botched holes.

In summary:

- One idea had been percolating for five years.
- Another had been percolating for six years.

- One idea was triggered by a video that someone shared with me.
- One idea was triggered after hearing a news report on the radio.
- One idea was triggered after seeing a news story on Twitter.
- Two posts were written based upon recent experiences.

I also added seven new ideas to my list of drafts. Two relate to memories that resurfaced this week that I'd like to write about sometime in the future:

- When I was nineteen, my then girlfriend and I would follow fire trucks to house fires in the middle of the night as a form of entertainment.
- When I was sixteen, I didn't have a roommate at band camp and was made to feel friendless and stupid until someone forced Keith Ducharme to room with me, which oddly made me feel even more friendless and stupid. Even crazier, it still bothers me to this day.

One idea originated with a statement made by skateboarder Tony Hawk on a weekly podcast that I listen to. One idea came to me while listening to a folk singer perform Johnny Cash's "Ring of Fire" at the Coventry Farmers' Market. One idea was prompted by a dream I had about my childhood clock radio. One idea is about the nature of surprise, highlighted in a short film called *Bench*. One idea describes an encounter with a person that I need to wait before writing about to avoid upsetting someone.

Movies. Music. Memories. Images. News reports. Podcasts. Dreams. Words and sentences spoken by people around me.

When you're a chicken, your world is expansive. Your influences are broad. Your passions are many. That is how I have managed to write a blog post every day of my life for almost two decades.

I am always in search of new eggs. You could be, too.

10 You Choose the Finish Line

"Truth is one, paths are many."
— Mahatma Gandhi

During my senior year in college, my adviser, a novelist and creative-writing professor, suggested that I take an advanced poetry class.

"Why?" I asked. "I don't like poetry. I don't want to write poetry. Poets make no money."

He explained to me that writing poetry might help me find clearer through lines in my fiction. Help me be more concise. I thought it was a dumb idea, but since he was my adviser, I agreed.

I enrolled in an advanced poetry class, not realizing that I was joining a dozen students who had spent the past three years together focused almost exclusively on the reading, writing, and memorizing of poems. They were students who spoke about metaphor with the seriousness and expertise of NASA engineers preparing rocket ships for space.

Ten minutes into the first class, I felt utterly unprepared and stupid. I felt like I didn't belong. Sensing my discomfort, my professor, Hugh Ogden, asked me to sit beside him. His actual words were "Honey, come sit next to me."

I did. A moment later, his dog lay down across my right foot. Hugh rubbed my back and told me that I would be okay.

He was wrong. I would be far better than okay.

It turns out that my adviser was only partially correct about what I might learn by taking a poetry class. Learning to read and write poetry did in fact teach me to find the through lines in my fiction. I learned to meander less, revise more, and let go of material that doesn't serve the story.

But what he and I didn't realize at the time was how the autobiographical poetry that I was writing that semester would become some of the first stories I would tell onstage years later. Not only was I finding ways to improve my fiction, but I was also taking my first steps into personal storytelling.

The most important moment for me came on the night that renowned poet E. Ethelbert Miller joined us. My classmates and I prepared poems for Miller, and he agreed to offer feedback and comment on each one. My classmates took this opportunity very seriously, writing long, epic poems filled with historical and literary references, complex rhyming schemes, and endlessly esoteric vocabulary. As each classmate took their turn reading their poem to Miller, I felt smaller and stupider.

Once again, I felt like I didn't belong. I felt like I had never belonged. All I wanted to do was find an excuse to leave class and never come back.

Unfortunately, I was still sitting beside Hugh. His dog was once again sleeping on my foot. My poem was sitting on the table in front of me, in perfect view of Hugh and my classmates. I was trapped.

When my name was called — the last of the evening — I grudgingly rose from my seat and read aloud this poem:

FOR MATHIEU

For the want of a quiet classroom
and a student who would remind me of me,
I saw red

instead of his button nose and freckled cheeks,
and in a voice that sounded criminal
as it echoed off the *Green Eggs and Ham* bulletin board,
I told him I'd be calling his mother tonight,
to tell her about his disrespect
for our nation's flag,
forgetting the thick, wet grass
that covered her grave.

The poem was about a moment that had happened just weeks prior. I was still student teaching — practicing being a teacher under the watchful gaze of an experienced teacher — when Mathieu, a first grader whom I couldn't manage effectively, interrupted my lesson for the umpteenth time and caused me to say those stupid, hurtful words.

When I finished reading, I sat down. My classmates stared at me with looks of confusion and pity. I felt so foolish. Each of them had read for well over a minute — most much longer — but my poem had clocked in at about twenty seconds.

I knew what they were thinking:

E. Ethelbert Miller came to our class, and this is what you chose to read to him?

Less than a dozen lines?

You purposely wrote in the language of a middle schooler?

I braced myself for Miller's feedback. Expected the worst. Prepared a heartfelt apology. Instead, Miller said that of all the poems read in class that evening, he liked mine best.

I was astounded. So, too, were my classmates. Visibly so.

Miller explained that although the other poems were exceptionally well written and possessed many of the qualities of excellent poetry, mine was the only poem that shared something of myself. "Matthew was vulnerable," he said. "That is one of the best things a poet can offer to a reader."

My heart soared. I felt like I belonged. I felt like I had finally been heard. For the first time in a long time, I felt truly good about what I was doing.

Fourteen years later, I would stand onstage at New York's famed Bitter End and tell the story of Mathieu for the first time in a Moth StorySLAM.

I won that night. Improbably, one of Mathieu's friends was in the audience. Within days, I had reconnected with Mathieu, who blessedly had almost no recollection of me at all. I essentially told an extension of the poem I had written for E. Ethelbert Miller. I spoke the poem in prose rather than verse. The medium changed, but the content basically remained the same. Since that night, I have taken almost all the autobiographical poems written in Hugh Ogden's poetry class and expanded them into stories for the stage and the page.

I never found success in poetry. Back in 2015 I actually combined some of the poems written in Hugh's class with some newly written poems and sent them off to my agent with hopes of becoming the next Billy Collins. Her response: "That's cute. Now write another novel, dummy." I paraphrase, but it's essentially what she said.

But what I did was take the content that existed in one form (poetry) and transform it into another (narrative). More importantly, I suspect that Hugh's poetry class helped me become the storyteller I am today. Vulnerability, brevity, and finding the through line of a story are all essential for storytelling success. I can't pinpoint exactly where those lessons first began, but I'm confident that Hugh's class assisted me mightily along a path I didn't even know I was walking.

My poetry professor made me a better writer of fiction and a better storyteller.

A Horizon of Possibilities

Choosing your creative outlet is an important first step as a maker of things. Most creative people begin with a vision of exactly what they will someday become: Novelist. Hairstylist. Filmmaker. Landscape architect. Designer of jeans. Muralist. Restaurateur. Florist. Pianist. Jeweler. Tattoo artist. Glassblower. Rocket engineer. Mime.

Nothing wrong with these visions. Nothing wrong with the realization of these visions.

When I was a teenager, I would tell people that I wanted to someday write for a living and teach for pleasure. I've nearly realized that seemingly ridiculous adolescent ambition. But exploring options, ignoring outward pressures, and allowing yourself to be ridiculous, experimental, and divergent can make all the difference when it comes to producing something great. Keeping an open mind in terms of what your finish line might be is critical to both learning to make something great and making that great something.

It's wrong to buy into the myth that the creative person is singularly focused on a defined end product. While this may be true for some, it's not uncommon for many to meander through a variety of disciplines along the way, finding different ways to express their creativity, and sometimes to shift the finish line entirely.

Your finish line should not be a fixed point in space but a horizon of possibilities. You should be moving forward, trying to get as close to that horizon as possible while leaving your actual end point flexible and possibly multitudinous.

• • •

Elon Musk, for example, is most closely associated with the automobile company Tesla and more recently with the aerospace manufacturer SpaceX, but his career path actually began in software. Chronologically, Musk's career path has been the following:

> In 1995, Musk cofounded the web-software company Zip2. This start-up was acquired by Compaq for $307 million in 1999.

> In 1999, Musk cofounded the online bank X.com, which merged with Confinity in 2000 to form PayPal. That company was bought by eBay in 2002 for $1.5 billion.

> In 2002, Musk founded SpaceX, an aerospace manufacturer and space transport services company, of which he is currently CEO and CTO.

In 2004, Musk joined electric-vehicle manufacturer Tesla Motors (now Tesla, Inc.) as chairman and product architect, becoming its CEO in 2008.

In 2006, Musk helped create SolarCity, a solar-energy services company that was later acquired by Tesla and became Tesla Energy.

In 2015, Musk cofounded OpenAI, a nonprofit research organization that promotes friendly artificial intelligence.

In 2016, Musk cofounded Neuralink, a neurotechnology company focused on developing brain–computer interfaces. That same year he founded The Boring Company, a tunnel-construction company.

Musk has also proposed the Hyperloop, a high-speed transportation system.

Musk was a physics and math major who first applied his talents to the internet, but he constantly evolved, finding new ways to apply his expertise and love for math, physics, engineering, design, and business to a variety of outlets. The finish lines constantly expanded and changed, but throughout his career, Musk consistently leveraged his skill set to build the things that interested him most.

Just imagine what the world might look like had Elon Musk decided to continue working in web development. Imagine a world where Musk's finish line never included automobiles and spaceships. Imagine where the world might be in a decade or two of Musk working on neurotechnology.

• • •

David Hockney became widely known in the 1960s as a painter and an influential contributor to the pop-art movement. Since then, he has continued to paint, but he has also become renowned for his work with collage, photography, stage design, and digital art. Hockney has experimented with painting, drawing, printmaking, watercolors, and many other media, including a fax machine, paper pulp, computer applications, and iPad drawing programs.

Hockney is an artist who made a name for himself as a painter but allowed himself to explore other adjacent outlets for his creativity. He's a man who works in a visual medium but who is constantly shifting his finish line.

But my favorite story about Hockney's willingness to experiment with form and alter his end product is this:

When the Royal College of Art said it would not allow Hockney to graduate if he did not complete an assignment that required a life drawing of a female model, he protested by painting *Life Painting for a Diploma*, a six-foot-by-six-foot image of a man in white underwear posing in front of a poster of a drawing of the human skeletal system. The poster is labeled PHYSIQUE, and written across the image are the words *life painting for a diploma*.

He also had refused to write an essay required for the final examination, saying he should be assessed solely by his artworks. Recognizing his talent and growing reputation, the Royal College of Art changed its regulations and awarded the diploma. Hockney forced the college to alter its required end point. He moved the finish line and forced *them* to conform.

• • •

The makers of things make their things, but sometimes they change what they — or someone else — thought those things might be. But we need not turn to billionaire inventors and world-famous artists for examples of the makers of things producing their work in a new form.

My mother-in-law Barbara Green began her career at Parsons School of Design as a graphic artist. For years, she and her husband Gerry owned and operated a company that designed and printed stationery, wedding invitations, and the like. Barbara did the design. Gerry did the printing. But she was also a painter and a knitter for many years, expanding into other visual realms to express her artistry.

My favorite part of Barbara's story is this:

Barbara taught herself how to use a computer by digging out a brand-new Apple from the closet at the museum where she was working after she and Gerry sold their printing company. No one at the museum had the knowledge, skill, or inclination to try out the machine, so she read the manual and taught herself how to operate one of Apple's first desktop computers. She quickly became an expert in digital technology.

Without any previous experience in computer science, she found a new passion hiding in a darkened storage closet.

Decades later, when she turned sixty-seven, she discovered the possibilities of digital art using an iPad, much like Hockney did years before. Almost overnight, she has not only applied her design skills to this new digital medium, but the designs she creates — images of ebullient people (many modeled after family members), a stylized ABC book, and much more — are clearly reminiscent of the work she was doing decades before.

Compare her graphic designs from the 1980s and 1990s to her digital work today, and there is no doubt that it's the same artist. Same style. Same aesthetic. Same sensibilities. But instead of working with pen, pencil, and paper, she's now working with a stylus, glass screen, and code.

Same content. Same eye for creation. New finish line. Also, in Barbara's case, an eventual licensing deal.

• • •

Be like Barbara. Be open to new finish lines. Be willing to imagine new finish lines.

Your great American novel might very well become a great American musical. Your goal of becoming stylist to the stars might transform into stylish wig designer for cancer patients. Your death-metal band might someday evolve into acoustic folk. Your dream of sculpting marble might become a much more profitable career carving ice sculptures on wedding days. Your attempt to develop an instant avocado-ripening chamber might become a means of preserving fruits and vegetables for space travel.

These things happen all the time when people who want to make stuff don't fixate on making one single thing.

- Taylor Swift wrote and performed country songs for years. Today she is one of the biggest pop-music stars in the world.
- Ron Howard began his career as an actor. Most people have forgotten his acting career entirely and think of him solely as a director.
- The Beastie Boys started their career in hard-core punk but became legendary for their rap music.
- YouTube initially launched as a video-based dating service.
- Shopify launched as an online snowboarding-equipment store. The business failed miserably, but the web storefront they created to sell their merchandise is now worth billions.
- French artist Thomas Voillaume migrated from creating computer-generated images to building real-world installations.
- Aleksander Małachowski went from teaching engineering classes to making a name for himself in architectural photography.
- John Madden went from Super Bowl–winning coach to one of the most legendary sports broadcasters in the history of television. He was oddly more well known for his broadcasting career than his coaching career, despite his success on the sidelines.
- Matthew Dicks started writing a collection of amusing lists to make his colleagues smile. That finish line unexpectedly became his sixth published novel. Many of the jokes in that book have also been brought to his comedy sets. That finish line may shift again as a producer ponders the possibility of a film based on the book.

Finish lines are fine, but they need to be flexible. What you envision at first might not be where you finish when it's all over. The idea can stay the same. The content can remain the same. But the thing you make might not be the thing you thought you'd make.

• • •

Final case in point: For the past nineteen years, I've been writing a blog without missing a day, as you know (unless you've been skimming this book, you monster).

In 2007, a cabal of cowardly losers attempted to destroy my career by excerpting blog posts absent any context in an effort to get me fired, along with my wife and principal. You know this as well if you're reading this book chronologically (which you should).

In the fall of 2010, I brought this story to *This American Life*, a national radio show and podcast. After much discussion with the producers of the show, I decided to pass on the opportunity to do the story with *This American Life*. I worried that the producers might come to town and stir up a hornets' nest that was better left dormant at the time. They actually warned me that many hornets would be stirred.

In July 2012, I told a version of the story at a Moth Grand-SLAM championship in New York City. I won the championship that night, and the story later aired as a part of *The Moth Radio Hour* on NPR stations all over the country.

In 2016, I began writing a teaching memoir that I thought would include the blog incident in all its gory detail. Two years later, in 2018, I decided that the incident itself would be more than enough for a full memoir and began writing that memoir instead. Part of the writing of that book has included interviews with those involved, and those interviews continue to this day.

In January 2020, just prior to the onset of the pandemic in the United States, I texted my friend Kaia, a musical genius, during the intermission of the musical *Jagged Little Pill*, based on the music of Alanis Morissette: "I want to write a musical with you, and even though I can't sing, I want to perform it with you. Somehow without singing?"

She agreed, but she told me that I'd need to sing. She could help me make that happen.

After passing on an idea for the musical that centered on planning the murder of my stepfather (an excellent idea that I still intend to pursue someday), we ultimately decided on writing a musical based on the blog incident. That work continues as I write this book.

The finish line for this content has changed many times. It may change again. I expect it to eventually include a memoir and a musical. But I'm also remaining flexible and open-minded as new finish lines present themselves. Or occur to me. Or are offered to me.

I am working hard, moving forward in the direction of the horizon but keeping an open mind in terms of where the finish line on that horizon might ultimately be.

10½   Five-Year Plans Are Inviting the Universe to Drop a Piano on You

I played golf with a guy who works in the corporate world. He's got a degree in mathematics and an MBA from Harvard, but he also has a newborn son at home and wants to find a way to spend more time with his family. He's fed up with the corporate culture and has done well enough to make a career change without having to worry about finances for a while.

Teaching, he has decided, is the way to go.

Once he discovered that I was a teacher, he immediately began asking question after question about the profession, including the fastest way to earn a teaching certificate. I explained Connecticut's ARC program to him — a three-month process by which college graduates can become teachers in their areas of expertise that are also areas of need throughout the state, math among them. "You could start the program in June and be teaching in September," I said. "One of my best friends did exactly that. He left the corporate world in June and was teaching math in Hartford in September."

The man was enthusiastic about the process and asked around a dozen follow-up questions as we walked the course together. With each step, his enthusiasm seemed to grow. As we made our final putts of the afternoon and headed back to the clubhouse, he thanked me for the information and said, "That program sounds great. It's still a little pie-in-the-sky for me, but I think I'll make it part of my five-year plan."

Five-year plan? Really? One thousand, eight hundred twenty-six days to achieve a goal?

I don't understand people who talk about five-year plans. In the span of five years — from 2004 to 2009 — I went from being single and still dreaming about someday writing a novel to being married and having published my first book and already sold my second. My wife gave birth to our first child, and we purchased our home.

Can you imagine me making a five-year plan, not knowing about my future wife, my future daughter, and my future success in the publishing industry? In today's ever-changing world, five years is impossible to predict.

Instead of a five-year plan, how about a six-month plan? Or a three-month plan? In five years, this corporate guy's son will be entering kindergarten. He may have more children, planned or otherwise. His company could declare bankruptcy. The United States could be at war with Canada.

Five years is a lot of time. If he's serious about wanting to change his life, spend more time with his family, and find a way to make a difference in the world, why wait five years? Having an intimate and personal understanding of how perilous and fragile life really is, I wanted to tell this guy to ditch the stupid five-year plan, go home, and sign up for the damn program.

The assumption that you'll even be alive five years from now seems like hubris to me. There is no telling. Planning to spend more time with your family five years from now is tempting fate. Just as you're finally ready to make your move, a bus may come along and run you over.

I wanted to shake this man and tell him that the time is now.

I didn't. In the end, this guy seemed too invested in this five-year plan to be deterred by my few nuggets of wisdom, but I am left wondering where he will be in five years. Will he be the teacher that he wants to be? Will he be spending more time with his family? Will he have left in his wake the corporate culture he so despises?

Who knows? It's five years away! But I can guarantee that none of these things will come to pass in this year or the next. That's the thing about a five-year plan. It allows you to do nothing for a long time.

Forget the five-year plan. Someday is today.

11   Make Terrible Things

> "Just because we do bad things
> doesn't mean we are bad people."
>
> — Unknown

"Don't let perfect be the enemy of good."

A popular expression. Also a stupid expression. Do me a favor: When you hear someone profess this ridiculous idea, reject it immediately. Disregard it. Refute it. Stand opposed to it with every fiber of your being.

It's no good. The expression should instead be this: "Don't let perfect be the enemy of progress."

"Don't let perfect be the enemy of good" establishes an expectation of good, when in truth, creative people — the makers of stuff — make terrible things all the time.

We must.

Creation is hard. It is messy and ugly and fraught with struggle and failure. It's an oftentimes miserable journey littered with cast-offs, botched experiments, fitful starts, unmitigated disasters, and utter failures.

We must accept this if we want to make something good. We

must be willing to fail again and again and again in order to find our way to goodness and, sometimes, greatness.

There is nothing wrong with making something that is terrible as long as you are moving forward, making stuff, and trying like hell to succeed. The only real failure for any creator is to stop making stuff.

Case in point: As you read about in chapter 8, I became a wedding DJ back in 1997 because my best friend Bengi didn't like the disc jockey at his own wedding. He thought we could do a lot better. We had spent the three years following high school living together and hosting parties every weekend for as many as one hundred people at a time. Bengi thought that we could translate those skills and experience to the wedding industry.

So knowing nothing about the wedding industry, wedding music, sound equipment, or lighting, we moved forward. We made progress. Rather than thinking or debating or strategizing, we just *did*. By the end of the month, we had purchased equipment that we still couldn't use and had booked our first wedding: one for a friend of a friend. We agreed upon a price of zero dollars.

It did not go well. The photographer complained that I was standing so close to the bride and groom that I kept showing up in their photos like some bizarre third wheel. We couldn't mix songs to save our lives. We had no knowledge of the songs that inspired people to dance. We didn't understand the delicate balance between fast and slow songs.

It was not our best wedding. It was serviceable at best. Not terrible but definitely not good. But we moved on.

The next wedding was much worse. We plugged in our speakers incorrectly, using the wrong cables, making it impossible to play the music loud enough and causing the lyrics of certain songs to drop out completely. I also failed to play the bride and groom's correct entrance song after accidentally sliding the crossfader over and failing to notice when the left CD player refused to play. One of our microphones ran out of battery power in the midst of the best man's toast.

This was absolutely our worst wedding ever. When the guests

ask the DJ to turn up the music and the DJ can't actually make the music any louder, the DJ has failed. When you need to pretend that the Beatles' "Twist and Shout" is a karaoke version because the lyrics have inexplicably disappeared, you are a bad DJ. It was an atrocious performance.

Twenty years later, I was sitting across from fellow storyteller Jeni Bonaldo at the Kripalu Center for Yoga & Health in the Berkshires. I wasn't there for the yoga, of course. The lack of scoring or competition of any kind, as I've said, makes yoga entirely unappealing to me. I was teaching a weeklong storytelling workshop, and Jeni was assisting. She also did a little yoga dancing on her breaks, much to my amusement.

In the midst of our conversation, she somehow mentioned the name of her cousin, who just happened to be the bride at that worst wedding ever. It turns out that Jeni was also at that wedding. She was seventeen years old at the time and doesn't remember anything going wrong that night. She then texted with her cousin to see what she recalled from the wedding, and even the bride had no recollection of our failures.

This is the beauty of making terrible things. No one remembers them. They are almost always forgotten. You need not worry. Even when the mistakes are remembered, mistakes happen every damn day. Your failures are commonplace at best.

By our one hundredth wedding, Bengi and I were operating our company at an exceptionally high level. We learned by doing. We solicited advice from people in the industry whenever possible. We experimented and adjusted. We continued making progress. Never stopped. Continued to make mistakes but pressed on.

• • •

You must be willing to fail. You need to accept the fact that you will likely make terrible things before you make good things.

Ira Glass of *This American Life* probably said it best:

All of us who do creative work, we get into it because we have good taste. But it's like there is this gap. For the first couple years that you're making stuff, what you're making isn't so good. It's not that great. It's trying to be good, it has ambition to be good, but it's not that good....

And if you are just starting out or if you are still in this phase, you've got to know it's normal and the most important thing you can do is do a lot of work. Do a huge volume of work. Put yourself on a deadline so that every week or every month you know you're going to finish one story. It is only by going through a volume of work that you're going to catch up and close that gap. And the work you're making will be as good as your ambitions.

I took longer to figure out how to do this than anyone I've ever met. It takes a while. It's going to take you a while. It's normal to take a while. You just have to fight your way through that.

"*The most important thing you can do* is do a lot of work. Do a huge volume of work." Make terrible things.

This is nothing new. In the early days, Walt Disney was fired from his job at a newspaper because his editor felt that he "lacked imagination and had no good ideas." He would go on to be rejected more than three hundred times by bankers who thought that his idea of Mickey Mouse was absurd. Disney didn't pay attention to the naysayers and went on to be very successful indeed. But that editor was probably correct. In his early days, Walt Disney probably "had no good ideas." He was probably making terrible things.

Michael Jordan was famously cut from his school's varsity basketball team in ninth grade. Do we think he was cut because he was playing brilliantly but went unnoticed by his coach, or was Jordan simply playing poorly as a fourteen-year-old boy? Jordan was cut because he wasn't good enough to make the team. His shooting, dribbling, and defense were bad. He was making terrible things.

Richard Branson, the now-famous founder of Virgin Group

and recent billionaire astronaut, first began his entrepreneurial career in 1966 with an attempt to breed and sell parakeets. When the birds began multiplying more quickly than he could sell them, he scrapped the business entirely. Next, Branson decided to grow and sell Christmas trees. Sadly, that business also failed after his rabbits ate his product. Richard Branson made some really terrible things before going to space.

After graduating college, I launched my career as a novelist with a book about a boy whose father was the corrupt sheriff in a small town in Minnesota, trafficking drugs across the Canadian border. About thirty thousand words into the story, I finally admitted to myself that it was terrible. Poorly conceived. Poorly written. Utterly predictable.

Thankfully that partial manuscript was written on a Brother word processor that still stored its data on removable disks, so that terrible story is gone forever. My next three attempts at novel writing still exist today. Each is about twenty-five thousand words long, and every single one of them is just as terrible as the first.

Before my first published novel, *Something Missing*, I wrote hundreds of thousands of terrible words. Pages upon pages of uninspired, unentertaining stories. I spent more than eight years writing bad fiction before finally stumbling upon a method and mindset that made fiction writing click for me. Had I not allowed myself to write poorly, I never would've had the opportunity to write well.

. . .

When we begin making things, we must give ourselves permission to make terrible things. Miserable, rotten, no-good things. Things that make us wonder if we'll ever make something good.

Judgment, taste, and self-assessment are critical to the creator's journey, but these tools should be applied only to the things we are making. Not to ourselves as the creators of the things.

The things you make can be terrible. They probably will be terrible from time to time, particularly in the beginning of your journey.

There is nothing wrong with stepping back and deciding that your spy thriller, your lemonade stand, your stained-glass window, your carbonated goat's milk, your short film, your escape room, your advertising jingle, or your corn maze is terrible.

This is a normal and essential part of the creative process. But that doesn't make you terrible. It doesn't make you incapable of making something great someday.

Judge the work. Critique the work. Despise the work.

Just don't judge yourself. Good people make terrible things. Talented, creative, brilliant people make truly terrible things.

Judge the work. Not the person. Despise the product but love yourself.

Then start again. Move forward. Make progress.

Create another terrible thing until you make a not-so-terrible thing. Maybe even something great.

11½ Rejection Is Expected, but So Is Persistence

Nobel Prize–winning novelist José Saramago submitted the manuscript of *Skylight* — his first — to a Lisbon publisher in 1953. Receiving no response, Saramago gave up fiction altogether. His wife says that her husband fell into a "painful, indelible silence that lasted decades."

Saramago returned to fiction in 1977 and would eventually write more than twenty novels before his death in 2010.

In 1989, having published three novels, he was at work on a fourth when the publisher to which he had sent *Skylight* wrote to say that they had rediscovered the manuscript and it would be an honor to print it. Saramago never reread it and said only that it would "not be published" in his lifetime. His wife published the book in 2014, after his death.

When I first heard this story, I felt great sympathy for Saramago. A publisher ignores his manuscript, not even bothering to decline the work, and an author loses twenty-five years that could have been spent writing. By all accounts, his first manuscript was excellent, and the book has received rave reviews, so it's not as if Saramago needed the twenty-five years for his talent to germinate. He was already brilliant in 1953.

He simply lost a quarter century of work.

That sympathy for Saramago lasted for about ten seconds. Then

I was reminded of all the authors I know whose first, second, third, fourth, and even fifth manuscripts were turned down by literary agents and publishing houses. Yes, as far as I know, all these people at least received some kind of response from the entities that received their work, but still, I know authors who struggled for decades with rejections before finally breaking through.

Saramago was ignored once and decided to quit. He took his toys and went home. My second reaction was decidedly less sympathetic.

I've read four of Saramago's books, including *Blindness*, which won the Nobel Prize in Literature and caused my wife to weep for a week while reading it. I'm not much of a fan of his work. I think he was an exceptionally talented writer, and I have enjoyed his stories a great deal, but Saramago forgoes the use of chapters and paragraphs almost completely in his books. His sentences can run on for more than a page. He goes pages and pages without the use of a period, preferring instead to use commas. He doesn't use quotations marks to delineate dialogue. In *Blindness*, he stopped using proper nouns completely. I can't stand any of it. I think it demonstrates a complete disregard for the reader and an unnecessary barrier to his stories.

Still, a small part of me wishes I could reach through time and tell him to strengthen his resolve and try again rather than waiting for twenty-five years before taking writing back up. I want to hug him and tell him that it will be all right.

Another part of me wants to kick him in the pants for acting like such a fool and not pressing on with his dream. Trying again. Refusing to give up.

Ironically, my friend who has read *Skylight* reports that Saramago was not using long sentences when he wrote it in the 1950s. Perhaps if he had found success with the book, he would've continued to write more conventionally and found a wider audience.

12   How Did They Do It?

"Find someone who has a life that you want
and figure out how they got it."

— LANA DEL REY

I was running on a treadmill at Bally Total Fitness in West Hartford, Connecticut, back in the spring of 2005 when my life was changed forever. I had just abandoned my third attempt to write a novel — a ridiculous story about a teenage savant and his pet ferret (no joke) — and was finally coming to terms with the reality that I would never become the novelist I had always wanted to be.

As hard as I tried, I just couldn't write good fiction. *I'll write for magazines*, I told myself. *Try my hand at a memoir. Maybe write a book on teaching. Wait for the day when a newspaper editor might offer me a weekly column.*

I was saddened by the thought that my dream was dead, but I was also ready to move on to something more fruitful and realistic. Forward motion. It made sense.

As I ran, I was listening to Stephen King narrate *On Writing*, his seminal tome on writing well. King was talking about the early days in his career, when he was writing stories for men's magazines and getting paid tens and hundreds of dollars at a time.

King was also a teacher, much like myself, earning $6,400 per year. His wife was working for Dunkin' Donuts. Between their two salaries and their two children, they were barely making ends meet. Living in a double-wide trailer. Unable to afford a phone. Unable to afford medication for their kids. Desperate times for two young parents, both of whom had dreams of publishing novels someday. King wrote:

> The problem was the teaching. I liked my coworkers and loved the kids — even the Beavis and Butt-Head types in Living with English could be interesting — but by most Friday afternoons I felt as if I'd spent the week with jumper cables clamped to my brain. If I ever came close to despairing about my future as a writer, it was then. I could see myself thirty years on, wearing the same shabby tweed coats with patches on the elbows, potbelly rolling over my Gap khakis from too much beer. I'd have a cigarette cough from too many packs of Pall Malls, thicker glasses, more dandruff, and in my desk drawer, six or seven unfinished manuscripts which I would take out and tinker with from time to time, usually when drunk. If asked what I did in my spare time, I'd tell people I was writing a book — what else does *any* self-respecting creative-writing teacher do with his or her spare time? And of course I'd lie to myself, telling myself there was still time, it wasn't too late, there were novelists who didn't get started until they were fifty, hell, even sixty. Probably plenty of them.

I slowed my pace as King read that passage aloud. By the time he had reached the end, I'd come to a complete stop. I couldn't believe it. Stephen King was talking about me. *Talking to me.* Absent the alcohol and cigarettes, I was coming perilously close to despairing about my future as a writer, too.

Like King, I was giving up.

Around that time of despair, King tossed his unfinished manuscript of *Carrie* into the trash, finding the story to be full of unfillable holes. He gave up on the story. Decided to move on to something else. But King's wife Tabitha removed the pages from the trash bin, read them, and told King to keep writing. She liked it. She saw potential where her husband had seen nothing but holes.

When he finally finished writing the book, it was the fourth novel he had completed. His previous three novels — *Rage*, *The Long Walk*, and *The Running Man* — would all eventually be published. But *Carrie* was the first. It represented his first big break.

King received a call from his wife one day while teaching at school, informing him that Doubleday had made an offer on *Carrie*: $2,500. Not a lot even by 1970s standards, but a publishing contract nonetheless. A much-needed break.

The paperback rights for *Carrie* would later sell to Signet for $400,000. A lot of money by any standard.

Listening to King talk about his journey, something shifted inside me. Standing on a treadmill in a Bally Total Fitness that no longer exists today, my life had changed in an instant. I suddenly saw a path to making my dreams come true. Someone not unlike me — a teacher with the dream of publishing a novel but despairing about his writing career — had found an unlikely path to success.

If Stephen King, formerly of a double-wide, telephone-free trailer, could do it, so could I. All I needed to do was keep writing. So I did. The path to my first novel was a circuitous one. It included two more false starts and nearly a year of writing Dungeons & Dragons adventures at the behest of my friend Shep, who perhaps recognized my need for an audience.

But almost exactly two years after that moment on the treadmill, in the spring of 2008, I received my life-changing phone call, also while teaching at school. It wasn't my wife who was calling — she was teaching in a classroom two doors down the hallway — but my literary agent, telling me that Doubleday had made an offer on my first novel, *Something Missing*. More than $2,500, too. Enough to pay off our wedding debts and put a down payment on a house.

Crazy, right?

Stephen King and Matthew Dicks, both at school, both in the

midst of teaching careers, when a phone call changed our lives. Both with offers from Doubleday.

Thank goodness Stephen King wrote *On Writing*. I found it just when I needed it.

Grit, Persistence, and Luck

Understanding how someone accomplished something can make an enormous difference in the life of a creator. By learning about the lives of people in a variety of creative fields, we can eliminate misconceptions and demystify the creative process. By learning about how the makers of things made their things, we can oftentimes see a path for ourselves.

It's good to know how hard it was for those who came before us. I think that we often see the creators of good and great things as somehow special — imbued with talent and power beyond our reach. Artists who ascended the mountaintop with grace and ease.

Sometimes this is true, but more often, it's simply dogged determination, a refusal to quit, a relentless drive to succeed, and dumb luck.

Knowing this can make our journeys easier.

Painter Frida Kahlo was in a serious bus accident at the age of eighteen. Confined to bed for three months following the accident, Kahlo began to paint as a means of passing the time. Her mother provided her with a specially made easel, which enabled her to paint in bed, and her father lent her some of his oil paints. She had a mirror placed above the easel so that she could see herself. Painting became a way for Kahlo to explore questions of identity and existence as her body healed.

She said, "I paint myself because I am often alone, and I am the subject I know best." She later stated that the accident and the isolating recovery period created a desire "to begin again, painting things just as I saw them with my own eyes and nothing more." Kahlo's moment of realization took place while recuperating in a hospital bed.

Zumba inventor Alberto "Beto" Pérez was a struggling fitness instructor and dancer who forgot to bring his regular music to an aerobics class one day. He happened to have cassette tapes of Latin dance music — salsa and merengue — and taught his class using them instead. In the improvised dance steps of that aerobics class, Zumba was born. Sometimes it takes an unexpected obstacle (and the combination of two different talents) to make something special.

Samuel Whittemore, age seventy-eight, was working in his fields on April 19, 1775, when he spotted a brigade of British soldiers sent to assist the retreat of forces from Lexington and Concord. Whittemore loaded his musket and ambushed the soldiers from behind a nearby stone wall, killing one. He then drew his dueling pistols, killed a second soldier, and mortally wounded a third. By the time Whittemore had fired his third shot, the British had reached his position behind the wall.

Whittemore drew his sword and attacked. He was subsequently shot in the face, bayoneted numerous times, and left for dead in a pool of blood. He was found by colonial forces, still trying to load his musket to resume the fight. Whittemore was taken to a doctor in the nearby town of Medford, Massachusetts, who declared that the man had no hope of surviving his wounds.

Whittemore promptly recovered from his injuries and lived another eighteen years, dying of natural causes at the age of ninety-six. He lived long enough to see the Constitution signed and the United States become a nation.

A monument stands in Whittemore Park at the northeast corner of Massachusetts Avenue and Mystic Street in Arlington, Massachusetts. It reads:

> *Near this spot, Samuel Whittemore, then 80 years old, killed three British soldiers, April 19, 1775. He was shot, bayoneted, beaten and left for dead, but recovered and lived to be 98 years of age.*

Sadly, they got his age wrong. More egregiously, they did not use an Oxford comma. Still, not bad for a man who would've qualified for Social Security sixteen years before the confrontation took place.

Whittemore was not exactly a creator in the traditional sense, but it's a lesson in never giving up. Never thinking it's too late. Never losing hope that you, too, can leave a mark. Grandma Moses would've been a more apt and obvious example of this, but I love the story of Samuel Whittemore and try to tell it whenever possible.

But how about this one: Estelle Getty, born on the Lower East Side in 1923, wanted to be an actress from an early age but never thought she was good enough to succeed onstage. Instead, she found a job as a secretary after high school, got married, and raised two children.

At age fifty-one, after her kids were grown, she decided to study acting. She considered quitting many times but loved the dream too much to turn her back on it. Eventually she met local playwright Harvey Fierstein and asked him to write a part for her in his next play.

He agreed, writing a role for her in *Torch Song Trilogy*. It ended up on Broadway.

Estelle Getty was well into her fifties when she was finally able to quit her day job and support herself as a working actress. *Torch Song Trilogy* toured America for four years. When the play made it to Los Angeles, she was seen by producers who were getting ready to launch a television pilot featuring four retired women living together.

At the age of sixty-two, Getty was cast as Sophia Petrillo in NBC's *The Golden Girls*. Three years later, in 1988, at the age of sixty-five, Estelle Getty won an Emmy for her role on the show.

Estelle Getty never gave up on her dream, even when she didn't believe herself capable of making that dream come true. She didn't give up when most actresses her age were being written out of television and film. It took her a lifetime to make her dreams come true, which is how long it sometimes takes.

Peter Roget was a British doctor, lecturer, and inventor who suffered from lifelong depression and retired at the age of sixty-one. In addition to his more traditional professions, Roget was also an obsessive list maker from the age of eight, explaining that making lists helped him cope with his depression. Following his retirement, Roget spent all his time making lists of words and organizing them into categories by meaning.

His catalog of lists was published for the first time in 1852 when he was seventy-three years old. It was titled *Thesaurus of English Words and Phrases Classified and Arranged so as to Facilitate the Expression of Ideas and Assist in Literary Composition.* It's better known today as *Roget's Thesaurus of English Words and Phrases.* Peter Roget found a use for his lifelong passion late in life and, in doing so, created something that still exists today. Something that I have used more than once while writing this book.

There are many paths to and timetables for success.

I was lucky to have been awakened to the power of the written word by Mr. Compopiano back in the fall of 1988.

I was lucky to find a way of writing novels while bored in Boca Raton on a Wednesday night in February 2005.

I got lucky when my friends convinced me to say yes to my own question and take a stage in New York City and tell a story about my life in July 2011.

None of the success that spiraled from these moments could have ever been predicted.

The path to success is rarely straightforward. Many of us need to get lucky along the way. Sometimes that luck comes in the form of a misplaced cassette tape. Other times you're lucky enough to be spotted onstage by an up-and-coming television producer. Sometimes it comes in the form of a spouse, plucking a partially written manuscript from the trash can, dusting off the cigarette ash, and reading what would one day become a bestseller.

Sometimes your misfortune can lead to your success, as it did for Kahlo in the form of a near-fatal bus accident. When the world handed her lemons, she made legendary lemonade.

Knowing that the paths of most creators are not linear, nor are they simple, can be enormously reassuring on those days when all seems lost and the horizon seems impossibly far away.

You're not special.

You're not a unicorn.

Neither blessed nor cursed.

You're just another creative soul, journeying on a long and windy path to making something good and maybe great. There is no telling how long it will take you and how many bayonets to the chest you will have to suffer along the way.

But cheer up. You're walking in the footsteps of greatness. Just keep walking.

Part 3

SUPPORT

"You can't do it alone, listen to me.
Everybody needs a home."

— Chic

13   Find Your People

"A friend in need needs a friend indeed."

— Karen Scalf Linamen

I wrote the first three chapters of my first published novel, *Something Missing*, while visiting Elysha's grandmother in Boca Raton back in February 2005. That trip changed my life.

Up until that weeklong Florida journey, I was starting every novel by planning it out as I'd been taught in college. I would plot out my story using Post-it Notes and a whiteboard, identifying set pieces, clever plot twists, unexpected turns, and critical character development. The whole story was laid out in front of me, before I ever started writing, in multicolored adhesive squares.

It turns out that I was excellent at purchasing Post-it Notes, but that was about it. The books were never good, and every one of them ground to a halt well before it was completed.

I was closing in on despair as our flight left Hartford, bound for Florida. When I arrived in Boca Raton, I discovered — much to my dismay — that Nana didn't have internet service in her home. She didn't have cable television. And even though Nana was seventy-eight years old at the time — the same age Samuel Whittemore was during his famous Revolutionary War skirmish — she was still driving, so Elysha and I didn't rent a car. Nana picked us up at the airport, which meant we were entirely at her whim for the week. Wherever Nana went, we went.

When you stay with Nana in Boca Raton, you rise early and eat breakfast at the club. While eating your eggs and toast, you discuss what you'll be having for lunch. You return to the club at noon for said lunch. While dining on sandwiches and soups, you discuss where you'll be going for dinner.

Then, around 4:30 p.m., you drive off the property — Nana still behind the wheel — to a restaurant in Delray that serves stone crabs. You enjoy a lovely meal, after which you return to the house for a quiet, relaxing evening.

"Quiet" and "relaxing" are not exactly my cup of tea. None of this suited me well. I was trapped in Boca Woods, an enormous walled-in community surrounded by golf courses and six-lane highways. I play golf, of course, but no one told me about the forty-five holes surrounding the property, so I had no clubs with me. I spent my week watching people play golf while I wished I could be playing.

Armed with a single book — Stephen King's *The Dark Tower VI: Song of Susannah* — and nothing more, I was out of reading material and anything else to do just three days into our weeklong vacation. But I had an idea for a short story that had been niggling away in my brain for the past couple of months.

My friend Justine had arrived to dinner one night upset because she had lost an earring. She had opened her jewelry box and discovered that one of her earrings had disappeared. "Maybe someone stole it," I said. "A clever burglar who stole one but not the other, so you'd never suspect theft." I suggested this theory to be amusing, but that idea — a burglar who steals things that go unnoticed — lodged in my mind. I thought it might make a good short story.

So on a Wednesday night, after Nana had gone off to an opera class and then a date with Joe, who was receiving treatment in the ICU of the local hospital (according to Nana, all her boyfriends were dying), I told Elysha that I would try to write a short story. "I've got nothing else to do."

But without Post-it Notes and a whiteboard, I just started writing, blindly plunging myself into the story. For the first time ever, I wrote without a plan. For the first time in a long time, I felt like I was writing something good.

By the end of the week, I had written the first three chapters of what I thought would be a long short story or maybe even a novella, but in the back of my mind, I started to wonder if this might be a novel. I had no idea where the story was going or what might happen, but I thought it was good. The best writing I had done in years.

Elysha read the first three chapters in Nana's kitchen on the Saturday morning before we flew home. She liked it a lot. So, too, did Nana, who warned me that if she thought it was bad, she would have to tell me as much.

So when I arrived back in Connecticut, I assembled a team of readers. People who would read along with me, chapter by chapter, offering me feedback, encouragement, proofreading and editing, and anything else they wanted to contribute.

That first team consisted of eight people, including Elysha and Shep. Some were trusted friends who provided outstanding feedback and advice. One served as a copyeditor, correcting grammar and spelling errors in the manuscript. One thought that everything I wrote was brilliant. She did nothing but compliment the hell out of me.

All of them were essential to my process. They told me when they were confused. They admitted when they were bored. They told me when I was funny and when I was trying too hard to be funny. Most importantly, I had an audience. I knew that someone was reading. Readers wanted to know what might happen next. They had strong feelings about the protagonist, Martin, and the decisions he made.

They became my team. My consiglieri. My people.

Seven books and a decade later, I now have a database of beta readers. I choose my readers based upon the book I'm writing and their availability. When I wrote *The Perfect Comeback of Caroline Jacobs*, a story about a mother and a daughter, my team consisted of seven women and one man. When I wrote *Twenty-One Truths about*

Love — a book in the form of the lists of a former teacher turned bookstore owner — half of my readers were teachers. When I wrote *Memoirs of an Imaginary Friend* — a book that I thought might cross over into the YA market — my team included a teenager for the first time.

After I turned in the first half of this book, the editor, Georgia Hughes, emailed me to say she had started reading: "Just a quick note to say I've read some of the manuscript and so far, I'm loving it." I was thrilled. It made my heart soar. I dove back into the manuscript with renewed energy and enthusiasm.

First-Look Audiences

Feedback is critical. Having a group of people on your side — receiving feedback and knowing someone is invested in your work — is everything. Simon & Garfunkel once sang "I Am a Rock" about a man who is an island unto himself:

> I have my books
> And my poetry to protect me
> I am shielded in my armor
> Hiding in my room
> Safe within my womb
> I touch no one and no one touches me
> I am a rock
> I am an island.

This was actually my personal theme song when I met Elysha. It's since been replaced by "Can't Keep It In" by Cat Stevens.

But Simon & Garfunkel were liars when they wrote that song, because even they were not alone. Simon had Garfunkel. Garfunkel had Simon. The two eventually went their own separate ways, but when they were singing about being an island, they were decidedly not alone.

They had each other.

Creation in a vacuum is a difficult thing. Eventually you need to hear from people you trust, and oftentimes the sooner, the better. This is terrifying for many creative people, because showing your work before it is complete — and sometimes even after it's complete — requires an enormous amount of vulnerability and courage.

Too bad. If you struggle with this, get over it.

If you want to make things that other people will want to see or hear or consume, you need to know what they think. The door can remain closed while you work, but eventually it must be opened to others. The sooner you can open that door, the better.

Identifying and assembling the right "first-look audience" for your work is critical to your success. It can mean the difference between moving forward and stalling out. It can transform self-doubt into hope. It can turn surrender into conquest. It can turn problems into solutions.

I was in the midst of writing *Twenty-One Truths about Love* when I thought I might be losing my story. The protagonist, Dan, was planning a robbery out of desperation and fear, but I couldn't think of something for him to reasonably rob. I needed to find something for Dan to rob that had a decent chance of success and a large enough payday to warrant the risk. I needed a relatively safe, profitable target for Dan.

With the advent of security cameras, it was hard to come up with anything that Dan might rob without being caught on film. And with the increased use of credit and debit cards, I couldn't think of anything short of a bank or armored car for Dan to rob with a payout worth the risk. But Dan wasn't exactly the bank- or armored-car-robbing kind of guy. He was desperate, but not exactly a criminal mastermind.

For three months, I stalled, searching for a target. Then one day in October, I took my brother Jeremy to a New England Patriots game. Sometime in the third quarter, with the game well in hand thanks to the greatness of Tom Brady, he asked me what I was working on. I hadn't really told many people about the book, and because it was being written in list form, no one had actually read anything yet, but sitting in section 331, row 29, seat 5, I decided to open the door and tell my brother in seat 6 about the book. I described the characters, summarized the story, and then explained my and Dan's problem: "What can you rob in today's world that will result in a lot of cash and reasonably low risk?"

Jeremy answered instantly: "A bingo." He was so quick and certain of his answer, I wondered if he hadn't been planning a robbery like this himself.

He explained that bingos are often held in places like VFW halls, Elks lodges, Daughters of the American Revolution meetings, churches... all easy targets, and they all deal in cash. Just like that, my problem was solved.

Solved because I opened the door. Added my brother to the team. Invited him into my creative world.

The more people we involve in the creation of our things, the more likely our problems will be solved.

Accountability

Finding your team and involving them in your creative process can also add a much-needed layer of accountability to your productivity.

If no one is reading your manuscript, it's easy to get lazy when things get hard.

If no one is listening to your song, it's easy to abandon it when it becomes a struggle.

If no one is listening to your podcast, it's easy to never edit and publish.

If you never preview your musical for an audience, it's easy to avoid scheduling an opening date.

If you never step up to that open mic and tell a joke, it's easy to put off your career in comedy to another day.

One of the biggest stumbling blocks for creative people — the potential makers of things — is a lack of accountability. Since most creators are not working for someone else, they decide on timetables, completion dates, criteria, rubrics, and more.

The artist decides when to paint.

The musician decides when to compose.

The entrepreneur decides when to write their business plan.

The poet decides when to write.

The dress designer decides when to sew.

The cake decorator decides when to bake.

When you are your own boss, as many creators are, you're not required to insist that your employee — also you — get anything done. The boss isn't required to make the employee accountable, because they are one and the same person. As a result, nothing gets done. Or nothing gets done on a timely basis. Procrastination, often fueled by fear and uncertainty (and that damn need for perfection), rules the day.

Years ago, I spoke about one of my books at a senior living facility. All the men fell asleep within fifteen minutes of the start of my talk, but the women listened attentively, asked good questions, and were engaged throughout. After I was finished speaking, a woman approached me and Elysha, who was accompanying me that day, and said, "I have a story that needs to be written. A real doozy. And you know what? I'm going to write it down someday now that I've heard you speak."

I was flattered, of course, but I had to ask: "How old are you?"

"I'm eighty-seven," she replied. "Why?"

"Well," I said, gingerly, "I think you should probably get started. You're eighty-seven years old. You don't have much time left."

Elysha elbowed me, hard, and the woman was clearly displeased with my remark, but here's the truth: that conversation took place more than a decade ago, which means that woman is probably dead today. Do you think she wrote her story?

I don't. I don't think you think so, either.

Don't Run Out of Somedays

For most of us, the reality is this: We assume that we will make our dreams come true someday, but then we run out of somedays, and we die. Sometimes we are hit by a bus. Sometimes we're shot by a stray arrow. Sometimes cancer sneaks up on us. A shark eats us. We fall into a volcano. We are hit by lightning.

Sometimes we just get old and die. I'm almost certain that woman died without ever sharing her story with the world.

Bad for the world. Worse for her.

But what if there was a writing group in her retirement community that met once per week to share their work? What if she had been assigned a date and time to share her work in progress with the group? What if the group had generously offered feedback, both positive and constructive, to the woman? What if she had found her own team of fellow writers and readers to encourage her, challenge her, and nudge her along?

Would that have increased her chances of writing her story before she ran out of somedays? I think so. I think you think so, too.

My daughter Clara is currently writing a novel. She won't let me see it, which infuriates me beyond belief, but she has two partners in crime — Livia and Sasha — who read her work often. Livia offers feedback, and Sasha is writing a novel of her own, so Clara and Sasha exchange manuscripts and discuss their progress.

When I asked Clara when her book will finally be finished so I can read the damn thing, she said, "Midwinter. February."

"How can you be so sure?" I asked.

"That's what I told Livia and Sasha."

Accountability. My twelve-year-old daughter gets it.

Build Your Team

Ever since 2010, I have been posting my yearly goals on my blog and on social media as a means of holding myself accountable. I repost my goals monthly along with my progress so far.

In 2021, the year that I'm writing this book, I have a total of fifty-three goals spread out among six different categories. That's admittedly a lot of goals, but I believe in setting a very high bar and accepting failure along the way.

In fact, my success rate over the years has been thus:

2010: 44%
2011: 62%
2012: 30%
2013: 60%
2014: 60%
2015: 59%
2016: 59%
2017: 71%
2018: 50%
2019: 48%
2020: 54%

That works out to an average of 54.3 percent.

You wouldn't think that posting goals online would be a meaningful way of holding myself accountable, but those monthly progress updates are some of my most widely read posts, and over the years, countless numbers of readers have actively involved themselves in my creative process. I receive emails from folks I have never met telling me how much they enjoy tracking my progress throughout the year and how much they appreciate my willingness to publicly fail in the completion of so many goals. Many have even assisted me in completing my goals in both small and enormous ways.

Knowing that readers are paying attention, knowing that they are invested in my success, and knowing that they sometimes offer to assist me on my journey means the world to me. They hold me accountable.

These are also my people. My team of unseen, relatively unknown partners in my journey. They motivate me to do more. It's a simple way of holding myself accountable for doing what I said I would do.

Choose Your People Wisely

You need to ensure that you find the right people to support you, too. Not every potential supporter is a good supporter. Some are entirely unhelpful. Others are downright toxic.

Years ago, I joined a writers' group at a local library, eager to connect with people who shared similar passions. As I left for the first meeting, Elysha hugged me and said, "Have a great time, honey. I'm so excited for you."

I returned two hours later, dejected and disappointed. About ten minutes into the meeting, the group realized who I was — the local author with two published novels under his belt — and immediately turned venomous. They wanted to know if my success was the result of knowing the right people, making connections via my college professors, or hiring a New York City publicist to draw attention to my work.

"None of those things," I said. I explained that I had spent three years writing my first novel, then I mailed it off to more than a hundred literary agents around the country, hoping to find one who liked my story. After dozens of rejections, I finally found someone who wanted to work with me. Taryn Fagerness. My literary agent and friend to this day.

Six months later, I had sold my first book.

No one seemed happy with this response. The meeting went downhill from there. Lots of side-eye and passive-aggressive commentary. By the time I left, I vowed never to return.

We need our people, but we also need the right people. Honest, supportive human beings who are invested in our success. Folks who lack envy. People who genuinely love you.

Cut out those who don't fit the bill.

Foolishly, despite vowing not to, I returned to that same writing group two years later, hoping for better results. Nothing had changed. I was treated just as badly the second time as I was the first.

That's fine. I have Elysha, Shep, Taryn, David, Jeni, Amy, Kaia, Erica, Joey, Lionel, and the rest.

Maybe Clara, someday, if she's ever willing to share.

14 Put Your Eyes on the Prize

"Success comes when we wake up every day
in that never-ending pursuit of why we do what we do."
— SIMON SINEK

Someone once asked me why I became an elementary-school teacher.
I listed the many reasons why my lifelong dream was to teach human
beings much smaller than myself:

- I wanted a job that made a real difference in the world.
- I like kids a lot. More than most adults. I love their
  honesty, sense of wonder, and desire to have fun whenever possible.
- School was always a safe place for me as a child. A
  home away from home. I wanted to create the same for
  children who need it today.
- I love the rhythms of the school year. The brand-new
  class each September. The way holidays are treated sacredly in schools. As Plato said, the "lifestyle choice"
  that school offers.

Once I was finished listing my reasons, Elysha added, "He also
hates authority. He can't stand being told what to do. Teaching, for

the most part, is done without any supervision, so it's perfect for him."

I was stunned. This had never occurred to me, but from the moment she said those words, I knew that it was true. Even with the modicum of supervision I receive, I am still a teacher who constantly bends and sometimes breaks the rules.

Know Why You Do What You Do

Why is this important? Knowing why we do the things we do can be enormously instructive about how we live our lives and move forward into new, creative realms.

You may recall me mentioning that ten years into my teaching career, I started to wonder if I might want to make another one of my childhood dreams — becoming an attorney — a reality.

Then I remembered what Elysha had said: I hate authority. I knew right there and then that I could never be an attorney.

I don't even own a tie anymore. Just the idea that a dress code would be imposed on me would be untenable, let alone all the procedural necessities and niceties of a courtroom. Lawyers live by an onerous, seemingly unending set of rules on a daily basis. They are required to be deferential to authority. I couldn't do any of that and still be happy.

But that didn't mean the dream entirely died. Rather than diving into a profession that would not suit me, I shifted the dream, allowing me to avoid supervision but still fulfilling at least part of it. In the past five years, I've worked with attorneys quite a bit, helping them craft opening statements and prepare witnesses, and teaching them to tell stories in the courtroom. I've worked with the bar associations of several states, taught classes at the University of Connecticut School of Law, and worked on retainer for a law firm during an especially challenging case.

Prior to the pandemic, I traveled to Indiana to teach storytelling strategies to more than three hundred prosecutors in Indianapolis, including the state's attorney general. That was an especially challenging assignment given that when I was arrested and tried for a crime I didn't commit, it was thanks in large part to an especially aggressive prosecutor. I felt like a long-tailed cat in a room filled with rocking chairs.

I'm not a lawyer, but I get to enjoy some of the appealing aspects of working as an attorney absent any authority figures or the need to wear a suit. My hope is to someday consult with the Innocence Project, helping those who have been wrongfully convicted. That might be even better than becoming an attorney.

As I recounted in chapter 2, a few years ago I also considered changing over from an elementary-school teacher to a high-school English teacher, and I even began taking one of the two classes needed to extend my certification. But as I talked to fellow high-school teachers, I not only learned about the time commitment that would be required but also started to understand what it would mean to leave the school where I have worked for the past quarter century.

I've established a reputation in my school and its surrounding community. I've earned the respect of parents, my colleagues, and my principal. I've proved myself to be trustworthy and effective. As a result, no one really bothers me very much. Other than the occasional moment when my boss needs to stop me from stepping over a line or bending a rule too far, I have an enormous amount of autonomy in my workplace.

If I were to switch schools and positions, that would likely change. That simple awareness that I learned from Elysha — I became a teacher because I can't stand authority — has helped guide my life and career in directions that suit me best. Knowing why I do what I do has spared me some major missteps in life. Knowing why you do what you do can also make the path forward much clearer.

Elysha taught third and fifth grade for many years and was perfectly happy in those positions. She loved teaching children ages eight to ten. Then she stayed home for about ten years, raising our children.

When it was time to return to the classroom, she didn't simply jump back into what she was doing before. Instead, she asked herself why she wanted to be a teacher in the first place and what had appealed most to her about teaching. After some soul-searching, she came to the realization that as much as she enjoyed working with children, she also loved helping parents support their children through their educational journey. There is no better grade to do this than kindergarten, when parents are often navigating public school for the very first time.

As a result, Elysha became a kindergarten teacher. She went from teaching children how to multiply and write poetry to teaching children what the letter *B* sounds like and how to take turns without killing one another.

She couldn't be happier.

Dig Deep

Asking yourself why you do what you do can make the path clear. Understanding why you do the things you do can help guide you to the life you most desire. Even more important, knowing why you do what you do, and keeping those reasons at the forefront of your mind, can also be exceptionally motivating. Even inspiring. And the more tangible reasons you can find for wanting to be successful, the more inspiring it can be.

Try this: Ask yourself why you are chasing your dream. Whether you want to be a filmmaker, the designer of roller coasters, the inventor of a new type of pizza, a classical composer, a rocket builder, or a cat trainer, what are your reasons for chasing that dream?

Dig deep.

Look into your past.

Find the best and worst of your motivations.

When I asked myself *Why do I want to be a storyteller — on the page or the stage?* the reasons, after some soul-searching, were many:

- I want to earn a living in a career that allows me almost complete control of my time.

- I want an opportunity to be financially independent.
- I want to be known in this world.
- It's fun for me to write and speak stories — both fiction and memoir.
- I'm absolutely consumed with thoughts of death and terrified by the prospect of ceasing to exist, so by putting words on a page, I hope to somehow live beyond my years.

All that is real and absolutely true, but then I really started to dig deep:

- I want to prove to all the teachers who failed to notice me that they made a mistake.
- I desperately want the attention of a mother who never seemed to have time for me (and has now passed away) and a father who left me at a young age and never really came back.

That last one came to me while speaking to about a thousand students in São Paulo, Brazil. As I began the question-and-answer session of my talk, a young woman asked, "You write books. Tell stories. Write a blog post every day. Write musicals. Poems. All of it. Why do you need to put so much stuff into the world?" The desire to garner the attention of a dead mother and absent father hit me for the first time in that auditorium, and I knew instantly that it was true. But there was more. When I dug even deeper, I found more still:

- I want to show Sean, Glen, Danny, and other childhood bullies that they did not win.
- I want to show the family members who didn't believe in me or didn't notice me that they were wrong.

This realization came to me a couple of years ago when my aunt Diane mailed me a packet of material that included political cartoons I had been drawing on an Easter Sunday when I was about twelve years old. As my relatives drank Sanka and talked about nothing, I was writing and drawing economic and political criticisms of so-called Reaganomics and the recent Soviet invasion of Afghanistan. Diane noticed me when no one else did, so after I left, she scooped up those cartoons and saved them for me. Seeing those cartoons decades later, I remembered so clearly how much of an outsider I felt like back then. I remembered desperately wishing someone would ask me what I was drawing and what I was thinking.

I tell stories because that wish never went away.

But there is even more:

- I want to show the cowards who years ago tried to destroy my teaching career with anonymous, libelous claims that I am still winning while they are still hiding in their pathetic little holes.
- I want to show the people who should've supported my career that I didn't need their damn help after all.
- I want to make Elysha cry again.

That last one is a biggie. After receiving the call from my agent telling me that a publisher had made an offer on my book — enough to make a real difference in our lives — I left my classroom in search of Elysha to tell her the news. I found her in a back hall of our school, heading back to her classroom. I stopped her in her tracks, told her the news, and watched as she collapsed to the floor in tears of joy. I've been trying to replicate that moment ever since. In addition to eliciting tears of joy, I'm also constantly, desperately trying to make her proud of the work I do.

Yet another reason: I'm still running away from the poverty, homelessness, and hopelessness of my youth.

The greater the number of reasons you have to achieve your goals, the greater the number of motivators you have to propel you forward.

Maybe I'm feeling a little listless one cold winter morning? I think about the bully who threw a music stand like a spear at my head because he thought it would be funny. Or one of those anonymous people who I know tried to destroy my career. Or maybe I implant the image of my future tombstone in my mind. Or I think about Elysha, still asleep in bed, laughing at a scene in my novel or nodding in agreement at an idea I have for a new story. I remind my-self of how we are all standing on the precipice of disaster, perfectly capable of losing a career and slipping into financial ruin overnight. Sometimes, I think about my father, absent from my life for the past four decades, hoping that someday I might write something that turns his attention in my direction.

You need to find your own motivators. The reasons you do what you do. Find the things that make you want to run through someone or toward someone or away from something.

Dig deep. Ask yourself hard questions. Give yourself the time required to find those answers, as uncomfortable or painful or heart-breaking as they may be. They can be the fuel that you will need on the days when your desire is low but your time is still ticking.

Choose Your Goals Wisely

Lastly, goal setting, like the kind described in the previous chapter, can help you enormously in terms of keeping your eyes on the prize. Maintaining a list, setting a time to review progress regularly, and building in some form of accountability has been a game changer for me and many of the people with whom I work. When you wake up every day without any question about what needs to be done and what steps are required to accomplish a goal, you are far less likely to find yourself procrastinating or filling your time with meaningless tasks and busywork. Add the element of accountability, and those goals will remain firmly fixed in your mind. Nothing slips through the cracks if others are paying attention, holding your feet to the fire, and supporting the cause.

But this will work only if you establish goals correctly, meaning they should be measurable, effort based, and attainable absent the necessary approval or actions of others. For example:

- My goal is to write a novel. Complete the assemblage of sentences that constitute a whole story. Whether or not a publisher decides to purchase that novel is beyond my control. I set goals that I can control through my own efforts, then I move forward.

- My goal is to pitch myself to MasterClass three times over the course of the year. Whether or not the production team at MasterClass is wise enough to hire me for one of their instructional videos on storytelling is beyond my control. My goal is to present the best pitch possible — then move on to the next goal.

- My goal is to send at least six letters to my father this year. My hope is that my father will respond, and we can reinvigorate our tenuous, inconsistent relationship. I have no control over the man who I wish would become a more important part of my life, so all I can do is send my letters and hope for the best.

- My goal is to finish writing the musical with Kaia. Whether she and I can find a theater to stage our show is irrelevant. Write the thing. That is something we can control.

- My goal is to produce twelve episodes of my podcast with Elysha, *Speak Up Storytelling*, this year. Setting goals for downloads would be ridiculous, since I can't influence this goal through my own effort. A higher-quality podcast may yield a larger audience, but that is not guaranteed. What I can guarantee is producing a specific number of episodes over the course of the year. The rest is left to fate. Or perhaps the hiring of a publicist, which could also be a goal.

When we judge our progress on our own efforts, we avoid assessing success and failure based upon things we cannot control. We keep our eyes on the prizes that can be won through our own hard work, focus, and determination. Stack up enough of those victories, and some of those dreams that require the intervention of others might just finally happen.

Answer the Why and the How

This is a chapter about two important questions: *Why?* and *How?* They are the two most important questions in need of answer in order for us to succeed.

The why ensures that we remain on the right path, pointed in the correct direction, avoiding pitfalls and obstacles that fail to align with our desires. The why also provides us with the much-needed motivation to continue on days when the work seems too hard or our progress is so insubstantial that we wonder whether we will ever succeed. Understanding what launched our creative desire — and piling up as many of those reasons as we can — will serve as a reminder of why we stepped onto this arduous path in the first place.

The how is the means of reaching our goals. It is the acknowledgment that long journeys require small steps. The how is the reminder to focus our energies on only those things that we can control. It's the understanding that we can't make this journey alone. We need others holding us accountable, rooting for us, and demanding that we keep working when quitting seems the more logical, sane choice.

You must answer the why and the how — not just today but constantly and relentlessly. *Why do I do the things that I do?* must be a question that never-endingly rings in your mind. *What is the next step to reaching my goal?* is a question you must repeatedly ask yourself.

Answer the why and the how, and you'll discover how easily all those other answers suddenly fall into place. Answer the why and the how, and you will find yourself excited about getting out of bed every morning, motivated for a multitude of reasons and knowing exactly what needs to be done.

Most people feel neither excited nor motivated when they open their eyes at daybreak. Most people wish for an extra hour in bed and wonder how they will fill the empty hours of their day.

Creative people — makers of things and dreamers of dreams — can't afford this dithering nonsense.

Answer why and how, and the course of every day will be clear, and the reasons for embarking upon it will be abundant.

14½ Leave Performative Productivity to the Female Lions

There was a time when scientists believed that the female lion was the hunter and the male lion lounged around all day, waiting for the female to bring home the bacon. This assumption was made based upon scientific observation. It was not hard to see. Female lions chased and killed their prey, and male lions did not.

I wasn't sure how I felt about this.

Part of me was annoyed with the male lion for disparaging our sex by acting like a lazy, good-for-nothing freeloader. The lion is supposed to be the King of the Jungle, but he more closely resembled Archie Bunker.

But another part of me was impressed by the male lion's ability to avoid hard work and allow someone else to do it for him. As a person who believes in delegating responsibility whenever possible, I found that the male lion's approach to hunting appealed to my ongoing desire to increase productivity. He wasn't exactly writing a novel, building a business, or making art, but perhaps rolling in the mud, splashing in rivers, and endless napping are the lion's equivalent of those things.

So I was conflicted. I wasn't sure how I should feel about the male lion.

Not anymore.

Further research into lion behavior, conducted partly through the use of infrared drones, has discovered that male lions are just as active when it comes to hunting as female lions. They simply hunt more efficiently.

Rather than chasing antelope on the savanna under the hot African sun, male lions hunt at night by locating a game trail and positioning themselves in an ideal spot for ambushing unsuspecting prey. They use considerably fewer calories in this type of hunting but are just as effective at finding and killing their prey as their female counterparts.

It turns out that male lions are actually better hunters than lionesses. It would be ridiculous for me to find joy in this newfound knowledge. Aside from our both being male, these lions and I have nothing in common.

Still, I do. I love the metaphor that it offers: There are usually two (or more) ways to accomplish a goal, but so often, people choose the way that is more publicly demonstrative, visibly active, and unquestionably effortful. They want to be seen as busy even if their method of choice is not the most efficient way of getting things done.

Performative productivity, I call it.

"Look what I did!"

"Watch me working hard!"

"You can't doubt my effort now!"

The credit you receive should be derived from the results of your effort. Not the journey you took getting there.

The male lion was maligned for years for being lazy, but it turns out that he was simply doing the job more strategically, thus embracing my foundational belief: accomplish as much as possible, as efficiently as possible.

15 Party Often

"Remember to celebrate milestones
as you prepare for the road ahead."

— Nelson Mandela

My friend Jeni Bonaldo finished writing her first novel in the spring of 2021. I'm proud of her. She's an English teacher, the mother of two, a storyteller, an occasional, albeit enthusiastic, yoga dancer, and much more. She's not one of these writers who required a six-month sabbatical, an antique desk, and a constant stream of chai latte to get the job done. She made the time and wrote an excellent story.

Also, it's about damn time. I say this only because I've been encouraging (possibly strong-arming and allegedly badgering) her for the past couple of years about finishing this book. Sadly, she doesn't listen to me nearly enough, which puts her at an enormous disadvantage.

Two years ago, I was sitting backstage with Jeni at one of my storytelling shows. As Elysha began introducing Jeni to an audience of more than five hundred people — my friend's largest audience by far to date — I was sitting alongside her, allegedly badgering her about how important it was to make time for the book.

Don't waste precious minutes.
Stop making excuses.
You're not getting any younger.
Move your ass, dummy.

Finally, she turned to me and said, "Could you maybe yell at me about the state of my novel after I finish telling my story?"

Admittedly, it wasn't the best time to badger even the best of storytellers. No one needs to hear how disappointing they are just seconds before they are to bare their soul to a theater filled with expectant strangers.

Sometimes it's hard to be my friend.

But I find myself just as annoyed with Jeni today as I was that night backstage at Infinity Hall. I have yet to receive my invitation to her "I wrote a book!" party. It's possible that she didn't invite me because of past transgressions, but I suspect the truth is this: she hasn't planned this party yet, nor does she have any intention of doing so.

Creative people are notoriously unsatisfied with the quality and quantity of their work. Upset about their progress along the creative continuum. Disappointed with their distance from their end point. As a result, they fail to celebrate each and every step of the way. They do something as fucking stupendous as write a book — something people say all the time they will someday do, but then just die instead — but fail to celebrate that accomplishment with a hot-dog party, a celebration at the roller rink, or a parade.

It's hard enough to make something. Bringing your barbecue-sushi restaurant into existence is not easy. Chiseling marble is back-breaking work. Forging medieval pickaxes seems downright dangerous. Writing a novel is the dream of many but fulfilled by very few. Creating a visual record of Richard Nixon's illegal bombing of Cambodia in a parking-lot-size quilt isn't something done every day.

Makers of things deserve credit, but they deserve credit for each step along the path. Not only do they deserve credit, but they need it, too. They need to honor themselves and their efforts. Creation is often a lonely, unrecognized piece of business. We toil away in solitude as we make our things, advance our dreams, and blunder our way into the darkness. When we finally take a meaningful, well-earned step forward, we must pause for drink and dance. We must make merry. This is the fuel that will fire our furnace and keep us moving forward.

• • •

When I finished my first novel, Elysha and I went to dinner with friends that evening. I had not even begun the process of looking for a literary agent — had not even proofread the book — but I recognized that I had done something I had only dreamed of accomplishing for years. It deserved to be honored. I deserved to be honored.

On the evening when my literary agent, Taryn, and I formalized our partnership, on the very last day of my summer vacation, Elysha and I were joined by friends for an ice-cream-sundae celebration. Finding a literary agent who is willing to represent you is not easy. The accomplishment deserved to be publicly recognized with cookie dough, hot fudge, and smiles.

On the day of that fateful phone call informing me of the offer from an editor at Doubleday, Elysha and I celebrated with friends and colleagues at an after-school happy hour before I joined a different group of friends to celebrate by playing poker and listening to Springsteen into the wee hours of the morning. The next day, Elysha's parents arrived from New York to take us out to dinner. Her mother gifted me a sweater.

I could go on and on. Every step of the journey was marked by some type of celebration, usually involving food, friends, and family. My favorite celebration was the night Elysha and I were eating dinner in a Boston Market when Taryn called to inform me that Tom Cruise was reading *Something Missing* and was considering it for film. Upon hearing the news, Elysha and I threw away our fast casual dinner and immediately drove to Max's Oyster Bar for a much fancier meal.

Two months later, we were at home, preparing to eat a dinner that Elysha had just finished cooking when another phone call came informing me that Brad Pitt was now reading the book. Once again, our food was jettisoned into the trash bin, and we returned to Max's for another celebratory dinner.

I've since learned that "Tom Cruise is reading" really means some underling of Tom Cruise, 192 rungs down the proverbial ladder, liked the book and is trying to push it up the 192 rungs to Mr. Cruise, which is unlikely and more wishful thinking than anything else.

Still, celebrate when you can.

. . .

I've met authors who have told me that it's bad luck to celebrate before their book hits the bookstore shelves. I once met an author at a literary retreat in Vermont who told me that she would celebrate only when her novel hit the bestseller list. I know an entrepreneur who won't celebrate the launch of her business until she's earned her first million dollars in sales.

It's as if creators are embarrassed to celebrate until everyone around them deems it time to celebrate. They are unwilling to stand on a chair or grab a megaphone or randomly dial strangers on the phone to announce their accomplishment.

This is a mistake. We cannot wait for the world to recognize our achievements. The past is littered with ingenious creators like Edgar Allan Poe and Eva Cassidy, who were never recognized for their greatness until well after their deaths. We can't depend on the world to take care of us. We must be willing to take care of ourselves. We must be willing to celebrate each step along the way.

We deserve the recognition. We need it to propel us forward.

The late author Howard Frank Mosher used to celebrate bad reviews by nailing them to the side of his barn and shooting them to pieces with his shotgun. Howard was a man who understood the importance of celebration.

We should not be ashamed or embarrassed to celebrate the steps along our path. The creative process is lined by milestones, and each deserves recognition. When football players win the AFC and NFC championship game — the last step before the Super Bowl — they don champion hats, receive a trophy, and drink champagne. Baseball and basketball players celebrate similarly. They do not worry about jinxing the next round of the playoffs. They don't wait until they win the World Series or Finals before popping the bubbly. They recognize that a big step has been taken. More steps lie ahead, but for a couple of hours, celebration is in order.

We must take a lesson from these athletes and do the same, even if that means hosting our own hot-dog party, purchasing our own "I got my business license, so I'm better than you" banner, or renting the roller rink for our "I dug the hole that will one day be my Jell-O pool" party.

So I await Jeni's invitation. It probably won't be a hot-dog party, but renting out the roller rink is entirely possible and might even fit her gestalt. A woman who yoga dances is probably into "couples skate." She wrote a book, damn it. The story is good. With any luck, I'll be writing a blurb for it someday.

Then again, she doesn't listen to me as often as she should, so perhaps she's holding off on celebrating until she wins the Pulitzer.

That would be so Jeni. Don't let it be you.

16 Feed Yourself a Compliment Sandwich

"Talk to yourself like you would to someone you love."

— BRENÉ BROWN

Five years ago, I was teaching a storytelling workshop to a group of formerly incarcerated men who now work inside schools, helping teenagers stay out of trouble. During lunch, one of the men approached me and asked, "So where did you do your time?"

I explained to the man that I had spent time in jail but had never been in prison. He paused, looked me over carefully, then said, "That's funny. You have a prison look about you."

I can't explain it, but I was thrilled to hear this. It was probably the idea that I looked tough enough to have survived prison. I texted several friends and described the moment, and every one of them agreed: one of the best compliments of my life.

Back in 1988, I was playing *Donkey Kong* in the Half Moon Arcades in Weirs Beach, New Hampshire. Half a dozen buddies and I were on vacation in the little town on the edge of Lake Winnipesaukee. We spent our days playing video games and sitting on the beach and our nights looking for girls.

Jeff "Coog" Coger was the best video-game player of our group.

His hand-eye coordination was incredible, and his instantaneous understanding of the nuances of every game was miraculous. Coog is also a black belt in karate whom we referred to as the "Skaggy-Bearded Ninja," so I guess his affinity for gaming sort of made sense.

On the last day of the vacation, our friend Tom approached me as I was dodging barrels and scaling scaffolding in an effort to defeat Donkey Kong and rescue Pauline. Tom watched me play for a bit, then he leaned in and whispered, "If you and Coog start playing a game on the same day, Coog is definitely better than you. Better than all of us. Doesn't even matter what game we're playing. But if I gave you and Coog a week to master the game, my money would be on you."

I can still hear Tom's words in my mind today, clear as a bell. Ridiculous, but also one of the best compliments of my life.

About two months after that fateful phone call announcing my first book deal with Doubleday, the first of three checks arrived in the mail from my publisher, representing one-third of my advance. Standing in the kitchen of our apartment, Elysha and I opened the envelope together and stared at the largest check we had ever seen. It was a simple, rectangular piece of paper that represented the elimination of a mountain of wedding debt and a down payment on our first home.

It was a piece of paper that would change our lives forever. Elysha hugged me and whispered, "You saved us." *Something Missing* is dedicated to Elysha. The inscription reads: "You saved me first."

But her words, spoken in that kitchen, might be the very best compliment that I have ever received.

I could continue listing compliments offered to me over the years by friends, family, colleagues, students, and more, but here's the thing: I couldn't go on forever. I'd probably run out of compliments pretty quickly.

This is the problem. People say joyous, ebullient, incredibly observant, deeply meaningful things to us throughout our lives, and for a fleeting moment, our spirits are lifted. Our motivation increases. Our feelings of self-worth soar. We feel as if we could fly. Then those compliments, save a few of the more memorable ones, are lost forever. Discarded into the trash bin of history. Forgotten like so much of our lives.

It's ridiculous. People say wonderful things to us. Sometimes they tell us something we already knew but are thrilled to hear that someone else noticed. Sometimes we're told something that we had never noticed about ourselves before. Sometimes we discover that we are appreciated, respected, or admired in ways we could never have imagined. Sometimes we are offered truly profound insight into ourselves that we might have spent our entire lives failing to see.

Sage wisdom should be labeled as "unforgettable." Yet three weeks or three months or three years later, the words are utterly forgotten. We retain a small collection of kindnesses bestowed on us over the years but allow the rest to fall away, then we wonder why we can't marshal the enthusiasm needed to move a project forward. We can't understand why we lack the motivation or drive to succeed. We can't imagine how we might continue on when the slopes seem so steep and the destination seems so far away.

We're offered fuel for our fire all the time, but instead of holding on to it, we allow it to slip through our fingers, forgotten and useless. As creators, we are going to face a ton of doubt and uncertainty along the way. Naysayers will stand in our path and lecture us on the foolishness of our dreams. Our work will be scrutinized, criticized, and utterly dismissed. We will be subjected to enormous amounts of negativity. It's hard enough to make something out of whole cloth. The critics along the way can sometimes make it feel impossible.

As a result, we must hold on to every ounce of positive energy. We must hoard the good to counteract the bad. Cling to the light for use on our darkest of days.

So there are two things I do whenever I receive a compliment (verbally or via email, text message, or comment on social media): I preserve the content, and I schedule its return.

Preserving Compliments

Apps like Evernote or Notion work well for preserving compliments, or perhaps you simply create a Word or Google doc where you can copy and paste the ones received by email or text message or (in the cases when the compliment was spoken to you) transcribe what was said. Find a place that works for you. For me, that place is Notion, an app that lives on my phone, on my desktop computer, and in the cloud, making it accessible no matter where I am. Wherever you choose, begin to gather all the positivity you receive in one place. Include past compliments as well. The ones you are fortunate enough to remember. The very first compliment on my list says this:

> On January 1, 1988, I was sixteen years old. I was standing on a bridge in California, strapped to a bass drum, ready to march in the Rose Bowl Parade. Two teenage girls were sitting on the curb nearby, waiting for the parade to start. After giggling a bit, they managed to get my attention and tell me that I looked a lot like Tom Cruise. I was clearly better looking in 1988, the sun was probably in their eyes, and Tom Cruise had not yet lost his mind.

That was one of the first compliments I can remember that made me swoon. It certainly doesn't apply to me today. Time has been kinder to Tom Cruise than me, but reading those words, I found myself right back on that bridge in my mind's eye, ridiculous shako perched atop my head, bass drum strapped to my body, listening to two California girls speak words that made me feel like I was walking on air for the entire parade.

Not every compliment on the list is a story, of course. When recorded in real time, they are either much shorter or simply the contents of an email or text message. Scrolling randomly through the list, they look more like this:

- "Guatemalan immigrant turned spousal- and sexual-abuse victim advocate spends two hours with me, crafting the outline of her story, and when we are done, she says, 'This was one of the best days of my life.'"
- "Hi, Mr. Dicks, I just wanted to say hello. I really miss having you as a teacher.... I was reading your book the

other day and really remembered you. My best school
days were in your class. Aashni"

- "My sister & I LOVE your blog, it's actually improved
  our relationship, we're in contact with each other so
  much more consistently to rave (or rage) about your
  words, it's been just great. LM"

I've been collecting compliments since 2009, so the list has grown
quite long. You'd be surprised how often someone says something
kind to you over the course of a decade or more. This is important,
because as a creator, you will need this list. Sadly, human beings are
wired to remember and retain the negative over the positive.

For a long time in human history, remembering the negative
encounters was important. In a world where you must remember
which berry tasted delicious and which one killed Uncle Frank, focusing on the negative made sense. When you're attempting to survive in a life-and-death world where predators lurk around every
bend, starvation is a week away, and writing has not been invented,
remembering the negative encounters might very well save your life.

But in the world where lions and tigers are no longer a threat
and a bag of Doritos is lurking around every corner, this inclination
to remember the negative does us little good. Nevertheless, we are
still far more likely to remember a negative statement than a positive
one. Studies have shown that a person needs to hear at least 5.6 positive statements in order to counteract a single negative one.

Since you are unlikely to achieve that 5.6-to-1 ratio organically,
you must manufacture the ratio by collecting the positive statements
of folks who would otherwise be forgotten and use those words on
those days when:

- you awaken lacking the enthusiasm to dive into the day.
- some monster has hindered your momentum with a
  few words of criticism or doubt.
- you start to wonder whether the work you are doing is
  worthy of continuing.

- it feels like the world has decided to place its boot on your neck and remind you of how little power you really have.

In these times of need, this collection of compliments might just save you.

• • •

Back in the fall of 2011, I received another fateful call from my literary agent, Taryn, also while at school, informing me that the third novel I had written, *Chicken Shack* (a working title), had been rejected by my publisher and every other major publisher in New York.

I had just spent a year writing a book that no one wanted. I had labored over character and plot and produced a story that I thought was very good, but everyone who mattered disagreed. After publishing two novels and feeling like I had finally launched my career as an author, I suddenly felt like it was over before it had really begun.

Doubt almost instantly found a foothold in my psyche. I was no longer a good writer. For a fleeting moment, people had thought of me as someone worthy of time and investment. I was the kind of author whose books deserved to be placed on the shelves of bookstores and libraries around the world. Then the world just changed its mind.

This also meant that money was going to become tight for Elysha and me. She was still at home, now pregnant with Charlie, and my book contracts were essentially replacing years of her salary while she gestated, birthed, and raised our children. Without another payday in the near future, I couldn't see how we would make ends meet on one teacher's salary.

I felt as low as I had felt in a long time.

"What now?" I asked Taryn.

In her characteristic no-nonsense way, she said, "Well, you just need to write the best book of your career."

When I hung up the phone, I sat down at my desk to pull myself together before calling Elysha with the bad news. But before I made the call, I opened the Word doc that contained my list of compliments at the time. It was much shorter back then, comprising mostly emails from grateful students and parents, but there were some compliments from readers, too. Compliments that are still listed today, telling me how much Martin from *Something Missing* and Milo from *Unexpectedly, Milo* had meant to them. Notes of appreciation and admiration.

They didn't wipe away the self-doubt and fear that I was feeling on that day, but they made a dark day a little bit brighter. They reminded me that I was capable of writing stories that readers loved. They gave me a little hope.

• • •

This is why we must preserve the positivity that we receive in this world. There are too many days when the universe kicks us in the teeth, leaving us flailing and floundering in pools of doubt and despair. A list of compliments, deployed at just the right time, can be a life preserver for us.

Even on days when our enthusiasm is high — like this day, as I write these words — these compliments can be incredibly useful. As I copied and pasted Aashni's compliment into this manuscript, I found myself thinking about her — now twenty-something and living her life — and remembering how lovely it was to receive that email when she was still a high-school student.

As I copied and pasted LM's compliment into the manuscript, I found myself wondering what she and her sister might think of today's blog post about showing our children *Ferris Bueller's Day Off* for the first time.

As I posted the compliment from the Guatemalan immigrant turned victim advocate, I realized that I have no recollection of that person. She is lost to me, but her words have returned, and they made me feel great.

Compliments are always helpful, even on the days when we don't feel like we need any help. The world is too full of kindness for us to not allow the kindnesses we're offered to echo in our minds again and again.

Don't allow another compliment to pass by unrecorded.

Scheduling the Return of Compliments

Even on a day when we don't need to counteract negativity, a little added positivity, particularly when it arrives unexpectedly, can be wonderful. This is why I also do the second of two things with these compliments: I schedule their return.

When I receive a compliment via email, I add it to my list of compliments, but then I "snooze" it for another day. "Snoozing" an email is a feature available on most email platforms that allows you to forward a message to the future. It's especially useful when you need the information contained in the email on a certain day but don't want it cluttering your in-box until that day. But I also "snooze" my compliments into the future. I forward them to a future version of myself who will see them with fresh eyes and perhaps a desperate need for some positivity. By forwarding these emails to my future self, I receive them again and have the opportunity to experience the warmth and goodness of reading them a second time, unexpectedly.

The world is filled with far too much negativity. In an effort to increase the amount of positivity in my life, I make these compliments count twice.

The mail application that I use had a "random" snooze feature, which allowed me to snooze my compliments to an unknown day and time. I loved this. Fire off some kind words to some mysterious date somewhere in the future.

That random feature has since been removed (I was probably the only person who had ever found a use for it), so now I close my eyes and randomly click the months and days on my email's calendar. I could be sending some emails a decade or more into the future, but I love that.

Positivity on the way, someday, hopefully just when I need it.

• • •

As I was finishing this chapter, I found myself texting with my friend Jeni about the movie *Ferris Bueller's Day Off*, which, as you know, Elysha and I just watched with our kids for the first time. Jeni thinks Ferris was a terrible friend who didn't respect his friend's boundaries or have compassion for his possible mental illness. I think Ferris was exactly what Cameron needed.

In the midst of this debate, Jeni realized that she was only five years old when *Ferris Bueller's Day Off* came out.

"I was fifteen years old," I texted back. "I'm ten years older than you? Weird. I don't feel ten years older than you."

"I'm mature for my age, and you're not," Jeni replied.

"That's not what I was thinking about," I said.

"Do you think I look old?" she asked.

"Not that, either," I texted. "I was thinking in terms of spirit. Energy. Approach to life."

"Yes," Jeni said. "You live life like a young person in all the best ways."

In a chapter about holding on to compliments, I received another compliment for my list, and this one is special because I know how much it hurts Jeni to compliment me. It annoys the hell out of her to say anything kind about me.

This is because I'm her Ferris Bueller, of course. Disrespectful of her boundaries, perhaps, but exactly what she needs.

17 Know Your Story. Tell Your Story. Listen to Your Story.

> "Remind yourself of your badassery."
>
> — Unknown

Years ago, I was standing at the photocopier, waiting for copies of a spelling test to emerge from the machine, when one of my colleagues asked if I had any plans for the weekend. I told her — and everyone else in the room — that my weekend was not looking good. "Two weddings. Friday and Saturday night. What the hell was I thinking?"

Back then, I was still spinning discs and leading hordes of inebriated wedding guests through the "Chicken Dance" and the "Macarena" nearly every weekend. I didn't exactly hate the job. I owned the company with my best friend Bengi, as you know, and we worked together, side by side, most weekends, making newly married couples and their guests happy. It wasn't a bad way to spend a Saturday night.

But in June, as wedding season was heating up but summer vacation had yet to arrive, the job was a lot harder. Teaching children all week and working as a wedding DJ on the weekend could be exhausting. Thus my complaint that day about my weekend plans.

At the end of the school day, as I was packing my bag, one of the teachers who had been in the copy room and had heard my complaint knocked on my door. "Can I talk to you for a minute?"

She sounded serious, so I invited her to take a seat.

"Listen," she said, "I'm sure this weekend is going to be hard for you, but you need to remember that most of the teachers in that room today are just squeaking by. If they want to vacation in Aruba or buy a new car or even go out for a fancy dinner, they need to save for weeks or months or even years to make that happen. Most of them are on a fixed budget. The same paycheck week after week. But you'll probably earn a couple thousand dollars this weekend. Maybe more. Not everyone can do that, Matt. I'm sure that being a DJ is hard at times, but watch what you say when you're around people who can't do what you do. Some of us think you're pretty damn lucky."

I have never forgotten that advice. I think about it all the time. My colleague was preaching gratitude, and she was right. I should've been more grateful for the skills, good fortune, and wherewithal I had to launch a successful business that paid well and worked in concert with my teaching career.

She had a point. I was capable of earning thousands of dollars in a single weekend if I wanted to, which is not possible for most people. I had more financial flexibility than many of my fellow teachers. Complaining about it was bad form. I sounded like an ungrateful, selfish jerk.

But what I also heard was this: *There was a day when you thought that being a wedding DJ might be both fun and a great source of extra income. You knew nothing about the wedding industry and even less about the responsibilities of a wedding DJ. You barely knew the music that needed to be played to get people to dance. But just a couple of years later, you and Bengi were booking clients, turning away business, and constantly raising your prices. You had quickly gone from knowing nothing about the wedding industry to becoming one of the most sought-after DJ companies in the state.*

Good job, Matt.

Know Your Story

Gratitude is a good thing, but knowing your story, telling your story, and listening to your story is just as important on those days when things seem hard or disastrous or impossible. As human beings, we so often climb enormous mountains of struggle and strife, reach the summit, but never bother to look back and admire our journey.

We can inspire ourselves by remembering how far we have come, how much we have accomplished, and how improbable our journey once seemed. We can inspire ourselves by telling the stories of our struggle and success.

For some of us, this can admittedly be more motivating than others. At the times when doubt and uncertainty creep into my mind, I can immediately go back to my darkest days, homeless, indicted for a crime I didn't commit, the victim of an armed robbery that would leave me for decades buried under the weight of post-traumatic stress disorder.

I can clearly remember the day when I thought that in order to survive the winter, I would need to move south. Homeless and hopeless, I reasoned that my only alternative to a freezing New England winter spent on the streets was the warmth of the Florida sun.

When I think back on those days and tell myself the story of my climb from the pits of despair, nothing seems as hard anymore. Whatever obstacle or critic has fractured my self-confidence is washed away when I take a moment and acknowledge what I have already overcome to make my dreams come true.

I do the same thing on a day when I climb out of bed, wishing I didn't have to go to school and teach. On those difficult mornings, I tell myself the story — aloud, if possible — of a time in my life when all I wanted to do was teach, but even that modest dream seemed unreachable. The idea that I, facing a felony charge and prison time, might stand before children someday and teach them how to read and write seemed ridiculous and impossible.

Suddenly the prospect of putting on pants and teaching children doesn't seem so daunting. It feels like a gift. In truth, it's a dream come true.

Tell Your Story

As the makers of things, we often face a long road. Hard days lie ahead. Even today, after I've made my dreams of teaching and writing a reality, hard days still stand in my way. It's the simple truth of the creator: we are only as good as our next thing. I've published seven previous books — more than I ever dreamed possible — but none of them seem to matter very much anymore. If *this* one flops, I am a failure.

On those days, I need to hear my story. I need to look back on the mountain I have ascended and remind myself of all I have already accomplished, regardless of the success of this book.

The parent of a student can express disappointment in a decision I made in the classroom, and suddenly, the last twenty-three years of a successful, award-winning teaching career can fall away. I almost instantly find myself feeling like a fraud. A teacher of smoke and mirrors rather than skill and substance. My years of excellent performance reviews feel like nothing. My recognition as Teacher of the Year is suddenly irrelevant. The wedding that I officiated for my former student suddenly feels like less of an honor. All the students and parents who reach out to me over the years to thank me for my work feel tiny in the face of one parent's stinging criticism.

It's in that moment that I must stop and tell my story.

Maybe I begin that story on my first day in an elementary-education class at the University of Saint Joseph — an all-women's college at the time that I had managed to attend by exploiting a loophole in a consortium of colleges — thrilled to be learning about the theories of Piaget and Harold Bloom and dreaming of one day having a classroom of my own.

Maybe I begin that story during my job interview with Plato Karafelis, wondering whether I might be able to land my dream job in what appeared to be my dream school.

But maybe I simply tell myself the story of a recent text message, sent by the parent of two students, Max and Molly, who passed through my classroom a long time ago.

The text read: "Max played Molly's boyfriend tonight in chess, and he said, 'Wow, you are so good at chess.' Max said to me, 'Mr. Dicks taught me.' #teacherlove"

Stories need not be enormous or earth-shattering in order to remind us of how far we have come and how much we have done. I read the text message, tell myself the story of those Max-and-Molly days, insert the story of the time Max overturned his kayak and needed me to save him, and tack on the Razor scooter that Max gave me on the last day of school (the one Charlie rides today), and I'm suddenly awash in good feelings.

Tell these stories to my own children, which I did, and I feel even better.

As a professional storyteller, I tell stories about my life all the time — often to hundreds of people at once — and I am convinced that the storytelling that I do has altered my spirit considerably. When you take the time to find and tell the stories of your struggles and successes, you are going to feel better about yourself, your past, and your future prospects. I believe that this is an essential part of every creative person's life.

But I also believe that the most important audience we have is ourselves. Even if we're a professional mime or a mountainside gardener or an enthusiastic hermit who never plans to speak to other human beings, the stories we tell about ourselves to ourselves can make all the difference.

Choose the right stories. Find the stories — both large and small — of overcoming the odds, knocking down obstacles, or slaying your proverbial dragons, and tell them to yourself. Go read *Storyworthy* to learn to find and tell them well.

At the very least, learn about my process called Homework for Life — via the book or my TEDx Talk on the subject. Nothing will be more important when it comes to finding and telling your story.

The secret is this: You must view your life story as a journey — an adventure — worthy of investment, excitement, and continuous forward movement. Rather than looking at your life through the small lens of the immediate moment or an ominous future, you must expand your view to all that came before. Take credit for your achievements. See these days that you live as scenes in a greater story that you can tell yourself.

And speak those stories aloud whenever possible. Say them to yourself whenever you can. This is important, too. Positive self-talk — when spoken out loud — can turn feelings of doubt and despair into something far more productive. In many ways, our conscious self and our unconscious brain are two entirely separate entities, forever disconnected but constantly striving to be more connected. Our unconscious brain, therefore, is paying attention to what we see and do at all times and responds accordingly, even if we don't actually mean what we say.

Sounds crazy, but it's absolutely true.

In essence, we can alter our mood by simply pretending that our mood is different than what it truly is. For example, research has shown that when we squint in exceptionally bright light — like the bright light of a winter's day — our brains often interpret that persistent squinting as either sadness or anger. So even if we are filled with joy, our brains think that we are sad or angry and will cause us to feel that, too.

You look sad on the outside, so your brain makes you sad on the inside.

The same holds true for the way you walk. Your brain interprets a slow pace as sadness or lethargy, and it interprets a quick pace as happiness and industriousness. Therefore, adopting a persistently quicker pace when you walk will make you feel happier and more productive.

Listen to Your Story

It's even more important to remember that your brain is always listening, too. It hears the words you say — whether or not any truth is behind those words — and will alter your mood based upon what it hears. If you continually describe yourself as a failure, a disappointment, or an impostor — even if you don't really believe it — your brain will believe it, and it will be on alert for anything that confirms what you are saying. To counteract this spiral, it's imperative that people who are trying to make things use as much positive self-talk as possible.

The monsters will tell you how bad you are. Critics are hiding behind every corner. Naysayers are not hard to find. Since they will offer you plenty of negativity, you must spend your time reminding yourself of how well you're doing.

This positive self-talk can come in the form of simple, positive affirmations. "Good job, Matt" is something people hear me say to myself all the time, because I believe in crediting myself for doing well.

Emptied the dishwasher in near record time? "Good job, Matt."

Survived a meeting without becoming too obstructionist? "Good job, Matt."

Spent fifteen minutes petting the cat? "Good job, Matt."

Helped Charlie with his homework? "Good job, Matt."

Finished a chapter of this book? "Good job, Matt."

Our brains are listening to us for clues about who we are, how we feel, and how we are doing. If we speak kindly and generously to ourselves — aloud — our brains will hear that and respond accordingly.

If that's not crazy enough, here's something even crazier: knowing this truth enhances the effect even more.

For example, it's been shown to be extremely good for the mind to spend time in nature. Simply lying beneath a tree and looking into the branches for fifteen minutes can alter our brain chemistry in enormously positive ways. But knowing that staring into a tree will make you feel better will make you feel even better. Knowing that you are doing good for yourself actually increases the good that you are doing for yourself, so we must consciously, purposefully speak well of ourselves whenever possible.

Be kind to your brain so your brain will be kind to you.

Personal mantras work, too. I have a collection of personal

mantras that I speak aloud constantly and speak silently to myself even more. The most prevalent is one told to me as a middle schooler by one of my teachers: "A positive mental attitude is your key to success."

I wish I could remember who said it, because it's been with me ever since, and it's true: a positive mental attitude really can be your key to success. It's been one of the defining traits of my life.

My former principal used to refer to me, sarcastically, as Mr. Sunshine. A colleague recently became irate with me for always answering the question "How are you?" with an enthusiastic "Great!" Jeni Bonaldo has accused me of toxic positivity.

But you know what? A positive mental attitude *is* your key to success. I've said it to myself — out loud and in my head — thousands of times over the past four decades. More than once per day. Is it a surprise that I believe it? My brain has listened to these nine words endlessly.

Other mantras that I speak often include:

"It's a town full of losers, and I'm pulling out of here to win." — from Springsteen's "Thunder Road"

"What one man can do, another can do." — from the 1997 film *The Edge*

"He who avoids complaints invites happiness." — Abū Bakr (I couldn't remember where this one originated, so I had to look it up. Turns out it's attributed to the father-in-law of the Islamic prophet Muhammad, as well as the first caliph of Islam. No recollection of where I read or was told this mantra, but it's been in my head since college, and I've always liked it a lot. Complainers are the worst, so this one pops into my mind whenever I find myself on the verge of complaining.)

"When they said 'Sit down,' I stood up." — from Springsteen's "Growin' Up"

"Rage against the dying of the light." — from Dylan Thomas's "Do not go gentle into that good night" (I have the entire poem memorized, thanks to Hugh Ogden, and I recite it to myself often, but this is the line that returns to me when I feel my effort is waning.)

"The hard thing and the right thing are usually the same thing."— Me, spoken through Budo, a protagonist in *Memoirs of an Imaginary Friend*

"Teach 'em." — Steve Brouse, my friend and colleague, who said this to a teacher who was complaining that her students didn't already know something

All these personal mantras fit perfectly into the story that I am constantly telling myself and others. Whether it's the story of my very first author appearance (when the very first question asked of me was "What role do your ex-girlfriends play in your fiction?"), or it's the story of the evening I sat in the front row of the Playhouse on Park alongside my creative partner Andy Mayo and watched professional actors speak and sing lines that I wrote, or it's the story of my proposal to Elysha or the birth of my children or the phone call with storyteller Erin Barker that ultimately led to this book, I am constantly, incessantly reminding myself of the great moments of my life through story. These words are the fuel to my fire. The reminder that I have ascended to great heights before. Done the impossible.

I once beat Tom Reed Swale in a round of golf.

I wrote an internationally bestselling novel.

My daughter told her seventh-grade English teacher (but not me) that I was inspiring.

I made Samantha Bee laugh.

I officiated my ex-girlfriend's wedding, Elysha's ex-boyfriend's wedding, and my ex-wife's ex-husband's second wedding.

I convinced a dozen disenchanted rabbis of the power of storytelling by filling them with whiskey and planting them around a campfire.

I pole-vaulted thirteen feet in the district championships.

I convinced Elysha Green to not only date me but marry me.

Dragons are easier to slay when you have slain one before. They are even easier to slay when you remember slaying them before. When the story of the battle and your eventual victory is alive in your heart and mind, the next battle does not seem too difficult anymore.

If I did that, I can do this.

That is why we tell our story. To ourselves, for sure, and maybe to the world.

Part 4

LIVING THE LIFE

"I told the universe (and anyone who would listen)
that I was committed to living a creative life not in order
to save the world, not as an act of protest, not to become
famous, not to gain entrance to the canon, not to challenge
the system, not to show the bastards, not to prove to my family
that I was worthy, not as a form of deep therapeutic emotional
catharsis...but simply because I liked it."

— ELIZABETH GILBERT

Creativity Cannot Abide Preciousness

"Don't be fancy, just get dancy."

— PINK

I'm sitting beneath a small, leafless sapling on a concrete median in the middle of a parking lot in West Hartford, Connecticut. My computer is resting on my lap, and I'm typing away when I hear someone call my name. I look up and see the parent of a former student approaching. She's pushing a cart filled with groceries and waving at me.

"Are you okay?" she asks.

"I'm fine," I say. "I'm writing."

"In the Whole Foods parking lot? On the ground?"

I shake my head and point to the building behind me. "No. I'm early for my dentist appointment. So I thought I'd squeeze in a little writing."

"Here?" she says. "On the median?"

"I didn't want to sit in my car," I say. "It's too nice a day. And the waiting room is even worse. All those chairs. Why so many chairs?"

She shakes her head and laughs. "I never envisioned you writing your books in the middle of a parking lot."

"Envisioned" is why I remember that moment so clearly in my mind's eye. It's the problem that faces so many people trying to create things and make their dreams come true: they envision a creative process that is idealized, unrealistic, cinematic, and inefficient.

If you want to make your dreams come true, a concrete median with a struggling, leafless sapling makes a perfect place to write a couple of pages before having your teeth cleaned. Any place that contains a reasonable amount of oxygen and terrestrial gravity works just fine. A concrete median is admittedly not ideal, but people who wait for the ideal circumstance in order to create usually die before their dreams are ever realized.

An author once told me about a writers' retreat in upstate New York where each writer is given a small well-appointed cabin in a forest glade in which to work. Breakfast and lunch are left in picnic baskets outside the cabin door, and in the evenings, writers gather for cocktails, a gourmet dinner, scintillating conversation, and a late-night campfire. Apparently a lot of sex, too.

It sounds idyllic. It also sounds a little silly. A little much for my taste.

Don't get me wrong: I wouldn't complain if you want to gift me a week at this writers' retreat. I'll happily spend a few days in the woods on your dime, but I suspect that I could get a lot more work done by eliminating the four-hour drive to and from upstate New York and just sticking my ass on a parking-lot median instead.

If you want to make things as desperately as I do, you don't need picnic baskets full of warm treats, idyllic mountaintop settings, and whiskey-fueled campfires. I wrote the majority of this book at the end of my dining-room table, opposite my wife's laptop, surrounded by folded laundry, small piles of books, and sleeping cats.

Other locations included the desk in my classroom, a table on my deck, a flight to and from San Francisco, a fourteen-hour layover in the Detroit airport, several aging picnic tables adjacent to Little League fields, and a pavilion on the edge of Dunning Lake, where my family and I spend many a summer day.

Another author I know escapes the interruptions of her husband, children, and dogs by renting a room in a Holiday Inn Express less than a mile from her home for the weekend. She orders room service and writes until she is exhausted, then she collapses on the bed and sleeps. When she wakes up, she orders breakfast and resumes writing. No picnic baskets. No woodland settings. No roaring campfires. Just a cheap, clean room and a couple of days of peace and quiet.

This strikes me as far more sensible.

Not Every Thing Needs to Be a Thing

My friend Rachel recently told me about the joys of drinking a glass of bourbon while in the shower. This is, of course, a ridiculous idea.

Not ridiculous in concept. Even though I don't really drink anymore (and you know how I feel about showering), I certainly understand the desire to combine two passions in an effort to enhance an already beloved experience. In this way, the joy of a glass of bourbon paired with a shower is understandable. Sort of like watching my favorite movie while riding the exercise bike or devouring bacon-wrapped chicken at a tailgate before heading into the stadium to watch the Patriots beat up on the Jets.

As a concept, bourbon in the shower is fine. Not my thing but probably lovely for a certain type of person. But bourbon in the shower is indicative of something that seems to be gaining purchase in society that I would like to take a stand against: making something out of everything.

It's happening all around us, and it must stop.

Can you remember a time when guacamole was prepared in the restaurant's kitchen and delivered to your table by a member of the waitstaff rather than at your table by a member of the kitchen staff, momentarily stifling your conversation so you can watch someone do their job in a display that's ultimately meaningless and slightly awkward?

Remember when wedding receptions didn't require a signature drink named after the bride and groom?

Remember when soccer was played on fields within your town limits and terms like *travel soccer* and *weekend tournaments* had not yet been invented? Remember when hundreds of dollars were not spent on hotel rooms so kids can run around on a grassy field just like the one down the street from their own home?

Every thing doesn't need to be a thing. It's getting ridiculous.

As a maker of things, you don't have the time to embrace ornamentation, ostentatiousness, unnecessary complexity, and purposeless expense. If you're trying to make things, a glass of bourbon in the shower might not be the best way to spend your time. Take your shower, get dressed, and then, if you want a glass of bourbon, drink one. Don't turn the act of washing your body into anything more than it is.

Get in. Get out. Get dressed.

Be happy that you're able to shower at all. More than half of the world's population still doesn't have access to hot water for showering on a daily basis. A shower is already a thing. It's an amazing thing. You don't need to add bourbon to the mix to make it any more precious than it already is.

Preparing guacamole at the table is absurd. We get excited about watching avocados being smashed before our eyes because we think it denotes an exceptional level of freshness and offers an artisanal flair. It doesn't.

Having your guacamole prepared in the kitchen one minute earlier achieves the same damn thing but doesn't interrupt the conversation with a preposterous, artificial, ultimately pointless moment during dinner.

Signature wedding drinks are created by caterers and bartenders who know that guests will consume these drinks in large amounts, thus allowing them to manage their inventory more effectively and maximize profits. Brides and grooms embrace the concept of these signature drinks — sometimes spending hours deciding upon the name for each one — because they apparently think they aren't going to get enough attention on their wedding day already. Signature drinks have become such a thing that magazines and websites are now dedicated to the challenge of "perfecting the art of naming your signature drink."

It's apparently an art now. Not only is it an art but apparently an art that can rise to the level of perfection, despite the fact that a week after the wedding, no one who attended could tell you the name of the bride and groom's signature drink.

And a year later? Even the bride and groom can't remember their signature drink.

Similarly, and perhaps even worse, people have come to adore the art that baristas design in their latte foam, because if anything in this world has ever been made into a thing, it is coffee. Drinking a cup of coffee is no longer a means of quenching your thirst, warming up on a chilly day, injecting caffeine into the bloodstream, or even savoring something that tastes good. Coffee has become a ritual for people. The coffee culture has taken something that was once small and simple and turned it into something of enormous import and great meaning. Coffee is no longer a hot, tasty beverage that people enjoy in the morning. It has become a means by which people define themselves. It is a constant, incessant source of conversation. It is precious and artisanal and Zen, and latte art reinforces these silly beliefs.

Admittedly, I have never tasted coffee. This was a conscious decision on my part after serving coffee to customers at McDonald's as a teenager. I witnessed the complexity and level of effort required to make a satisfying cup of coffee, as well as how often coffee seems to disappoint people. Is it the right temperature? Do you have the correct sweetener? The correct amount of the correct sweetener? Do you have half-and-half? Skim milk? Whole milk? A flavored creamer? The correct flavor of creamer? The correct amount of the correct flavor of creamer? Do you have the right flavor of coffee? The right roast? How long ago was it brewed?

I'm not saying that drinking coffee is a bad thing. I'm suggesting that if you spend time preparing, drinking, and speaking about a beverage that perpetually disappoints you, you may have a problem. Not every thing needs to be a thing.

Showers can just be soap and shampoo and water.

Coffee can simply be a beverage.

Soccer can be a sport that kids play after school and on Saturdays on the field around the block or even across town.

We are all important enough already. Life is sufficiently complex. There is already great meaning in simple things if you pay attention. There is no need to make food or drink or sports so ostentatious and grand that we impute undeserved meaning to them.

Things are already things. See them as such. Embrace them for what they already are.

• • •

This is important to you as a maker of things, because all too often, people who want to lead a creative life become ensnared in the perceived trappings of the creative life instead of the hard reality that gets things done. They forget that almost every person who ever created anything great did not have six hours per day at a farmhouse table made of reclaimed birch in a Manhattan Starbucks alongside a tall almond-milk latte, heated to 153 degrees, easy on the foam.

Creation requires going into the mines. Digging deep. Working hard. Getting your hands dirty. If your act of creation is an image fit for Instagram, you're probably doing it all wrong.

In the late 1980s, with a busy job as a lawyer and a wife and kids at home, John Grisham started to write his first novel. Every day for a span of three years, Grisham woke up at 5:00 a.m. to write a page of what would eventually become the bestselling novel *A Time to Kill*. His second novel, *The Firm*, was the breakout success that enabled Grisham to quit his day job.

Author Jeff Goins explains that Grisham became a writer by "stealing away a little time, thirty minutes to an hour each day. That was it. With a growing family and a new career, it would have been reckless to quit law and become a fulltime author. In fact, that wasn't even his goal; he was just writing to see if he could do it. He took one step at a time, and three years later he had a book."

On a delayed train from Manchester to London's King's Cross station, J.K. Rowling came up with the idea for her Harry Potter series. Over the next five years, she outlined the plots for seven books in the series, writing in longhand and amassing scraps of notes written on different papers. A single mom surviving on government benefits, she wrote when her child was asleep, at home, and in cafés, on an old-fashioned typewriter.

Back in 1976, Steve Jobs, Steve Wozniak, and Ronald Wayne started a business out of Jobs's parents' garage in Cupertino, California, putting together one of the first prototypes of their Apple personal computers. Though starting a business in a garage seems sexy today, there was nothing sexy about a garage in 1976. It was simply the cheapest solution to the problem of space.

Warren Buffett, CEO of Berkshire Hathaway and one of the wealthiest people in America, still lives in the same home in Omaha, Nebraska, that he bought in 1958 for $31,500. Buffett and I start our days similarly: a five-minute commute to work with a stop at McDonald's for breakfast.

Buffett purchases used cars and clips coupons, and when his first child was born, he converted a dresser drawer into a space for the baby to sleep instead of spending money on a bassinet. When his second child was born, he borrowed a crib rather than buying one.

Warren Buffett does not believe in ostentatiousness, pretentiousness, or extravagance. He spends his life building his company, increasing shareholder value, playing bridge, strumming a ukulele, and singing.

A true creator. A maker of things.

Remember: The thing you are making should be precious. It should be fancy-pants beyond compare. This makes sense. It's the thing that represents — it's the end product of — your effort, talent, and vision. Your art, your business, or your invention is deserving of every ounce of your attention and should be treated as supremely precious, but the act of making it — the location, timing, and process — should not.

The making should be ordinary. The results should be extraordinary.

18½   No Room for Pretty When It Comes to Productivity

Long ago, in some forgotten past, there was a person — probably a teacher — who looked at their bulletin board and said, "You know … if I put some borders around this bulletin board, it might look cute."

So that's what they did. They added borders to a bulletin board — probably cut from construction paper or wrapping paper — and the rest is history.

Or more likely…

Long ago, in some forgotten past, a product-development manager in a company that manufactures school supplies said, "I know! We'll fool teachers into believing that bulletin boards require thematic borders to be complete!"

So the company began manufacturing and selling bulletin-board borders to guileless teachers who blindly thought, *Yes, it's true! I need a series of little pencils or balloons or images of the solar system framing the edges of this bulletin board, damn it!*

The result, sadly, is a bizarre and ubiquitous belief that bulletin boards require borders. In school, of course.

In the real world, bulletin boards already have borders. These borders are called the edges of the bulletin board. No one in the real world is disturbed or upset over a bulletin board's lack of thematic framing. No one is looking for the thing that displays information to be fetching or delightful. It's the stuff on the bulletin board that's supposed to matter. Not the stuff around the stuff.

I recently added a world map to a perpetually empty bulletin board in my classroom. The map actually serves a purpose. We use it to track featured locations on a daily news show. We add pushpins to the various locations around the world and then discuss these locations in detail.

Quick, contextualized lessons on geography and geopolitical history.

More than one colleague has noticed my world map and suggested that I add some borders around the bulletin board to make it complete. I pointed out each time that the bulletin board is already complete. It features relevant information that we use almost every day. More than I could say for a lot of *their* bulletin boards. My colleagues disagree. But more importantly, my students do not. I asked them if I needed to add borders to their bulletin board. As disagreeable as they like to be, not a single one of them thought that borders were needed. Many laughed at the notion.

So maybe there's hope for the future.

And don't even get me started on the inexplicable need to cover bulletin boards with colorful fabric or large sheets of colored paper. My students agree that the exposed cork surrounding our world map is just fine, too.

The lesson here is simple: Don't ever do something that will steal time and effort from your life just because everyone else is doing it. Also, don't ever do something that will steal time and effort from your life if it doesn't yield any meaningful results.

The absence of prepackaged artistic flourishes on my bulletin boards does not affect my students' ability to learn in any way. So why waste time on that when I could instead do something meaningful for a student?

19 Make Something into Something

"Inspiration is not garnered from the litanies of what may befall us; it resides in humanity's willingness to restore, redress, reform, rebuild, recover, reimagine, and reconsider."

— PAUL HAWKEN

I'm standing on a stage in a comedy club in Grand Haven, Michigan. My ten-minute set is coming in about two minutes too short. I could just stop talking and walk offstage. I'm not contractually required to fill all ten minutes, and I've been killing it so far.

Why push my luck?

But it's in these moments of uncertainty and improvisation that I seem to do my best work. My biggest laughs often come when I'm speaking off the cuff about something that has just come to my mind seconds before. In that moment of uncertainty, I start to talk about my father. I'm not sure why a man I don't really know — a man who apparently wants little to do with me — strikes me as fodder for something funny, but he does, and it works. I tell a quick bit about trying to impress my father at a young age by living dangerously.

The biggest laugh comes when I tell the audience that one of the ways my siblings and I earned our father's approval was by playing (and winning) "Who can stay in the dryer the longest?" Enduring a warm, dark, bruising tumble was the secret to my father's love.

Three months later, I expand that sixty-second bit into a six-minute story that I perform in a Moth GrandSLAM championship in New York City. Later that month, I write about that same story — expanding it further — for a blog post. Two months after that, I expand it further still by using it as the basis for a humor column in *Seasons* magazine.

Six months later, The Moth asks that I expand that story even further for one of their larger Mainstage shows, where I find myself performing for an audience of more than one thousand people at the Wilbur Theatre in Boston.

Seth Meyers takes the stage an hour after our show. We sell out the theater. He does not.

The recording of that performance at the Wilbur is later aired on The Moth's podcast and *Radio Hour* for an audience numbering in the millions. Two years later, Double Take Comics asks me to write story lines for their new Night of the Living Dead comic-book series. I take that same story and hand it off to a character in the comic just before he confronts a zombie horde for the first time. About a year after that, a version of the story is used as a plot point in my latest novel.

The story is eventually featured on our *Speak Up Storytelling* podcast. The video recording of my performance at the Wilbur is published to my YouTube channel. It's a story I often tell when speaking to high-school students. It's an example I use in my book *Storyworthy*.

Someday I hope to tell it to my father as a means of bridging the inexplicable chasm between us.

It started with a single joke — no longer than sixty seconds — improvised on a stage in Michigan on a Tuesday night, yet the mileage I've gotten from that content has been incredible.

Maximizing the Mileage of Creative Content

As creative people, we must be the collectors, the preservers, and whenever possible, the transformers and expanders of our ideas and content. We need to be supremely flexible in terms of how we view the path of our creative life and the things that we make. When we learn to unshackle our ideas from their original conceptions and allow them to collide with the world, we can find ways to transform them into something new, and the results can be extraordinary.

Audiences can expand. Profits can increase. Creativity can flourish.

Successfully creative and entrepreneurial people turn the things they make today into the creative fodder of tomorrow. This often means expanding beyond our initial image of who we might be and what our content might look like. Rather than becoming locked into a single vision, we must be willing to transform our ideas into the form that will reach the most people possible and maximize our ideas and hard work in as many ways as possible.

For me, this has meant taking ideas for novels that my agent and editor didn't like and turning them into screenplays, musicals, or picture books instead.

It's meant taking the idea for a novel and fusing it with an idea for a different novel while also adding a personal story to the mix to create my next book.

It's meant taking a collection of oral stories from my childhood and combining them into the meat of my first middle-grade novel.

It's meant taking the poems that I wrote back in Hugh Ogden's advanced poetry class and turning them into stories that I tell onstage.

It's meant writing screenplays based upon my published work and unpublished short stories.

It's meant taking stories told on stages around the world and using them as the centerpieces for keynotes, commencement addresses, inspirational speeches, and TED Talks.

It's meant taking the work that I've done on marketing and advertising campaigns and transforming those experiences into the lessons of tomorrow's clients.

It's meant that I've had to expand my identity beyond novelist to columnist, screenwriter, playwright, comic-book writer, storyteller, comedian, consultant, speechwriter, speaking coach, public speaker, entrepreneur, and business owner.

As the makers of things, we must view these things not only as the things we made but as the inspiration or seeds for the next thing. Content — whether it be stories, sculpture, graffiti, costumes, quilts, jokes, novelty socks, balloon art, fireworks displays, murals, songs — is our most precious and valuable commodity. Making something from nothing is miraculous. Whenever possible, we must find ways to reimagine, reconsider, rebuild, or repurpose that miracle to serve our creative needs again and again.

My wife baked a braided challah a couple of years ago. Actually, she baked three braided challahs because it was early in the pandemic and her fifty pounds of flour had finally arrived. She took inert ingredients and transformed them into a something that was entirely unlike the somethings that made the thing. And it was delicious. Miraculous.

The kids and I ate two of the loaves because we love her challah, but a person can only eat so much bread in a forty-eight-hour period, even in the midst of a pandemic. There were also muffins, cakes, and bagels to eat. My wife stress-bakes.

So with the last loaf of bread — the one we hadn't eaten quickly enough for her liking — Elysha made French toast. Bread pudding. Croutons. French onion soup. Meatballs.

She took the thing she made and reimagined it as other things. She didn't allow her initial vision to stop her from making something new.

For the artist, this might mean photographing an original painting for an Instagram feed. Offering the image as an NFT. Creating prints of the original for sale. Depending on the specificity of the image, perhaps using it in the creation of a meme, a poster, or the graphic on a mug. Maybe the artist turns the image into a jigsaw puzzle or collaborates with a poet to bring words and image together.

For the documentarian, this might mean posting shorter,

self-contained segments of the movie online to promote the film and also share the content in briefer, more manageable pieces. Maybe it means writing a magazine piece based on the documentary content or developing lesson plans to go along with the film to promote its use in public school or higher education.

For the baker, this might mean writing a cookbook that includes some of their most original recipes. It could mean partnering with a deli to provide the bread for sandwiches, teaching baking classes, or turning unsold bread into French toast. Bread pudding. Croutons. French onion soup. Meatballs.

• • •

The trope of the starving artist is a trope because it's real. The makers of things are often hungry for a very long time. It's not easy to create something new and then convince other human beings to support the creation of that thing.

We need every edge we can get. We need to exploit every opportunity available to us. We need to look at the thing that makes us special — the stuff we make — as an enormously valuable resource that can and should be exploited whenever possible.

Art is only inert when we think of it as inert.

A joke is only a joke when you stop looking for its next iteration.

Flour is only flour when we think of it as flour.

Braided challah is only braided challah when you think of it as one thing instead of the many things it can become.

Your job as a creator — a maker of things — is to make your thing, but then put that thing on a proverbial shelf in your brain. Not on some shelf in a dusty pantry at the back of your brain but on display in a place of prominence and importance. Keep it in a place in your mind (or, if it's small and tangible, on an actual shelf in your home) where you will come across it often. Rather than forgetting about it and moving on to the next thing, imagine it as a glowing bauble, looking to become something new and different and maybe even better.

Making something is hard. Moving from nonexistence to existence takes an act of enormous will and extraordinary energy. It's an accomplishment of epic proportions.

This is not an exaggeration.

Once there was no book, but now there is a book. Pages and a cover and everything.

Once there was no business, but now there is a business. Products and customers and maybe even a storefront.

Once there was no quilt, but now there is a quilt. A warm, soft means of making a sofa look good and retaining some memories in the process.

Each of these is an astounding turn of events.

If you can then make your something into something else, or allow your something to become the inspiration for something else, then even better. You deserve as much mileage from your somethings as possible. That mileage will only come with the awareness of and an eye to any road ahead.

20 · Don't Be an Asshole

> "Be a good person, it is easier
> than pretending to be a good person."
>
> — NITIN NAMDEO

Years ago, a woman handed me the first three chapters of her manuscript as I signed a book for her during one of my author appearances. Then she asked — a little too aggressively — if I would read the first fifty or so pages and let her know what I thought. I agreed.

Today I might be less inclined to simply accept an unsolicited manuscript, but I admired her gumption. I told her it might be a while before I could get to it, given I was in the midst of finishing a book of my own, but I would eventually email her with my thoughts.

Two months later, on a Sunday afternoon in October, the Patriots were blowing out their opponent in a lopsided matchup, so halfway through the fourth quarter, I turned down the volume on the TV and started reading her manuscript.

I liked it immediately. The concept was original and brilliant, the writing was sparse yet deep, and best of all, it was funny. Absolutely hilarious. I took some notes in the margins as I read and planned to write to her the next day. Maybe even pass the manuscript on to my agent with the writer's permission.

That same evening, the woman wrote to me, demanding that I destroy her manuscript immediately. She accused me of being "just another one of those authors" who says one thing but does another. She was angry, disappointed, and what's worse, vindictive.

Against my wife's better judgment, I wrote back, trying to sound excited about her manuscript. I told her that earlier that afternoon I had just finished reading her pages and had many great things to say about the story. I essentially ignored all her rude remarks, pretended they were never said, and attempted to give this talented writer a second chance.

She replied almost immediately, accusing me of lying to her. I actually replied a third time, once again ignoring her rudeness and trying to bridge the gap between us. The woman was an authentically good writer, and I felt obligated to give her every chance I could. She responded with a tirade of profanity.

I didn't bother replying again. I tossed the manuscript into the trash and moved on.

This wasn't the only time I've dealt with an irate writer. Two years after the previously described disaster, I received this email from a man I had never met before:

> I play poker in Las Vegas, and not a week goes by that someone doesn't say that I'm the politest poker player. Poker is a nasty, brutal game, but it doesn't mean I have to be like all the others.
>
> Most people mistake politeness for weakness.
>
> I am not a writer, and doing this is hard for me. I have attached my personal project on winning, poker, aggression, OODA loops, women, the marines, alcohol, loneliness, insanity, hell, and my 2 cents on all of the above.
>
> Enjoy the quotes.
>
> Back to my cave of darkness.

Two days later, the same person sent me a follow-up email:

> I know how extremely busy you are — so to take time and reply with such an awesome and considerate email is something I will always remember.

OH I FORGOT — YOU COULDN'T EVEN BE BOTHERED TO HIT REPLY AND SAY THANKS FOR YOUR INTEREST OR DROP DEAD.

I know it would have taken maybe two seconds.

Oh well, just another dick.

Will ignore you in the future.

Correspondence like this is always surprising, but tragically, it's also more common than you might think. I make myself fairly available to the public, so as a result, people who are anxious to succeed often reach out to me in desperation.

Many of them are assholes. They feel entitled to my time and energy. They make assumptions about what they deserve or what they are entitled to. They become angry when I don't offer assistance or advice in the time frame they have deemed appropriate. They become enraged when my responses are not detailed or specific enough.

They get angriest when I tell them that I found my literary agent by sending one hundred unsolicited letters to one hundred different agents around the country, along with a portion of my manuscript, and I was preparing my second batch of hundred letters when I finally got an offer of representation.

No, I didn't "know someone."

Yes, you need to write the book first.

Yes, you really need to write the book first.

So many people who reach out to me are looking for some magic pill. They think I have the secret password that will allow them to crack the publishing industry. They ask me for the name of my agent, when her name is easily found on the contact page of my website.

I understand why they are upset and frustrated when they lash out at me. I remember what it felt like to write something good and wonder whether it would ever see the light of day. I understand the emotions behind their words. But strategically speaking, it makes no sense to spew vitriol at me. Burning bridges is never a good idea. You never know when someone might prove to be helpful to your career. You can be angry, outraged, or incensed, but you need not lead with these emotions when writing to someone whose help, or lack of help, didn't meet your standards.

It only makes you look like an asshole. Contrast the previous emails with my correspondence with Caleb and John that I'm about to share.

A few years ago I spoke at a local library about my books and writing. Sitting front and center in the first row was a young man who wanted to be a writer. He was on the edge of his seat, ready to absorb all that I had to say. He listened intently, asked lots of questions, and at the end of my talk, introduced himself to me.

Since that day, Caleb has sent me samples of his work from time to time, and when I have the chance, I will read his pages and send him back some feedback. He's young, but he's already showing the signs of a promising writing career. He has chops.

Equally important, he's polite. He's socially adept. He understands that I get exceptionally busy and sometimes can't read everything. Whenever he sends me something, he includes a small amount of writing and opens with the sentences "No problem if you can't get to this. You have a life. I get it."

I don't always respond to Caleb's writing, but I'm far more likely to respond to him than others because he is polite, empathetic, and not an asshole. The way you say something can make all the difference.

Recently, I received an email from someone asking me to listen to and respond to a recording of their story. This is something I am routinely paid to do these days, so it was a bold request. The writer was essentially asking me to work for free. The email read like this:

Dear Matt,

My name's John and I'm a foreign language teacher from Italy. I'm one of your fans, and you, your stories, and your book *Storyworthy* have had a great impact on me on many levels. Homework for Life — I have that spreadsheet, too, now! I'm getting in touch to ask you if you'd be interested in listening to one of my stories in which I try to use your techniques.

I wrote it and recorded myself telling it. This is my cheap way to podcast. :) I hope you'll notice the influence you had on me by the way I tell this story (focus on small daily moments, using the present tense, starting the story near your 5-second moment). If you don't see this, it's entirely my fault! :)

I'm not after any sort of detailed feedback, Matt, but I was just wondering if you think I'm on the right track or not.

Hope to hear from you and have a great day.

Thank you,
John

Did you see what John (not his real name) did? Not only did he indicate his sincere investment in my content, but his question was a simple one: "Am I on the right track?" John is aware of the constraints on my time and asked me to answer a simple question rather than making an appeal for extensive feedback.

It was a presumptuous request, but it was also nominal in its specifics and was exceedingly polite.

Will I respond to John? I already have. How could I not respond to such a well-phrased request?

Let Kindness Pave the Way

The life of a creative person becomes a lot easier when the people in power want you to succeed. You need to be exceptionally good and exceptionally lucky to be an asshole and still be successful. In the absence of a benefactor, a trust fund, or incredible talent, let kindness pave your way.

My literary agent, Taryn, was standing in my backyard one day a few years ago, talking about my work and our next steps, when she said, "Listen, the one thing that I want you to remember is to not be an asshole. Your editors like you. You have the reputation of being easy and fun to work with. It makes it a lot easier to sell your books."

I've never forgotten those words.

I was speaking to a storyteller during the pandemic, commenting on all the corporate clients I work with regularly on storytelling, marketing, advertising, and communications. I know many storytellers who would like to get this kind of work but just can't. I wondered aloud why.

My storytelling friend, whom I first met in one of my workshops, answered immediately: "You understand customer service. You know that a little bit of kindness and generosity can go a long way. I suspect it's all those years managing McDonald's restaurants. You learned how to treat employees well to get them to work hard for you. You know how to accommodate a customer so they leave with a smile. Not everyone gets that. That goes a long way with corporate clients, nonprofits, universities, and people like me."

In other words, I'm not an asshole.

Being an asshole may admittedly get you something in the near term, but creators must play the long game. We need to keep our eyes not on today's horizon but on the thousands of horizons beyond this one. This can be something as simple as asking my editor's assistant for my editor's favorite coffee order so that each time I visit her New York office, I show up with some caffeinated goodness (despite my own personal aversion to the stuff). But this can also mean understanding the importance of flexibility, collaboration, and cooperation in all creative endeavors. As an author, I recognize the enormous team of professionals who help bring my books to the masses, so I find a way to thank as many of them as possible for their efforts. I can't always find all of them — the men and women working in the pulp factory are beyond my reach — but my editor, copyeditor, proofreaders, cover designer, marketing and publicity teams, and all the assistants I can identify and connect with are thanked whenever possible.

It also means keeping your less-than-kind comments to yourself or expressing them at designated times and in designated places.

. . .

Years ago, I lost a Moth GrandSLAM championship to a competitor whose story was more than three minutes over the allotted time. This should've been the kiss of death for the storyteller in terms of the competition, but somehow, some way, the judges still gave her a score that was one-tenth of a point better than my own.

Needless to say, I was annoyed. After the show, a prominent member of The Moth's staff approached me and told me that I should've won. "Even if her story was better, you can't be long by three minutes and still win," they said. I nodded politely, thanked them for their kind words, and talked about how much I had enjoyed my competitor's story.

I really did enjoy the story. It was just too damn long to be declared the winner.

Later, I found out that my conversation with that prominent Moth staffer was overheard by others, and the complaints about the length of my competitor's story were falsely attributed to me instead of the staffer. As a result, word spread that I behaved like an ungrateful jerk that night, and at least one Moth producer placed me in the proverbial storytelling doghouse for a while as punishment.

Now I was really annoyed. Even more annoyed than I was at losing the championship, which, for a person as competitive as me, is really saying something. What annoyed me most was that I specifically, deliberately, relentlessly avoid situations like this.

Yes, it's true. I complained about losing that championship. And yes, it's true: I stated many times that I was the rightful winner of that GrandSLAM. But I didn't speak a word of this publicly (until now). I have a strict policy that prevents me from complaining about storytellers and/or their stories until I'm in the privacy of the car with Elysha or a trusted friend. I never complain about or speak poorly of a story in public because I don't want to be perceived as a whiner, a sore loser, or, worst of all, an asshole.

This isn't always easy. Envy is a powerful force in the minds of many creative folks, myself included. In a world where opportunities are limited and power structures create unfair advantages, feelings of jealousy and anger are common.

A fellow comedian gets a spot that you think you deserve. A start-up receives funding from an angel investor, but your company does not. A gallery features your friend's collection of sculptures but passes on your own. A film studio decides to make *The Revenge of the Return of the Rebirth of the Night of the Still Living Dead* instead of your more sophisticated film about an orphaned boy and his orphaned tortoise.

Envy is real and many times unavoidable, but the way you express it — in terms of space, time, and audience — is entirely under your control. Complain about the injustice of the world, but complain about it privately. Complain about it to a loved one or a creative partner. Avoid complaining to the people you may need in order to climb the mountain. Avoid complaining to the people climbing alongside you. Avoid complaining whenever it sounds like sour grapes.

Comedian Marc Maron spent much of his career in a state of bitterness and anger. He only managed to overcome those feelings later in life after launching a podcast and spending the first couple of hundred episodes talking with the people toward whom he had felt (and sometimes still felt) animosity.

"Are we okay?" Maron would ask at the end of these oftentimes cathartic episodes.

Back in 2017, after Maron had scored interviews with the likes of President Obama, Lorne Michaels, and Amy Poehler, he said, "I'm happy with my success, but I was certainly driven by envy and spite for most of my life. Validation is shifty in this business; if you're not capable of saying, 'I'm doing a good job,' how do you determine what it means to be successful? My envy and insecurity pushed other people away."

As creators, we cannot afford to push people away. We need as many people as possible on our team. We need help. We need support. We need allies.

We can't afford a single enemy if it's avoidable.

• • •

One of the easiest ways to enlist support is to acknowledge your good fortune and express gratitude whenever possible. Even the biggest pain in the ass can enlist the support of others when they are willing to credit the contributions of people or the universe to their success.

In the fall of 2018, I was speaking about the importance of storytelling to an auditorium filled with high-school students. After completing my remarks, I asked for questions. A young man in the front row raised his hand and said, "I don't mean this as an insult, but your life has been awful. Like really, really bad. How did you manage to survive all that stuff and stay positive and become who you are today?"

Not only had the young man heard some of my stories over the course of the previous hour, but he and his class had studied my biography online. Watched many videos on my YouTube channel. Read my storytelling book. Even subscribed to my blog. He didn't know me well, but he knew about some of the struggles of my past with which you are now also familiar. Kicked out of my childhood home at eighteen. Arrested and tried for a crime I didn't commit. Jailed. Homeless. Died twice (from a beesting at twelve and a head-on collision at seventeen, both requiring paramedics to perform CPR to restore my life). Victim of a violent armed robbery. Shared a bedroom with a goat. Worked fifty hours a week while completing two full-time degree programs. Slandered on a public scale by an anonymous-coward contingent in an effort to destroy my career. A lifetime of PTSD. Left-handed.

All that messy stuff that has been my life.

There were many things I could've said to that young man. I could've spoken about my desire to do great and interesting things. I might've mentioned an ongoing, overwhelming existential crisis that has made me relentlessly focused on forward movement. I could've talked about how the struggles of my past have granted me enormous perspective today, so I'm able to shrug off many of the problems that paralyze others. I could've talked about the structure and strategies for productivity and efficiency upon which I have constructed my life. I could've discussed how living well is the best revenge — a fact I think about every day when I step into my classroom, knowing cowards once tried to prevent it from ever happening again.

Instead, I said this: "I never forget how lucky I have been."

The auditorium erupted in laughter, and I understood why. At that moment, I seemed anything but lucky.

I pressed on. "No, I'm serious. I'm an exceptionally fortunate person. Think about it. I'm a white, straight man living in the United States. Do you have any idea how many advantages those simple things have afforded me? If I was Black or gay or a woman, my road would've been a hell of a lot harder. If I was born in Mexico or Afghanistan or Ethiopia or Syria, this life that I enjoy today almost certainly would not have been possible."

I paused to allow this to settle, then I continued. "In addition, I'm healthy — both in mind and body — and reasonably intelligent. I grew up in Massachusetts, which is near the top of the country in public education. I've deliberately avoided illegal drugs for my entire life, but I could've become addicted to alcohol like so many. But I didn't. I got lucky. And my heart stopped beating and I stopped breathing twice in my life, and both times, trained medical personnel saved my life with CPR. How lucky is that?"

More laughter. But also nods from the audience.

I finished with something like this: "I'm not saying that your road will be easy, but if you're a white, straight, American man, you have the easiest road of anyone anywhere. I hear this nonsense about reverse racism. I hear young white men complaining that they are the victims of a system designed to stack the odds against them. These are stupid people. Try being Black or Hispanic for a day. Try being someone who isn't cisgender. Try being a woman. Try being physically disabled or struggling with a mental illness. White, straight, healthy American men have no idea what kind of discrimination and hatred and harassment and obstacles people unlike us face every day. Yes, I've had a tragically eventful life at times, and yes, I had to fight like hell to get where I am today. I was relentless and positive and forward-thinking and willing to do whatever it took to survive and thrive, but no one was holding me back because of the color of my skin or my sexual orientation or my gender. My biology has afforded me enormous privilege, and I'm quite certain that more than anything else, that has been the greatest factor in my success."

And I believe it. For all the things I have done in my life to be successful, my status as a white, straight, physically and mentally healthy American man has been most important.

The student who asked the question, a Black teenager, walked over and hugged me.

Express some gratitude. Acknowledge your good fortune.

It's hard for anyone to think of anyone as an asshole when you do this.

20½ · 9 Rules for Making You More Efficient with Email and Less of a Jerk Face

"I don't believe in email. I'm an old-fashioned girl.
I prefer calling and hanging up."

— SARAH JESSICA PARKER

1. Email is often a means of informal communication. As such, you can dramatically decrease the amount of time spent on email with short, efficient replies like "Thanks" and "Understood" and "Agreed." Dispense with formalities whenever possible and increase efficiency.
2. Blind carbon copy (bcc) is often the tool of the passive-aggressive coward. Before including an email address in this field, always ask yourself why you are using it. If you're trying to hurt or embarrass someone or conceal something, knock it off, jerk face.
3. Never send an email written to express your anger or disappointment with someone. Those emotions are better conveyed over the phone or in person, where unnecessary aggression and excessive vitriol cannot be shielded by the passive-aggressive nature of email. In other words, don't be a coward. If you're upset, pick up the phone.

4. "I sent that angry email because I express myself better in written form and was too enraged to speak" is never an excuse for violating rule #3.

5. If you receive an angry email, pick up the phone and respond immediately. The faster, the better. The best way to handle a passive-aggressive person is in an aggressively direct manner. Angry email senders tend to be people who do not handle conflict well and therefore hide behind technology. Pulling back the technological curtain will be uncomfortable for them and will often knock them off their position.

6. In-box zero should be your goal, if only for productivity and efficiency purposes. Leaving email in your in-box forces you to look at it every time you access your mail application, which takes time and energy. It's akin to sifting through the same growing pile of mail every day to find a specific letter or bill. In-box zero will eliminate the time required to take action on incoming emails by not adding them to an already enormous pile.

7. Use a mail application that allows you to schedule a time when you want an email to hit your in-box. Turn email into something that you receive when you want to receive it. I often reschedule incoming email for a designated time during the day when I plan to read and respond, thereby keeping my in-box empty and enjoying the benefits of rule #6. If I receive an email pertaining to taxes, I reschedule it to hit my in-box on April 1. If my fifth-grade team receives an email requesting action on our part, I reschedule it to hit my in-box in twenty-four hours in the hopes that one of my colleagues will handle the request before I need to.

8. Respond to emails that require action as quickly as possible, and always within twenty-four hours. Failing to respond to an email — even if your response is "I'll get back to you tomorrow" — projects the image of a person who is overwhelmed, disorganized, and inefficient.

9. Choose subject lines for your emails that will allow your readers to identify the general purpose of the email without actually opening it and will help you search for that email in the future.

21 Eat a Lot

"Content isn't king. It's the kingdom."

— LEE ODDEN

Elysha was recently commiserating with a friend. Her friend's husband frequently disappears into their basement for hours at a time, reading books and magazines, while she takes care of their four young children.

"I have a similar problem with Matt and his headphones," Elysha said.

The headphones in question are small, wireless, and affixed to my head almost always. They are sitting atop my head as I write these words. With the touch of a button, I can be listening to a podcast, an audiobook, or music, and admittedly, I often am. I'm listening to Aretha Franklin right now.

Ironically, Elysha gave me my first pair of wireless headphones years ago for Christmas. Since then, I have gone through dozens of pairs. At the moment, I'm wearing the Levin wraparound sports wireless headset with built-in microphone. I have the one pair atop my head and two more sets, fully charged, in my backpack, just in case.

I highly recommend them. And Elysha is right. I am constantly listening to something. If I'm not engaged in conversation, I am probably playing a book or podcast. As you might imagine, this unquestionably leads to moments when Elysha is speaking to me, but I can't hear her because I'm listening to a novel or a book on the history of the English language or a podcast on finance, history, screenwriting, social science, technology, design, and more.

It's frustrating for her, I know. When it happens, I feel like a jerk. Much of the time, I'm engaged in an otherwise mindless task like washing the dishes, cooking dinner, or folding laundry, but still, it would be nice to be able to speak to your husband without having to raise your voice or flag him down like you're signaling a jet on the runway at LaGuardia.

I know. It's not great. Yet after bemoaning my headphones and my constant use of them, my wife said this to her friend: "But it's also changed our lives."

Despite the annoyance that my headphones create from time to time, Elysha also recognizes that a great deal of my creative ideas are born and fueled from my constant consumption of content. She knows that the endless stream of words that flow from my headphones into my ears has resulted in some of the most important leaps forward in my career as a maker of things.

She's absolutely correct. My incessant content consumption changed our lives. And that doesn't even include the books I'm reading, the newsletters delivered to my in-box on a daily basis, and the websites I frequent.

The audio content alone that I consume has been instrumental to my creative life: The ideas for three of my six published novels (and my unpublished novel) originated from my listening to podcasts. The idea for one of my plays came from listening to a podcast. The topic for one of my more popular TEDx Talks took shape when I was listening to a book and despised the ideas being proposed by the author so much that I needed to find a way to refute them.

Storytelling

Listening to The Moth's podcast back in 2009 led me into the world of storytelling, which has completely transformed our lives like nothing else. The podcast sent me to New York City to perform for the first time, where I won my first storytelling competition and then kept on winning. Part of my success admittedly came from years of experience writing stories, publishing novels, emceeing weddings, and analyzing films, but it also came from listening to The Moth's podcast for two years before ever taking the stage. By listening every week without fail, I soaked in all that great storytelling DNA and learned many of the secrets of telling a great story without even realizing that it was happening.

Soon I was performing on stages in New York, in Boston, and then around the world.

Less than two years after I told that first story, Elysha and I launched Speak Up, a Hartford-based storytelling organization that helps people find and tell their best stories. We began by producing shows in theaters throughout Connecticut, and by telling my own stories in those shows, I began receiving requests from audience members that I teach workshops on the craft. Those workshops eventually led to my career in consulting and coaching.

Though I couldn't possibly foresee this future, listening to The Moth's podcast ultimately launched my career in marketing, advertising, speechwriting, and filmmaking. It led me to work with hospitals, attorneys, entrepreneurs, documentarians, television writers, the clergy, and the children of Holocaust survivors. It's led me to share the stage with some of the best performers in the world and meet some of the most interesting people who populate my life today.

Business and Investing

Listening to podcasts on business, the stock market, and retail investing led me to become an investor myself. In addition to market-beating gains in the stock market for the past four years, I have acquired knowledge about business that has been an invaluable asset when consulting in the corporate world. My knowledge of markets, competitors, trends, and more allows me to move with ease in this world while bringing a perspective on communication that executives don't often possess.

One CEO said to me, "The Venn diagram of storytelling and business is usually two very separate circles with lots of space in between. You've somehow managed to overlap them quite nicely for yourself."

I did so by listening a lot. Reading a lot. Committing myself to the study of something entirely new. And I didn't do so with an eye toward consulting. I was genuinely interested in the economy and investing after years of listening to podcasts like NPR's *Planet Money* and *Freakonomics*. I was chasing after a subject that I wanted to know more about, finding books on the subject, and seeking out trusted resources. I mentioned this interest to my friend Tony while tailgating at a Patriots game one day, and he pointed me to podcasts like *MarketFoolery* that focus solely on investing.

Three years later, after hundreds of hours spent listening and nearly as many hours spent reading, I made my first stock purchase: Visa, Mastercard, PayPal, and Square. The "War on Cash" basket recommended by Jason Moser of The Motley Fool.

It's paid off very well.

Four years later, my portfolio consists of about twenty-five different stocks, and I have knowledge of many, many more companies and markets.

What began as curiosity about the economy and investing has become an enormously valuable tool when helping clients communicate about their business.

Comedy

Listening to podcasts hosted by comedians and about comedy finally convinced me to take the stage and try stand-up, and the experience

I gained telling jokes onstage has directly translated back into my storytelling, my coaching, and my consulting. I'm constantly being hired to punch up a speech, infuse humor into a marketing campaign, and teach comedy techniques to storytellers. I'm not the funniest comedian by a long shot, but I've become a student of comedy, and my access to the storytelling, corporate, and film worlds has made my skills very valuable. Even though my initial plunge into comedy was not done with an eye toward my business, the lessons I've learned have been enormously profitable. But it all began with something I simply wanted to learn more about.

Screenwriting

Listening to the screenwriting podcast *Scriptnotes*, recommended by a friend and hopeful screenwriter, convinced me to begin writing screenplays of my own. Though I have yet to sell a screenplay, I am currently working with producers on adapting one of my novels for the screen, and the experience I've gained while writing, developing, and pitching stories for the screen has helped me tremendously in the writing of my plays and musicals, which *have* been produced. Listening to *Scriptnotes* also led to the development and launch of *Speak Up Storytelling*, the podcast that I produce and host with Elysha that reaches tens of thousands of people every month in countries around the world.

• • •

It's rare in this world for a new idea to emerge from the ether, uninspired or uninformed by something else. Nevertheless, warnings against being a generalist have persisted for centuries.

The phrase "jack-of-all-trades, master of none" is a popular one spoken by those who espouse a singular focus, but the original phrase was "A jack-of-all-trades is a master of none, but oftentimes better than a master of one." In other words, learn a lot about a lot.

This makes a great deal of sense. Many of the most successful people — both today and in the past — have demonstrated interest in more than one subject: Charles Darwin, Elon Musk, Steve Jobs, Richard Feynman, Ben Franklin, Thomas Edison, Leonardo da Vinci, Marie Curie, and many, many more. A study of the most significant scientists in all of history uncovered that fifteen of the twenty were polymaths — people possessing knowledge in a wide range of fields, including Newton, Galileo, Aristotle, Kepler, Descartes, Faraday, and Pasteur.

The founders of five of the largest companies in the world — Bill Gates, Steve Jobs, Warren Buffett, Larry Page, and Jeff Bezos — also polymaths.

Creative people understand that inspiration can come from almost anywhere, so the more content you consume, the more interests you cultivate, and the more things you learn, the more likely you will find a new idea. You must be someone willing to immerse yourself in a large and wide variety of content, not limiting yourself to your field or your personal areas of expertise. Diverse and seemingly disparate ideas can collide and form something new and beautiful, but it can only happen when you commit yourself to ongoing, continuous, relentless learning.

In his book *On Writing*, Stephen King wrote, "If you don't have time to read, you don't have the time (or the tools) to write. Simple as that."

And it doesn't ever end. Or at least it shouldn't ever end.

My study of business and markets continues on a daily basis. Since I began performing stand-up, I've only expanded the number of podcasts that I listen to on the subject and watch far more comedy than ever before. I still listen to The Moth's podcast and *The Moth Radio Hour*, in addition to a number of other storytelling podcasts. I've read books on the subject of storytelling for business, becoming a student of the work of Nancy Duarte.

My studies continue, but they expand as well. I'm always looking for the next frontier. My current interests include the science of the brain. I'm fascinated by what causes people to retain some memories while losing others, and I'm curious about how much information the brain holds that we simply can't access. I'm interested in ways in which brain chemistry is altered by human speech, as well as the methods by which learning and retention can be improved.

I'm also reading about gene therapy and developments like CRISPR's gene-editing technology, and I'm immersed in the technical aspects of cinematography — including lighting and sound — for a new project I'm working on.

I'm even learning about aviation via YouTube channels, though I have no intention of ever flying a plane. Why? I'm interested. And I never try to predict where an interest may or may not lead.

Will any of these new interests transform my life in the way The Moth's podcast or my study of markets and investing has?

I'm not sure, but it's also not the point. As a creative person — a maker of things — I know that one of the best ways of developing new ideas, identifying new connections, and expanding my potential skill set is by constantly pursuing new learning in whatever direction my interests may point me. There is no predicting what new bit of knowledge will open a new door and expand your universe, so I simply chase my interests and consume new content, wherever my curiosity takes me.

If you don't have time to learn something new, you don't have time to make something new.

Not as elegant as Stephen King, but just as true.

22　Pessimists Die Knowing Only That They Were Correct. Optimists Thrive.

"Do you think that I count the days? There is only one day left,
always starting over: it is given to us at dawn
and taken away from us at dusk."

— JEAN-PAUL SARTRE

Here comes a hard truth.

I know. Why end with a hard truth?

I opened this book asking for you to fill your heart and mind with hope. Remember that? It feels like a long time ago for me, but who knows? Maybe you powered through the book in a single day. If so, good for you. Unless, of course, you ignored your family or some other important responsibility in the process. If so, go repair the damage after reading this chapter and the afterword — don't sleep on the afterword. It's a good one.

So if things went according to plan, you began reading this book with hope in your heart, and the lessons, strategies, and suggestions that I've offered have been received with an open mind and a willing spirit.

Maybe you're excited about the path that lies before you. Maybe you can't wait to get started. If I did my job, you're well equipped with the tools to launch your creative journey, or relaunch your creative journey, or perhaps jump-start the journey that you've been on for a while.

I hope so. I started by asking you to find some hope for our journey together.

Now I find myself hopeful for you. I hope like hell for your success.

But as I said, I have some hard truth for you now. Ready?

Here it is: People quit on their dreams all the time. It's easy to give up. Very few people on this planet make their honest-to-goodness dreams come true. Most settle for second or third tier at best. More often than not, they settle for nothing at all. They move through this life without direction or ambition, falling into the path of least resistance. They travel like water down a mountain, meandering meekly to the bottom.

Then, one day, they look back on their lives and wonder why they allowed so many opportunities to slip through their fingers. They can't understand why they surrendered so easily. How did they give up on their dreams so quickly and without so much as a fight?

Then they die.

Most people live a life like this. Most people suffer this fate. They die with regret.

I don't want this fate to befall you. I don't want you to end up wishing you had more time to finally do something. Yearning to turn back the clock. Angry with yourself for all that you could've done but failed to do.

I've given you tools to avoid this fate. Tools to increase your chances of realizing your dreams. Methods to bolster your creative capacity, your spirit, and your stick-to-itiveness. They will all help. I promise you.

I have one more thing to offer you. This last one might be the most important of all. The thing you will need every day to keep moving forward: optimism.

There are two types of people in this world: optimists and pessimists. Some people claim to be realists, but you need to understand two important truths about realists:

1. They are not optimists.
2. They are simply pessimists who are too afraid or too embarrassed to acknowledge who they really are.

As a creative soul, a maker of things, and a person pursuing your dreams, you can't afford to be a pessimist. Too many negative forces are already aligned against you. Creating new things is hard. Making your dreams come true is already an uphill battle. Along the way, there will be people who find your progress threatening to their own ego. They will try to impede you whenever possible as a means of self-preservation.

There will also be competition. People trying to achieve the same or similar goals. People vying for limited resources and space that you want and need.

There will be bad luck. Stupid people. Bureaucracy. Traffic. Blizzards. Broken bones. Paperwork in triplicate. Slow mail service. Flat tires. Bad hair days. Mosquitoes. Hangnails. Broken shoelaces. Potholes. Cavities.

A lot of stuff will get in your way. It will sometimes feel like the universe is pitted against you.

That is why you need to be an optimist. You must believe that things will turn out right.

Even if a pessimist is proved correct in their doomsday prediction, the only advantage they will possess is the smug self-satisfaction that comes with being correct. But being smug and correct about negative outcomes is the goal of soulless ghouls, chronic complainers, jealous siblings, bullies, frenemies, and other varieties of awful people.

Happily, pessimists are wrong more often than not. Martin Luther King Jr. wisely pointed out, "The arc of the moral universe is long, but it bends toward justice." Humanity marches forward in fits and starts, but progress is unrelenting. Research also shows that optimists are happier and live longer, because even when the planet is struck by a pandemic, optimists experience the pandemic only for its duration. Pessimists worry about it for years before it ever arrives, and worry like that can wear you down quickly. Assuming the best allows you to avoid the pain of assuming the worst, even if the worst is on its way.

History is filled with artists, writers, scientists, designers, entrepreneurs, and other creative souls who toiled for years before finally achieving greatness. While overnight success and the instantaneous realization of your dreams is preferred, it's unlikely — so only those who believe in their craft, themselves, and their future will persevere.

When I began writing this book, I asked Elysha, "What do I do that has allowed me to succeed?"

Her answer was instantaneous: "You believe that everything will work out, then you work it out."

You must do the same. When you feel like you can't, try what I call "throwing my present to the future."

• • •

It's early June. Two weeks left in the school year, but summer has already arrived. The school bell is minutes from ringing in the start of the day, but it's already ninety degrees outside. Even hotter in our non-air-conditioned school.

Except for a select few offices, of course. Those spaces absent of children. Let the kids and their teachers bake while the suits stay cool.

One of my colleagues pokes her head in the classroom and begins to complain about the heat. I cut her off. "Listen," I say, "in less than eight hours, the school day will be over, and in less than two weeks, the school year will be over and we'll be heading into summer vacation. Pretty soon today's temperature will be meaningless to us, so let's just make that moment now. Let's pretend it's 3:30 or June 15 already, since both will be here soon enough. Let's not waste time and energy on complaining about something that we won't care about soon."

To my colleague's credit, she smiled and said, "Okay. But I'm eating lunch in my car with the AC running."

Smart lady.

"Throwing my present to the future" is based upon the assumption that many of the problems we face today are temporary, fleeting, and ultimately forgettable, but in the moment, they can feel awful, momentous, and painful. In these cases, I try to avoid those negative feelings by acknowledging that the problem will be irrelevant in a day or a week or even a month and then pretending that the next day, week, or month has already arrived.

The future is often better than the problematic present, so maintaining an awareness of that more pleasant future and assuming the emotional disposition of that future version of yourself can alleviate the short-term suffering caused by troublesome but temporary struggles.

I use this strategy all the time. I believe that everything will work out, then I work it out. When throwing my present to the future, I work out the problem in my mind first before working it out in real life. I remain optimistic that the toils and troubles of the present will appear trivial in the future. I work hard to maintain that optimism in the face of disaster.

There's also nothing wrong with feeling great about yourself. Look around. How many people do you know who are truly chasing their dreams? I don't need to look very far to find a whole lot of people working in careers that they stumbled into because it was convenient or easy or afforded them a good salary. It's not hard for me to find people who spend their days at jobs they do not love and their evenings in front of the television and do little else to fill their hours.

Unhappy people are everywhere. They are like weeds.

I see a hell of a lot of people living ordinary lives, but very few grew up dreaming of one day being ordinary. Yet here they are. Everywhere. Ordinary.

I see these people. I look hard at them, because they serve as reminders to me that if I had chosen the easier pathway, that could be me, too. *Good job, Matt!*

Even if I'm falling on my ass or landing on my face, at least I'm failing while trying. Climbing and slipping and falling but then

picking myself up and trying again. If you're chasing your dreams —
if you're trying to make great things or carve a new path or bend the
universe to your will — you're already doing better than most of the
human beings on this planet. Many live in circumstances that tragically don't allow them to chase their dreams. Others have the means
and ability but simply don't.

Kurt Vonnegut once posed the question: "Who is more to be
pitied, a writer bound and gagged by policemen or one living in
perfect freedom who has nothing more to say?"

Many people are living in perfect freedom but have absolutely
nothing to say. Truthfully, most people are average. It's the mathe-
matical definition of the word. If you're reading this book, climbing
a mountain, and truly chasing the dream, you're doing better than
most.

You're above average. Probably a lot better than just above average.

Remember that. It will help. I promise it will.

But maybe don't say it aloud very often. No reason for the world
to think you're an arrogant jerk. As I've said, there are already too
many pitfalls awaiting you. But nothing wrong with holding your
head high, believing in the future, and, most importantly, believing
in yourself.

• • •

As I approached the final pages of this book, I wasn't sure how to
end this last chapter. What parting words should I offer you? What
collection of sentences would mean the most to you?

I asked Elysha if she had any thoughts, but before she could
answer, Charlie said, "Super Cow."

"I should end with Super Cow?" I asked.

"Yes," he said. "Super Cow."

Charlie has always loved cows. He has always loved to moo.
"Super Cow" was not surprising coming from him. But you know
what *is* surprising?

I agree. *Super Cow*. It's perfect. Let's make those two silly words our secret mantra. The two words you and I will use when the struggle is mighty and the finish line seems impossibly far away. Let "Super Cow" remind you of all that you have already done. All the skills and strategies that you have acquired. All your previous accomplishments.

Super Cow.

Creator
Optimistically
Winning

I don't really need the acronym to love the idea, but if you needed a little more meaning, there you go.

Super Cow.

Say it aloud. Say it loud. Shout it, if possible.

At the very least, "Super Cow" will make you smile on those toughest of days.

At best, it will remind you that there is a nine-year-old possible future guitarist, current Little League outfielder, and avid Minecraft builder who believes in you and wants you to do great things. He really does. He loves to watch human beings excel. There isn't a jealous bone in the boy's body. He wants nothing but the best for you.

I do, too. I really, really do. I'm rooting for you. I am in your cheering section, making a hell of a lot of noise on your behalf.

I can't wait to see what you will do. What you will make. How you will change your life. How you might even change the world.

Your future is bright. I know it. Make sure that you know it, too. Remind yourself every day of how extraordinary you are.

Believe that everything will work out, then go and work it out.

Get moving. Remember: someday is today.

Now go kill it.

22½ You Can't Change Unless You Change

The question I get asked most often is "How do you get so much done?" I'm always willing to offer advice on becoming more productive and more efficient, and people are typically receptive to my suggestions.

Occasionally, however, people become annoyed and frustrated with my suggestions because they involve changing a habit or routine. I find this odd. How do you expect to become more productive and efficient without instituting a certain degree of change in your life? I honestly think these people wanted me to give them a magic pill.

The most frequent comment I receive from these annoyed folks is this: "I don't have time to do that." Which is to say: "I don't have time to save time so I would have more free time to do the things I want to do."

This also strikes me as odd. I offer a strategy that admittedly might take some time to implement, but upon completion of the implementation, the person would then have even more free time, yet the person can't see how the initial investment would offer an enormous return. These people would prefer to continue to waste time and operate inefficiently rather than dedicating a small amount of time in an effort to stop wasting time.

But I see this unfortunate pattern frequently. These are the folks who allow chores to pile up and become all-day affairs rather than taking the small amount of time required to stay on top of things. These are the people who won't spend the two or three minutes getting organized but will then waste half an hour as a result of their disorganization.

I think that in the end, some people are resistant to change, even if the change promises a better, more productive, more efficient life. It's hard for them to see beyond their own lives, and it's exceptionally hard for some to break the habits and routines they have established.

But telling me that you don't have time to save time? To be more productive?

That is ridiculous.

Don't let yourself lapse into such a protest.

Afterword

by Matthew Shepard

Matthew Dicks is not a crackpot. I think it's important to clear that up.

He may come across as eccentric in how he organizes and manages his life. You may be thinking this very thing after having read this book.

But annoyingly, *it works*.

I say "annoyingly" because those of us who know Matty (or Matt, as the case may be) also know that he can come across as, well, let's say "a bit much" sometimes. And we know that he believes fiercely that he is, by and large, in the right on many things. This makes it all the more irritating to many of us close to him when those things, like what you've read here, prove to work out.

He does everything I do, and so much more, because of the way he has developed strategies to conserve his time for things that matter. I saw early signs of this decades ago, even before Matty was a family man, when we would spend weekends playing various games and sports. While some of us would stay over at the host's house, possibly engaging in a bounty of post-activity refreshments, Matty usually drove to and fro (probably too fast, to be fair) to be able to maximize his time spent doing other, more productive things, yet he still never missed an activity or participated any less enthusiastically.

One year he attended our full weekend of nonsense, including hours of networked gaming and an all-too-violent "flag" football game, while also trying out wedding cakes with his fiancée. While he "Matt-ily" neglected to bring us — his closest friends — any cake, he otherwise did not stint on his attention to either activity.

It really is annoying to us friends when he's right.

To be fair, I know for a fact that I *could* do as much as he does, but unlike him — and I assume, unlike you, since you are reading this book — I am more of an anti-Matty. I was, in fact, shocked that I would be asked to comment on this particular book, as I have arranged my life very carefully over the past twenty-five years or so to get to a point that I can expend a minimum amount of effort on productive endeavors so I can spend more time on things others might deem frivolous. Many of our longtime friends, built more toward Matty's end of the productivity curve, would likely say I'm the eccentric one.

But the fact is that both Matty and I *have* those longtime friends, despite living at opposite ends of that curve. He's not some freakish workaholic loner, even by my admittedly slacker-esque standards. He has a loving family. He dotes on his wife and children. And he makes time for all of them — for all of us, really — while teaching, writing books, consulting around the globe, and doing however many of his other jobs he may have mentioned... because he makes it work for him.

He does exactly what this book describes so well.

Matty has one of the best life balances of anyone I know. I have enjoyed hours of tailgating, NFL games, and golf with him over the decades I've known him even while he was writing books, building businesses, winning storytelling competitions, penning columns, and everything else. Just as annoyingly, he applies his focus to golf as well, and my meager, unpracticed abilities and decades-old clubs are no longer enough to best him, even though he can still drive the ball only 150 yards.

But I digress, which happens a lot where Matty and I are concerned. The point I was making was that he manages to make the time for golf with me (and others far better than me), football, poker, and more, and seemingly never to the detriment of his other friends or his family. In fact, despite all his work and obsession over productivity, the people he cares about have always been his priority.

In that way, he's no different from you or me. Actually, in no way is he really different from you or me.

Okay, that's not entirely true. By and large, he's probably been far, far more of a disaster than most of us. This is a man who has such poor attention to some of the details of life that until very recently he literally didn't know what color his own house was, even though he's lived inside it for more than a decade. This is a man who once nearly electrocuted himself by putting the end of a plugged-in computer cord in his mouth so he could have both hands free. He thankfully escaped electrocution but concussed himself on the bottom of the desk he was working under as he leaped in — wait for it — shock. This is not some kind of genius.

So now you're probably thinking, *Wait, this is the guy I'm taking advice from?* But Matty has made a practice of learning, and experimenting, and he's figured some things out, usually the hard way, such as "Don't put electrical cords in your mouth," or simply because he had no choice.

If you're like me, you may have been fortunate enough to travel the traditional high-school-to-college route, supported by family in some way. Matty took — through no choice of his own — a far more circuitous route. He was generously gifted with dishes and a microwave on his eighteenth birthday — a subtle hint as to what his immediate future living arrangements would be. He found himself at various points shortly thereafter homeless, living in his car, and falsely jailed. I suspect this might be the source of his focus on the value of time, and especially quality time. It began with that time being taken from him, in so many ways. So he set out to get it back and make sure he never felt it was wasted again.

As you know well by now, he put himself through school, working full-time managing a McDonald's — the same company that led to that jail time (revisit that story in chapter 1 — it's well worth rereading). He completed two full-time degree programs, simultaneously at two different schools, and founded the DJ business that would lead to me meeting him (the marriage didn't work out, as he mentioned, but the friendship with the wedding DJs did). Today, as you also know, he performs onstage, consults on storytelling with corporations and universities, writes books, and more.

He maximized his time, and, quite simply, it made his life better. Any of us could do it, too.

Matty understands that the time we have with those we love is one of life's greatest gifts. So why not make every effort to maximize it where you can? It is amazing how much time we can make for the things that really matter.

As Matty's friend, I am absolutely a beneficiary of his methods, in that I get to hang out with him and discuss those very ideas. I may still not want to function at the level that you and he aspire to, but having known him, and having had the opportunity to discuss these concepts, has absolutely made me more conscious of what I *do* want and what I need to do to be there.

That is a gift we can all benefit from.

Matthew Shepard is a communications coordinator for a national nonprofit, proud father of an awesome daughter, enthusiastic New England sports fan, and poor but happy golfer. Matthew Dicks thinks he should really be doing more.

Appendix

Chapter-by-Chapter Action Plans

Here's the problem with a book like this: Half a dozen salient points will remain with you long after you've read the book (probably more given the extraordinary nature of this particular book), and some may already be making an enormous difference in your life. My production manager, Kaia, for example, told me that proofreading chapter 2 has already altered the way she views time and has changed her life considerably. She's getting more done and living life better thanks to reading the chapter and telling me where I sounded stupid. But what about chapter 9? Chapter 13? All of part 4? Those are important, too. Everything is important. I left all the unimportant stuff on the cutting-room floor.

So what follows are a series of action plans for each chapter. My goal was to provide you with ways of actively and immediately implementing the strategies of this book into your everyday life. Rather than placing these plans after each chapter and disrupting the flow the book (and my extraordinary eloquence), I've placed them here at the end. Now that you've learned everything that I wanted you to learn (and absorbed the wisdom of Elysha and Shep), it's time to put the lessons, practices, and methods discussed in these pages into action.

But this is important: don't judge the value or merit of each action plan.

Some may seem exceptionally useful and simple to implement. Others may seem more onerous and time-consuming. Still others might seem kooky or silly.

Forget all that. *Do them all.*

Don't assume that one isn't as useful or important as the next. Every action plan has been considered carefully, designed specifically, and tested by friends, colleagues, and even some strangers for its practicality and usefulness.

Everything works. I promise. Just do what I tell you to do. Please? Don't spend all this time with me, reading this book and learning my strategies, only to resume your life unaltered. This is your chance to make tangible, sustainable differences in your life using the strategies I have provided.

Your one-hundred-year-old self wants you to do this. Listen to that version of yourself. As you well know, there is great wisdom in that future version of you.

One other suggestion: Engaging in a process like this is often done best with a partner, so if possible, find someone to join you on your quest. Share the book with them (by which I mean purchase a copy for them to read, too) and engage in these action plans as a team. Accountability (as you now know) is often critical for compliance, motivation, and stick-to-itiveness.

Also, share your work with me! Send me photos of your chapter 1 action plan assignment via social media or email. Share your list of your chosen deletions from chapter 5. Invite me to your chapter 15 action plan event. Include me in any of the emails that I've asked you to send as a part of an action plan, and forward some of your team's responses.

I want to know how and what you're doing. I want to hear that you're making progress. I want to share your insight and success stories with others. I selfishly want to use your journey as an inspiration for my own.

Do it. Live it. Share it.

Now get started. Someday is today.

PART 1: TIME

Chapter 1: The One-Hundred-Year-Old Plan

*I need to look ahead and ask [the one-hundred-year-old] version
of myself — the one who understands the importance and preciousness
of time — how I should spend this hour, this day, or this week.
He is my trustworthy narrator. He is the one who knows
what is best for me.*

Action Plan

I want you to have a visual representation of the one-hundred-year-old version of yourself. Not some imaginary version in your mind. I want you to have a physical, stare-you-in-the-eye, unforgettable visage of the person you will someday be: older, wiser, and wrinklier.

For me, I have a perfect visual representation of that person in my mind's eye whom I call upon constantly, but I've been doing this for a long time. My image was born on the floor of a McDonald's restaurant in Brockton, Massachusetts, back in 1992.

You're new. You need reminders. Constant, relentless reminders.

If I didn't have that clear image in my mind already, I'd probably create a stick-figure drawing of myself, lying in a cozy bed, eating a cheeseburger alongside my cat and my surprisingly youthful-looking wife, watching the television show *Dexter*. Everyone says I need to watch that show. I'll probably get around to it by the time I'm one hundred.

My production manager, Kaia, would print out a photo of the late Broadway luminary Elaine Stritch. She sets high bars for herself.

My wife Elysha says she would print out a photo of Betty White. Sounds about right. My son Charlie says he would make an old-person Minecraft version of himself.

Maybe your visualization is of a grandparent or an elderly neighbor or the Metro-Goldwyn-Mayer lion or Harriet Tubman.

Choose one. Then make the image. Draw, print, paint, color, sketch, photograph, mold in mashed potatoes ... whatever it takes.

In fact, make more than one. Then stick them in all the places that your eyes land upon frequently throughout your day. The bathroom mirror. The refrigerator. The windshield of your car. Two little images, one on the top of each of your shoes. Stick one on the forehead of the person you love most. Put one in the shower.

The point is this: If you're going to look to the older version of yourself to make these critical decisions, you need to have someone to look to. A reminder of what I want you to do.

I'm serious about this. No joke. Don't think, *That's cute, Matt*, and move on. Stop reading and make your one-hundred-year-old self. Plant it in all the most frequently occupied spaces of your life.

Let it serve as a reminder that you need the wisdom of the much older version of yourself in order to make the best choices.

Then move on.

Chapter 2: 86,400 Seconds

I want you to stop thinking about the length of a day in terms of hours and start thinking in terms of minutes. Minutes matter.

Action Plan

It's time to inventory and account for your day. This is going to take some time and effort, but it is essential.

Step 1: Determine how many of your minutes are being used well.

Every day is composed of 1,440 minutes. Using the Chasing Zero worksheet provided on page 290 (or downloading and printing it from somedayistodaybook.com), you will be accounting for your time on a daily basis by subtracting the minutes spent on everything you do to fill your day. The goal is to subtract the minutes for each activity so that you ultimately reach zero at the bottom of the page.

From the moment you awaken, begin accounting for your day by tracking each activity and the time in minutes that it takes to complete it. Begin by converting the amount of time you slept into minutes. At the end of the day, subtract the total number of minutes accounted for from 1,440. Your total should be 0.

If your subtraction yields more than zero, you've spent time in a way you can't account for, so you need to figure out where.

Maybe you've forgotten the eleven minutes spent scrolling social media when you arrived home. Maybe you forgot to account for the time it takes every morning to walk the dog. It's possible that you forgot to record the eight minutes it takes your 1996 Dell Dimension desktop computer to boot every day.

Or perhaps there are things in your life that take more time than you thought. Maybe your six-minute shower is actually nineteen minutes long when accounting for toweling, applying of moisturizers, and staring at yourself in the mirror. Maybe you thought your commute to work was thirty minutes when it's really forty-one minutes. Maybe you thought that your trip through the Starbucks drive-through every morning took about three minutes, when in reality it takes ten.

You can't begin looking for ways to save time until you know how you spend your time.

Step 2: Evaluate the use of your time.
1. Is there something consistently on the list that should not be on the list because it's not yielding you anything positive in your life?
2. Are there things in your life that could take less time?
3. Are there things missing from your list that need to be added? More time spent with your cat? A weekly phone call to your sibling? A lot more sex?

Complete a Chasing Zero worksheet for every day of your week. Repeat frequently, if possible. The more data that you possess, the better. If you truly believe that time is your most valuable commodity, you must begin accounting for it with the same specificity and

CHASING ZERO WORKSHEET

Activity	Minutes Spent
Sleep	
Total minutes accounted for:	
Total minutes in a day	1,440
Minus total minutes accounted for:	–
Total minutes unaccounted for:	=

exactitude as you do your bank balance. We can't make great decisions about how we spend our time until we know how we spend our time.

Chapter 3: Sleep Correctly

My proposal is that you begin by increasing your efficiency of sleep. If you're forced to lie down and render yourself unconscious at least once every day, you should try to do it in the shortest, most restful way possible.

Action Plan

Complete the following checklists.

Checklist #1: Standard Sleep Practices

These are the steps that should be taken regardless of your investment in your sleep. Think of these as equivalent to brushing your teeth, wearing shoes, and smiling at babies. It shouldn't even be up for debate.

- ❑ Establish sleep and wake times that fluctuate by less than thirty minutes every day. Weekends and weekday times should be the same. Variation should be minimal.
- ❑ On evenings when you stay out later to enjoy a Springsteen concert, attend a Monday Night Football game at Gillette Stadium, or sneak into the midnight showing of *The Rocky Horror Picture Show*, try to keep your wake-up time as close to your regular one as possible, even if this means less sleep. Maintaining a consistent body clock is more important than catching up on two or three hours of lost sleep.
- ❑ Acquire a white-noise machine of some kind and begin using it immediately.
- ❑ Identify the locations in your body where you hold the most tension and relax them one by one before sleep. You can pinpoint these locations by beginning in your

toes and working your way to the top of your head, noting places in your body where tightness exists. Once those locations are identified, begin relaxing them first each night.

❏ Eliminate the snooze button from your life for the rest of your life.

❏ Engage in daily exercise. Begin with a brisk daily walk of ten to fifteen minutes. If a brisk walk is all you ever do in terms of exercise, that's fine. Fantastic, even. You're already doing better than most people.

❏ Lower your bedroom temperature to sixty-five degrees.

❏ Install f.lux on all phones and computers.

❏ Set an alarm to go off one hour before bed. When the alarm sounds, stop looking at phones and computers and stop all eating.

❏ Whenever possible, take a short, warm shower before bed.

Checklist #2: The Level-Up Challenge (Only for the Brave of Heart)

If you're serious about treating sleep as sacredly as it deserves to be treated, take these actions as well.

❏ Remove the television from your bedroom. Throw it away if possible.

❏ Begin a meditation practice. Download an app, subscribe to a podcast, and/or take a meditation class. Make it a daily practice that you can use in the evening to clear your mind of the terrors of existential dread (or whatever happens to keep you up at night).

❏ Stop reading in bed. Stop all activities in bed except for sleeping and sex. If you can move sex to a separate location (or many separate locations), do so. It will help with sleep, and it may improve your sex life, too.

Chapter 4: The Eagle and the Mouse

*The eagle knows not to invest your most precious resource in
things that are ultimately irrelevant. Don't waste time on things
that will mean nothing to you hours or days later. Don't spend
a minute on something that you will forget in an hour.
Don't even think about things over which you have no control.*

Action Plan

1. Make an honest, ruthless self-appraisal of all the things
    you do that don't need to be done.
    a. Look for things you think you need to do even
        though no one else is doing them.
    b. Look for things people scoff at you for doing.
    c. Look for things that make you feel guilty or silly
        for doing them.
    d. Look for things you do that no one ever notices
        you do.
        These are the places where you can often find
    wasted steps. Do your best to scrutinize your life care-
    fully. Don't be kind to yourself.
2. Ask five people who know you best to make a list of all
    things you do that you don't need to do. Tell them to
    be ruthless.
3. Ask the five colleagues who work with you most closely
    to make a list of all things you do that you don't need to
    do. Tell them to be ruthless.
4. If you have a partner, spouse, or roommates, ask them
    to make a list of all things you do that you don't need to
    do. Don't worry. They will be ruthless already.

Examine the lists. Consider removing any and all items from your
life, even if it's just to see what will happen.

What you will discover is this: the most common reaction other
people will have to your shedding an obligation is nothing.

If an item appears on more than one list, you must seriously consider removing it from your life forever. The more you remove, the better off you will be.

Chapter 5: Things That Don't Deserve Your Time

Time is the most valuable commodity on the planet,
and you have just as much of it as the wealthiest people alive.
Value it accordingly. Never waste it away.

Action Plan

There are many things that steal our time, but in today's world, few things are more destructive than the small computers that we carry in our pockets and still refer to as phones.

Therefore...

Inventory the apps on your phone. As you take note of each one, consider:

- Is it worthy of your time, or is it robbing you of your most precious commodity?
- Is it moving you in a positive direction and helping you achieve your goals?
- Has your life been better, worse, or about the same since downloading the app?
- Would you be embarrassed if someone found you using the app?

Assign a *yes* to worthy apps, a *no* to neutral or mixed-feelings apps, and a *hell no!* if the app is robbing you of your precious time, failing to move you forward in a positive direction, or making your life worse in some way. Delete the latter apps immediately.

Example

App	Yes	No	Hell No!
Personal email	✔		
Work email		✔	
Facebook		✔	
Venmo	✔		
Spotify·	✔		
Candy Crush			✔
Waze	✔		
TikTok		✔	
Weather	✔		

Chapter 6: Be a Criminal

If we want to make things happen, we sometimes need to be criminals.

Action Plan

In order to steal time, you need to be prepared to do so. Find yourself in a meeting or class that is meaningless to you? Discover that your aunt's birthday party is going to last a lot longer than anticipated? Realize that your doctor has no respect for your time? These are the moments when time can be stolen back but only if you are prepared to do something productive with it.

Your task is to assemble a burglar bag: a list of tasks and materials that can be used in instances like these.

For me, it was once an application to become a notary, a collection of lists that would ultimately transform into a novel, and spelling tests in need of correcting.

Today, I carry a stack of envelopes, each containing a card. The envelopes are already addressed and stamped. If I'm able to steal three minutes from an otherwise meaningless meeting or am left in a dentist's waiting room for fifteen minutes, I remove an envelope from my bag and write a short note to one of my students about their recent performance. Over the course of a month, every student receives a letter from me with almost no time commitment whatsoever on my part.

I write these notes using stolen time only.

I also have five poems on my phone I am trying to memorize and a series of jokes I am trying to improve.

I also have a folder in my bag containing a series of letters written to Elysha by a particular set of parents during one of her first years of teaching. The letters are hilarious, and I'm pondering turning them into a one-act play. I look at them from time to time and take notes on what they might become.

You need your own burglar bag: a collection of meaningful, productive things to do when you find yourself able to steal some time. This can consist of digital projects that live on your phone or physical objects you carry with you at all times.

You can't waste these stolen minutes wondering how you might fill them. You need to be prepared to use them the instant you've taken possession of them.

Chapter 7: Don't Lose Days to Rotten People

Negative people will bring you down. Positive people will lift you up.

Action Plan

Make a list of all the people in your life who steal time and energy from you. This list should include friends, neighbors, relatives, colleagues, clients, and customers. It can also include collectives of people, including organizations, businesses, zoning boards, the cable company, and any other entity that routinely creates strife in your life.

Anyone who spoils your mood, demands unnecessarily of your time, makes you uncomfortable, creates drama, steals or burns your property, or has kidnapped your guinea pig.

For each person, choose one of the four courses of action outlined in the book:

1. Forgiveness
2. Empathy
3. Elimination
4. Enemies list

Take the chosen action for each person.

If an action does not eliminate the drag that the person has on your life, shift to a different strategy. For example, trying to cultivate forgiveness or empathy for a rotten person is a noble choice, but if you find yourself unable, you may simply need to eliminate the person from your life.

Harsh, I know, but you deserve the best, which sometimes means eliminating negative people from your everyday life.

Example

Horrible Person/Group	Required Action
Alan	Elimination
Eric	Forgiveness (leaning toward elimination)
Ryan	Enemies list
The Concerned Parent Body of West Hartford	Enemies list
Mike	Forgiveness
Jas	Enemies list
Will	Empathy
Katherine	Forgiveness
Cynthia	Empathy

PART 2: TAKING THE LEAP

Chapter 8: Say Yes

The result of that simple yes is remarkable. That yes results in a possibility tree — the branching of new opportunities — of enormous proportions.

Action Plan

First, go back to that one-hundred-year-old version of yourself — the one on your fridge, the one dangerously plastered to the windshield of your car, the one that got moldy in the shower.

Then...

1. Grab some Post-it Notes.
2. Cut out a speech bubble for every one of those representations of your one-hundred-year-old self.
3. Write the word *Yes!* on each Post-it Note speech bubble.
4. Stick it to the image.

From this point forward, whenever you're asked to engage in a new creative endeavor, your answer is going to be "Yes!" Every opportunity deserves a yes, and every yes deserves at least three days before becoming a no.

After three or more days, if the yes still does not feel right, you may change it to a no.

Chapter 9: Be a Chicken, Not a Pig

Stuff begets stuff.

Action Plan

1. Make a list of every personal and professional interest you have had since you were a kid. Spend some time

making this list. Give yourself a week or more. Ponder the hell out of it.

2. Ask your parents, siblings, and partner for every personal and professional interest that they remember you having or speaking about in your life. Add these items to that list.

3. Post the list in a visible location.

4. Choose the first item to begin studying.

5. Download a podcast, subscribe to a YouTube channel, purchase a book, sign up for lessons, enroll in a class, or join a club related to the chosen subject. Great job! You've started something you've waited your whole life to begin.

6. Repeat frequently.

Chapter 10: You Choose the Finish Line

Keeping an open mind in terms of what your finish line might be is critical to both learning to make something great and making that great something.

Action Plan

1. Choose one of your creative pursuits — one that you are working on or one that you envision for your future.

2. Spend five minutes describing what the ideal result of this endeavor would look like. Write, draw, paint, sketch, or outline. Don't just think. Create a tangible representation of the result of this endeavor.

3. Now imagine every possible permutation of this endeavor, and do the same. Write, draw, paint, sketch, or outline. If your dream is to open a shop called Fancy Panties (one of Elysha's former dreams), possible permutations might include an online shop, a space inside Victoria's Secret, a company dedicated to the design

and manufacture of women's underwear, a sustainability business modeled after the bra company ThirdLove, a children's paper-doll cutout book that includes fancy panties, or the licensing of the name Fancy Panties for underwear already on the market.

4. Ask your five smartest friends for the permutations that they can also envision for your project. Include their ideas on the list.

5. Continue to add to this list as you pursue your dream.

6. Post it somewhere prominent as a reminder of what your creative pursuit might ultimately become.

7. Listen to the NPR podcast *How I Built This*. Nearly every episode demonstrates this concept in reality and will give you additional strategies for pivoting, reimagining, or reinventing.

Chapter 11: Make Terrible Things

Don't let perfect be the enemy of progress.

Action Plan

1. Get a box. Grab one of the many cardboard boxes that likely arrive at your home on a regular basis, or perhaps go to Etsy and purchase something a little more substantial. Label it *Terrible Progress toward Perfection*. Even better, purchase a bulletin board or a shadow box. Label it the same.

2. Whenever you fail — slightly or spectacularly — place a representation of that failure in the box or on display. This might be the actual failure itself, a photo of the failure, or a visual representation of the failure. Find a means of celebrating each addition to your box or

bulletin board. Maybe enjoy a slice of ice-cream cake. Send an email and photo to some of your closest friends with the heading "One fewer disaster away from success!" Host a naked dance party. Or maybe take Howard Frank Mosher's approach and stick a photo of your failure to the side of the barn and open fire with your shotgun.

Chapter 12: How Did They Do It?

It's good to know how hard it was for those who came before us.

Action Plan

1. Rather than asking what someone does for a living, ask them this: "How did you end up in your current profession?" and "What was the hardest thing that you recently faced professionally?" Make these the questions you ask everyone you meet.

2. If you're fortunate enough to encounter someone who has found success in your chosen pursuit, ask them to lunch, brunch, dinner, coffee, or a drink. Ask them to tell you their creative story. Record it, if possible.

3. Continue to listen to the NPR podcast *How I Built This*. Once again, nearly every episode demonstrates this concept in reality, and there are hundreds of episodes. You're not even close to finishing them all.

PART 3: SUPPORT

Chapter 13: Find Your People

*Feedback is critical. Having a group of people on your side —
receiving feedback and knowing someone is invested
in your work — is everything.*

Action Plan

Make a list of your friends, colleagues, and anyone close to you. Beside their name, list their skills. Update the list frequently as people enter and exit your life and add to their own skill sets.

Example

Name	Skill Set
Shep	English major, appreciates humor, honest, mixes positive feedback with a multitude of suggestions
Jeni	Storyteller, writer, brutally honest, my creative antagonist
David	Writer, deeply analytical, strong structural analysis, understands the depth and breadth of humor, does not get overly impressed with funny writing
Jeff	Not easily impressed, willing to read entire books in one gulp, large-picture feedback
Kaia	Younger than me and more aware of the many ways I may offend, possesses an excellent blend of artistic and practical skills, invested in my success, understands all my PTSD needs
Elysha	A solid writer, not easily impressed, nearly perfect taste, likes my sensibilities

Chapter 14: Put Your Eyes on the Prize

Asking yourself why you do what you do can make the path clear.
Understanding why you do the things you do can help
guide you to the life you most desire.

Action Plan

Complete a worksheet like the following for each of your creative
pursuits. Be open to adding to this list as you consider additional
reasons for your pursuits. Oftentimes the reasons for your motivations aren't immediately obvious and are multitudinous.

I have completed one of mine as an example.

Creative Pursuit	Reasons Why
Stand-up comedian	It frightens me, and I want to be brave in all things
	It makes me a better storyteller
	Mike Birbiglia is one of my heroes, and this will bring me closer to being him
	Making Elysha laugh keeps her from abandoning me for the likes of Ryan Reynolds or Senator Christopher Murphy
	Listening to people laugh at stuff that I made up in my head makes me feel fantastic
	Corporate clients always want to learn how to be funny

Chapter 15: Party Often

We must be willing to celebrate each step along the way.

Action Plan

Identify the first meaningful step in the pursuit of your creative goal. *Not* a significant milestone or extraordinary accomplishment. Just a meaningful step.

- For a novelist, this might be the completion of the first draft of a book or even the first chapter.
- For a storyteller, it might be the first performance of a story onstage.
- For a business owner, it might be the hiring of a first employee or an increase in hourly pay or the development of a new logo.
- For an artist, it might be the first purchase of clay. The mounting of canvas on a frame. The first song plucked from the strings of a ukulele.

Before moving on, plan your celebration *now*. When you reach that first meaningful step, how will you celebrate? Once it's decided, tell three people in your life.

During this planned celebration, identify the next meaningful step and plan that celebration.

Repeat forever.

Chapter 16: Feed Yourself a Compliment Sandwich

We're offered fuel for our fire all the time, but instead of holding on to it, we allow it to slip through our fingers, forgotten and useless.

Action Plan

Establish the collection place for all future compliments. A program like Evernote or Notion. A Word or Google doc. Ideally, it should be digital so that you can cut and paste compliments received via text message and email. It should also be easily accessible.

Once that location has been established, enter this as your first compliment:

> You're doing a fantastic job supporting yourself by creating a system for holding on to compliments long-term so that they can be a source of inspiration in times of need. Also, you deserve to hold on to these compliments. You deserve nothing but the best. Well done! — Matthew Dicks

Now enter any other previous compliments that you can recall, including compliments found in your past email and text messages.

Chapter 17: Know Your Story. Tell Your Story. Listen to Your Story.

We can inspire ourselves by remembering how far we have come, how much we have accomplished, and how improbable our journey once seemed. We can inspire ourselves by telling the stories of our struggle and success.

Action Plan

Purchase *Storyworthy: Engage, Teach, Persuade, and Change Your Life through the Power of Storytelling* by Matthew Dicks.

Self-serving? Perhaps. But I'm serious. You need to learn to find and tell your best stories, and this book, written by someone you know pretty well, will do the job. Also, if necessary, be a criminal. Steal it. Or go to the library and check it out.

I'm not kidding around here. Finding and telling your best stories is one of the best things you can do for yourself. So when you finish this book — or right now — get your hands on that book, or purchase and download the audiobook.

Start finding and telling your stories.

PART 4: LIVING THE LIFE

Chapter 18: Creativity Cannot Abide Preciousness

If you want to make things as desperately as I do, you don't need picnic baskets full of warm treats, idyllic mountaintop settings, and whiskey-fueled campfires.

Action Plan

1. Make a list of all the things you think you need in order to work.
2. Now cross off every item on the list that you don't actually need.
3. Make a new list of things you *actually* need in order to work, absent the niceties on the previous list. Post this list in all the places where you might be working.
4. Choose a place where you could never imagine working — your equivalent of a concrete median, beside a barren sapling, in the middle of a parking lot. Some apocalyptic landscape of a creative space. Uncomfortable and unimaginably uninspiring. Go work there for a period of time to prove to yourself that it's possible.
5. Take a photograph of yourself working in this hellscape. Print a copy and display it someplace prominently, both to remind yourself of what is possible and to let others know how remarkably committed you are to your creative pursuit.

Chapter 19: Make Something into Something

As creative people, we must be the collectors, the preservers, and whenever possible, the transformers and expanders of our ideas and content. We need to be supremely flexible in terms of how we view the path of our creative life and the things that we make.

Action Plan

This plan requires the list of people whom you assembled in chapter 13. You can email them, schedule a meeting on Zoom, or even make this action plan a part of your chapter 15 celebration.

Your message will be this:

> So I've made my thing. Opened my Fancy Panties shop. Recorded my polka–yacht rock fusion album. Woven those wicker chairs. Invented a new-and-improved cat litter. Designed and constructed the wedding gown of the future.
>
> Now what?
>
> That's the question I bring to you, my team of attractive geniuses.
>
> What else can this something be? How can I take the thing I've invested enormous amounts of time, energy, and possibly money into and make it something else as well?
>
> This step is often hard for the creator to see. Oftentimes it relies on luck and serendipity, which is lovely, but I'm trying to make it purposeful, too, by enlisting the creativity and multitude of experiences of y'all.

Encourage your team to make your something into something else.

Chapter 20: Don't Be an Asshole

Being an asshole may admittedly get you something in the near term, but creators must play the long game. We need to keep our eyes not on today's horizon but on the thousands of horizons beyond this one.

Action Plan

Seek out at least five people in your life with whom you have a great deal of contact. Try to find people in different settings of your life. People who see you in a variety of contexts and roles.

Engage your team from the previous action plan, too, if you'd like.

Send this email:

I'm engaged in an important creative pursuit, and I need your help. Fear not. It won't be too hard. It turns out — at least according to the bold and brilliant Matthew Dicks — that being an asshole can be an enormous detriment to my career. But here's the thing: assholes can't always see their assholery. So I need you to keep an eye on me. If I'm acting like an asshole to anyone, for any reason, I need you to let me know.

This is serious. Okay?

Also, you might want to purchase a copy of *Someday Is Today* and *Storyworthy*. Both written by Matthew Dicks. They might change your life.

You can leave that last part off if needed. Or bold it.

Chapter 21: Eat a Lot

As a creative person — a maker of things — I know that one of the best ways of developing new ideas, identifying new connections, and expanding my potential skill set is by constantly pursuing new learning in whatever direction my interests may point me. There is no predicting what new bit of knowledge will open a new door and expand your universe, so I simply chase my interests and consume new content, wherever my curiosity takes me.

Action Plan

Send this email to your team:

One of the best ways for creative people to become more creative is to expand their interests and knowledge across a variety of disciplines. The problem is that people tend to remain in their lane and rarely branch out into new realms. Oftentimes people can't even see what other realms might be worth exploring.

This is where you come in. Please take an hour, a day, a week, or a month to consider areas of interest and indulgence that you think I should pursue. This could be just about anything:

- A book I might never read
- A film I might never think of seeing
- A sport I should watch or play
- A podcast or YouTube channel that I should dip into
- A board game that I might love
- A person I should meet
- A cuisine I should try
- An interest of yours that you think should also be mine

What am I missing? Tell me. Please. One suggestion would be great. A dozen would be extraordinary.

Thanks so much, my friends.

Warmly,

[Your name]

Chapter 22: Pessimists Die Knowing Only That They Were Correct. Optimists Thrive.

As a creative soul, a maker of things, and a person pursuing your dreams, you can't afford to be a pessimist.

Action Plan

Choose three points in your life:

1. Your most challenging year in school
2. Your most difficult work experience
3. Your most heartbreaking relationship

If any of these things are happening right now, I'm so sorry. If so, choose your second-most challenging, difficult, or heartbreaking experience.

For each example, make a list of all the things that made that experience especially terrible.

Now ask yourself: *Do any of those things still exist today?*

The goal of this exercise is to remind you that regardless of the mountain of struggle that you currently face, this, too, shall pass.

The acne, endless amounts of homework, and adolescent thuggery of eighth grade no longer occupy your life. The boss of the pizza place where you worked in college who yelled at you and stole your tips is lost in the beauty of your rearview mirror. The weekend nights spent eating pints of ice cream, watching *Love Actually*, and telling people that you were spending time working on yourself after that especially hard breakup are no longer a blip on your radar.

It's easy to think that problems linger. Struggles never end. The pit of despair cannot be escaped. This exercise will remind you that you have been in bad spots before, but each time, you have risen above them and moved forward.

You got this.

Acknowledgments

Many thanks to the following people for making this book possible:

My wife Elysha, who has supported me, encouraged me, put up with me, and loved me more than I ever thought imaginable.

Clara and Charlie, my children, whose lives constantly and inevitably filter into my stories and work. They are joyous, hilarious, brilliant human beings who make me excited to climb out of bed every morning.

My in-laws Barbara and Gerry Green for continuing to fill my life with their enthusiasm, excitement, and unsolicited counsel. About once a month, Gerry will say, "Tell me something exciting, Matt! Give me some news!" He has no idea how long I have waited for someone to ask me a question like that.

Erin Barker, writer, storyteller, producer, artistic genius, and friend, who asked me three years ago to talk to her about productivity. We spent about an hour on the phone, discussing some of my strategies, and at the end of that conversation, she said, "You should write a book about this stuff." I took Erin's advice, and this book is the result.

Kaia Pazdersky, who began as a colleague, quickly became a friend, graduated into the caregiver of our children, and is now working as my production manager and collaborator on many projects, including this book. Her wisdom, eye for detail, and willingness to tell me when I've stepped over the line or on someone else's toes have been invaluable.

Matthew Shepard, who remains my first reader, my closest literary confidant, and the person who always sees what others do not.

Jeni Bonaldo, who has allowed me to write about parts of her life while pestering her constantly. People have worried that we don't get along, but our constant bickering and bantering is actually a sign of our close friendship. At least I think so. I don't care what Jeni thinks. An editor would be wise to request a copy of her first manuscript.

The many people who read portions of this manuscript and were kind enough to offer thoughts, including David Golder, Amy Mahoney, Erica Newfang, and at least two people whom I've forgotten.

Alex Freemon, my copyeditor, who has undoubtedly spared me many literary embarrassments. Copyeditors are the unsung champions of the literary world.

Managing editor Kristen Cashman, who parachuted into the book at the last minute and pulled things together, ensuring my blunders were kept to a minimum.

Tanya Fox, the proofreader of the final text of this book. For a perfectionist like me, even the smallest error makes me lose my mind. Knowing that a professional perfectionist read every line of this book allows me to sleep well at night.

Georgia Hughes, who has made this journey into nonfiction possible. Books like *Someday Is Today* and *Storyworthy* require an editor to step into the life of the author and not be repulsed by what they find. I feel so very fortunate to have such a skilled and generous human being finding some value in my thoughts and ideas and helping me to shape them into something more palatable for the reader.

Lastly, thanks to Taryn Fagerness, my agent, friend, and partner in this creative life. She found me in the slush pile years ago and changed my life forever. She makes my sentences better, my stories better, and as a result, my life better. It's not often that another human being can make your dreams come true, but she did, and I am forever thankful.

Notes

Chapter 1: The One-Hundred-Year-Old Plan

p. 14   *"Remembering that I'll be dead"*: Steve Jobs, "2005 Stanford Commencement Address" (prepared text, delivered at Stanford University, Stanford, CA, June 12, 2005), in "'You've Got to Find What You Love,' Jobs Says," *Stanford News*, June 14, 2005, https://news.stanford.edu/2005/06/14/jobs-061505.

Chapter 2: 86,400 Seconds

p. 46   *"A 2007 study published by a molecular biologist"*: Jessica Stillman, "This Wacky-Sounding Procrastination Cure Is Actually Backed by Science," *Inc.*, November 28, 2016, https://www.inc.com/jessica-stillman/this-wacky-sounding-procrastination-cure-is-actually-backed-by-science.html.

p. 46   *Getting into a freezing shower*: Carl Richards, "The Benefits of Getting an Icy Start to the Day," *New York Times*, March 14, 2016, https://www.nytimes.com/2016/03/15/business/the-benefits-of-getting-an-icy-start-to-the-day.html.

p. 47   *"Starting your morning by tackling challenges"*: Brian Tracy, *Eat That Frog!: 21 Great Ways to Stop Procrastinating and Get More Done in Less Time* (Oakland, CA: Berrett-Koehler Publishers, Inc., A BK Life Book, 2017), 27.

p. 49   *The average American spends 65.6 minutes*: Karen S. Hamrick et al., *How Much Time Do Americans Spend on Food? EIB-86*, US Department of Agriculture, Economic Research Service (November 2011).

p. 53   *"A new survey found that 49 percent of adults"*: Walt Hickey, "Beef, Books, Crooks," *Numlock News*, June 2, 2021, https://numlock.substack.com/p/numlock-news-june-2-2021-beef-books.

p. 55   *"Americans are obsessed with television"*: Teal Burrell, "I Gave Up TV, Then Qualified for Olympic Marathon Trials and Got My PhD," *Washington Post*, March 25, 2017, https://www.washingtonpost.com/national/health-science/i-gave-up-tv-then-qualified-for-olympic-marathon-trials-and-got-my-phd/2017/03/24/6d90aafc-ee38-11e6-9973-c5efb7ccfb0d_story.html.

p. 56   *"People who watch more television"*: Burrell, "I Gave Up TV."

p. 56   *the average American spent 145 minutes per day on social media*: "Social Media: Statistics & Facts," Statista Research Department, Statista, February 25, 2021, https://www.statista.com/topics/1164/social-networks/#dossierkeyfigures.

Chapter 4: The Eagle and the Mouse

p. 82   *"enough to last for the rest of my life"*: Elizabeth Snead, "Steve Jobs on His Issey Miyake Black Turtlenecks: 'I Have Enough to Last for the Rest of My Life,'" *Hollywood Reporter*, October 11, 2011, https://www.holly woodreporter.com/news/general-news/steve-jobs-his-issey-miyake-black -turtlenecks-i-have-last-rest-my-life-246808.

p. 82   *"You need to remove from your life the day-to-day problems"*: Michael Lewis, "Obama's Way," *Vanity Fair*, September 11, 2012, https://www.vanityfair .com/news/2012/10/michael-lewis-profile-barack-obama.

p. 82   *"I mean, I wear the same thing every day, right?"*: "The Reason Mark Zuckerberg Wears the Same Shirt Every Day," *Career Blog*, Workopolis, November 11, 2014, https://careers.workopolis.com/advice/the-reason -mark-zuckerberg-wears-the-same-shirt-every-day.

p. 88   *"Life is not lost by dying"*: Stephen Vincent Benét, "Stephen Vincent Benét Quote #1489262," Quotepark.com, last updated June 3, 2021, https:// quotepark.com/quotes/1489262-stephen-vincent-benet-life-is-not-lost-by -dying-life-is-lost-minute-by.

p. 91   *In a test of the spotlight effect*: Benedict Carey, "It's Not All about You," *Los Angeles Times*, January 13, 2003, https://www.latimes.com/archives/la-xpm -2003-jan-13-he-spotlight13-story.html.

p. 93   *"Everyone has too many clothes"*: Macy Cate Williams, "25 Life Lessons Written by a 104-Year-Old Man," POPSUGAR.Living, May 13, 2020, https://www.popsugar.com/smart-living/life-lessons-written-104-year-old -man-36166279.

p. 93   *"more than five" belts*: "Fashion Belt Market Size 2021 — Latest Research Report, Future Prospect and Forecast to 2026: Major Companies: Prada, Loewe, Wild Fable [Reports Page No. 116]," press release, WICZ Fox40 TV, November 30, 2021, https://www.wicz.com/story/45332625/fashion-belt.

p. 94   *"A new study published in* Nature": Walt Hickey, "Poison, Rivers, Anime," *Numlock News*, April 9, 2021, https://numlock.substack.com/p/numlock -news-april-9-2021-poison.

p. 95   *"Death is not waiting for us"*: Eric Barker, "The 5 Habits That Will Make You Happy, According to Science," *Time*, December 16, 2015, https://time .com/4149478/happiness-neuroscience-simplicity.

Chapter 5½: How to Ruin the World

p. 105   *1. Insist on doing everything through channels*: Robert M. Galford, Bob Frisch, and Cary Greene, *Simple Sabotage: A Modern Field Manual for Detecting and Rooting Out Everyday Behaviors That Undermine Your Workplace* (New York: HarperOne, 2015), 140.

Chapter 7: Don't Lose Days to Rotten People

p. 120   *A 2017 study found that working*: Dylan Minor and Michael Housman, "Sitting Near a High-Performer Can Make You Better at Your Job," *Kellogg Insight*, May 8, 2017, https://insight.kellogg.northwestern.edu /article/sitting-near-a-high-performer-can-make-you-better-at-your-job.

p. 123 *"It's one of your greatest gifts"*: Maya Angelou, interview by Oprah Winfrey, "Oprah Talks to Maya Angelou," *O, The Oprah Magazine*, May 21, 2013, https://www.oprah.com/omagazine/maya-angelou-interviewed-by-oprah -in-2013/5.

Chapter 11: Make Terrible Things

p. 173 *"All of us who do creative work"*: Ira Glass. "Ira Glass on the Creative Process," YouTube, April 2, 2019, https://www.youtube.com/watch?v=GHrmKL 2XKcE.

Chapter 11½: Rejection Is Expected, but So Is Persistence

p. 176 *"painful, indelible silence that lasted decades"*: Ursula Le Guin, "Skylight by José Saramago — Love, Life and Loss in Lisbon," *Guardian*, July 23, 2014, https://www.theguardian.com/books/2014/jul/23/skylight-jose-saramago -love-life-loss-lisbon.

Chapter 12: How Did They Do It?

p. 179 *The problem was the teaching*: Stephen King, *On Writing: A Memoir of the Craft* (2000; repr., New York: Scribner, 2020), 147.

p. 181 *"I paint myself because I am often alone"*: "Biography of Frida Kahlo," Frida Kahlo Foundation, accessed January 25, 2022, https://www.frida-kahlo -foundation.org/biography.html.

p. 181 *"to begin again, painting things just as I saw them"*: "Frida Kahlo," Design Santa Barbara, June 1, 2018, https://designsantabarbara.tv/episodes /design-santa-barbara-great-artist-frida-kahlo-frank-goss-and-ralph -waterhouse-with-your-host-michael-kourosh.

Chapter 16: Feed Yourself a Compliment Sandwich

p. 220 *Studies have shown that a person needs to hear*: Jack Zenger and Joseph Folkman, "The Ideal Praise-to-Criticism Ratio," *Harvard Business Review*, March 15, 2013, https://hbr.org/2013/03/the-ideal-praise-to-criticism.

Chapter 17: Know Your Story.
Tell Your Story. Listen to Your Story.

p. 230 *research has shown that when we squint*: Eric Barker, "The 5 Habits That Will Make You Happy, According to Science," *Time*, December 16, 2015, https://time.com/4149478/happiness-neuroscience-simplicity.

Chapter 18: Creativity Cannot Abide Preciousness

p. 242 *"stealing away a little time"*: Jeff Goins, *Real Artists Don't Starve: Timeless Strategies for Thriving in the New Creative Age* (Nashville, TN: Thomas Nelson, 2018), 101.

Chapter 20: Don't Be an Asshole

p. 259 *"I'm happy with my success"*: Marc Maron et al., "Marc Maron, Margaret Atwood and More on Envy," *Wall Street Journal*, August 29, 2016, https://www.wsj.com/articles/marc-maron-margaret-atwood-and-more-on-envy-1472484738.

Chapter 21: Eat a Lot

p. 270 *A study of the most significant scientists*: Mike Peckham and James Whitehead, "The Renaissance of the Polymath: And You Could Be One Too," PSA Training and Development Ltd., June 28, 2019, https://www.psa-training.co.uk/renaissance-polymath-one.

p. 270 *"If you don't have time to read"*: Stephen King, *On Writing: A Memoir of the Craft* (2000; repr., New York: Scribner, 2020), 147.

Chapter 22: Pessimists Die Knowing Only That They Were Correct. Optimists Thrive.

p. 274 *"The arc of the moral universe is long"*: Martin Luther King Jr., "Remaining Awake through a Great Revolution," address at Morehouse College Commencement," The Martin Luther King, Jr., Research and Education Institute, June 2, 1959, https://kinginstitute.stanford.edu/king-papers/documents/remaining-awake-through-great-revolution-address-morehouse-college.

p. 277 *"Who is more to be pitied"*: Kurt Vonnegut, *Bluebeard* (New York: Dell Books, 1988), 140.

About the Author

Matthew Dicks is the internationally bestselling author of the books *Memoirs of an Imaginary Friend*, *Something Missing*, *The Perfect Comeback of Caroline Jacobs*, *Unexpectedly, Milo*, *Twenty-One Truths about Love*, *The Other Mother*, and *Storyworthy: Engage, Teach, Persuade, and Change Your Life through the Power of Storytelling*. His novels have been translated into more than twenty-five languages.

He is also the author of the rock opera *The Clowns* and the musicals *Caught in the Middle*, *Sticks & Stones*, and *Summertime*. He is a columnist for *Seasons* and *Slate* magazines.

When not hunched over a computer screen, Matthew fills his days as an elementary-school teacher, storyteller, marketing consultant, storytelling and speaking coach, blogger, wedding DJ, minister, podcaster, and lord of Sealand. He is a former West Hartford Teacher of the Year and a finalist for Connecticut Teacher of the Year.

Matthew is a record fifty-three-time Moth StorySLAM champion and seven-time GrandSLAM champion whose stories have been featured on the nationally syndicated *Moth Radio Hour* and its weekly podcast. Matthew is also the cofounder and artistic director of Speak Up, a Hartford-based storytelling organization that produces shows throughout New England. He teaches storytelling and public speaking to individuals, corporations, nonprofits, universities, and school districts around the world. In addition, he is the creator and cohost of *Speak Up Storytelling*, a podcast about finding and telling your best stories.

Matthew is married to his friend and fellow teacher Elysha, and they have two children, Clara and Charlie. He grew up in the small town of Blackstone, Massachusetts, where he made a name for himself by dying twice before the age of eighteen and becoming the first student in his high school to be suspended for inciting riot upon himself.

You can find Matthew at **matthewdicks.com**.